Great American Mansions
and Their Stories

By MERRILL FOLSOM

HASTINGS HOUSE, PUBLISHERS • NEW YORK

For Elnor

Copyright © 1963 by Merrill Folsom

Second Printing, August 1976

Third Printing, January 1979

Published simultaneously in Canada by
Saunders of Toronto, Ltd. Don Mills, Ontario

Library of Congress Catalog Card Number: 63-19792

ISBN: 8038-2625-7
ISBN: 8038-2681-8 (pbk.)

Printed in the United States of America

GREAT AMERICAN MANSIONS
and Their Stories

John Ringling's Ca' d' Zan

CONTENTS

V

FOREWORD

In the heart of almost every man there is a special kind of mansion he dreams of building some day. Often the aspirations are achieved and the events that take place later within the walls are dramatic sagas of mansions and masters that stand in sharp focus as chapters of Americana. In this book, some of the typical and widely different sagas are related. Most of the mansions are large in size; all are large in social significance and all are assured of continued life.

The plaque on a building in Washington, D. C., is inscribed: "What is past is prologue." So it is with homes. Planners would be in a sad plight deciding where they were going if they did not know where they had been.

The development of mansions in the United States reached a peak when fortunes were amassed from newly born industries, before labor and the government were taking big bites. A mansion built without financial restraint invariably bore the indelible stamp of the owner's personality, aspirations and social outlook; often the desires of a woman also were reflected. Occasionally the completion of a Taj Mahal marked the climax of a man's business and matrimonial happiness, with a steady decline following.

Then, too, many a home demonstrated conclusively that man's ambitions exceed his capacities or his physical strength. Some mansions were not completed for thirty years; a few never were finished.

The builders were of all types. Some were educated and genteel, others were illiterate and uncouth; most had individual combinations of traits. One of the brand-new millionaires was asked if he wanted a Renoir painting in the library and he replied, "Sure, get him to paint the kids." The more scholarly millionaires, however, were great book and art collectors.

Something that most of the mansion builders had in common was a desire to impress friends and business rivals with homes more elegant than anything else in town. To complete the idea that conspicuous consumption of valuable goods was evidence of reputability, extravagant parties were given in the mansions. During one of them, gems were hidden in a pile of sand on the ballroom floor and every guest was given a small sterling-silver bucket and shovel to see how many of the precious stones he could find to take home. At other parties, shapely young girls swam in tanks of water in the center of banquet tables or, along with flocks of colorful birds, emerged from huge pies.

There was bragging about $60,000 antique beds, million-dollar private railroad cars and 250-foot yachts. While bread lines were on the streets, one New York party that cost $200,000 evoked sharp comments from both press and pulpit.

Fads in the designs of homes ran the gamut. Before the current trend toward modern houses there were copies of the châteaux of the Loire, the palazzi of Venice, the villas of Spain and the Georgian town houses and Gothic castles of England. A shift in style was the same as dogs barking when a postman came along the street; one dog barked and all the others in the neighborhood followed suit without knowing exactly why. The result in some mansions was a magnificent hash of Florentine doors, French tapestries, Tirolean cloisters, African marbles, English china, Dutch paintings and Oriental vases.

The struggle to get ahead of the Joneses continues but it is doubtful if any of the mansions of yesteryear will be duplicated. The day of wanting a home of 250 rooms and all the servant problems it entails is over. But millions of visitors every year are finding the mansions of the past fascinating and worth preserving.

MERRILL FOLSOM

NOTE

"Great American Mansions" and its sequel "More Great American Mansions" were written in the nineteen sixties. Some of the people in them have since passed on, a few of the mansions have changed ownership and use, inflation continues to alter admission fees and a very few of the buildings have been removed to make space for condominiums and roads.

Other changes continue inexorably. Marjorie Merriweather Post, dealt with in the second book, died recently, her fabulous Hillwood estate in Washington was rejected by the Smithsonian Institution because it had an endowment of only $10,000,000 for maintenance and her spectacular Mar-A-Lago estate in Palm Beach was accepted by the United States government only to have officials in a quandary now about how to use it.

But the mansions and the famous people who built and occupied them continue as part of the indelible web of American traditions and stories about them will survive for generations.

MERRILL FOLSOM
1976

GREAT AMERICAN MANSIONS
and Their Stories

Vizcaya's entrance loggia has an early Roman bath from Pompeii, surmounted by a statue of Bacchus and infants astride sea monsters.

A Bachelor's Paradise

Vizcaya, the Pleasure Dome of James Deering

MIAMI · FLORIDA

WHEN JAMES DEERING was a machinery salesman in Chicago he began thinking of some day having a splendorous home in a warm climate, with bright flowers all year and no blizzards to leave snow drifts at the front door. When he became a multimillionaire as a chief owner of the International Harvester Company, the doctors told him to slow down. He followed their advice by beginning a search throughout the world for a place to build the home of his dreams. He looked especially at the French Riviera, Monte Carlo, southern Italy, North Africa, Egypt and the semitropical resort areas of the United States.

Money was of no concern either in the search or in the purchase of art objects for the projected mansion. Before the first stone of the dwelling was laid Mr. Deering had bought enough paintings, statues, furniture, old roofs, tile floors and the entire interior walls, doors and ceilings of other persons' castles to fill several warehouses.

He acquired treasures of nineteen centuries, dating back to a Roman bath discovered in the ruins of Pompeii and including the interiors of châteaux on the Loire, *casas* in Spain and palazzi of Venice, Rome and Milan. He acquired former possessions of Marie Antoinette and Queen Isabella as easily as the ordinary collector would buy a Paul Revere teaspoon.

Mr. Deering located four gold gooseheads to use as water faucets in his canopied marble bath and he fell so much in love with the ancient red tile roofs of a Cuban village that he bought all the tiles for use on his home, but he never found a woman who met his exacting standards. In his leisure moments he preferred bourbon to women. His secretaries were men. He remained a bachelor all his life. So, unlike most mansions, his dream-home of sixty-nine rooms and eighteen baths was influenced neither in design nor management by a woman's thinking.

Mr. Deering was an elegantly dressed little man, with mixed-gray hair, pince-nez, penetrating pale-blue eyes and a kindly voice. He often carried a Malacca cane. He generally wore pearl-gray suits, occasionally switching to white linens. He owned 600 neckties.

Mr. Deering named his home Vizcaya. He never told how much it cost him but he was reported to have spent $9,000,000 for its 190 acres, which he bought in 1912; for its construction, which began in 1914 and continued through 1916; and for its furnishings, which he collected for twenty-five years. By any yardstick the costs today would be at least $18,000,000, but anyone now can enjoy it for $1.25; it has become the Dade County Art Museum.

Visited by more than 110,000 persons a year, the mansion is considered more of an art treasure itself than a museum, and its ten acres of formal gardens are among the finest in the nation.

The guides on sight-seeing boats from Miami Beach tell lively stories to wide-eyed tourists about the "wild parties" Mr. Deering gave at Vizcaya. Actually, the man had few close personal friends, his parties were as genteel as those in the White House and on most nights everybody had to be in bed at 10:30 P.M. His favorite remark was "My, my, my! Isn't it pretty!" There were signs posted on walls of the servants' quarters that read: "There will be no whistling in the palace when Mr. Deering is in residence." This ban on whistling among the twenty-five household servants and fifty gardeners was no extreme hardship, since Mr. Deering was "in residence" at Vizcaya only ninety days a year and spent the remainder of the year at his homes in Paris, New York City and Chicago.

As a site for his palace Mr. Deering chose the flat Florida jungle, mangrove swamp and low limestone cliffs on the shore of Biscayne Bay, near the southern boundary of Miami. Henry M. Flagler's railroad had reached there and Miami had grown from an Indian trading post into a burgeoning community of 10,000 persons — the nucleus of the present population of 300,000.

Mr. Deering kept 1,000 masons, carpenters, artists and metal craftsmen at work on his palace for two years. He insisted that it should incorporate the best of

Vizcaya's tea room has eighteenth-century wallpaper, lighting standards, furniture, a marble floor and gateway from Italian palaces.

the Italian, French and Spanish palace-fortresses of the seventeenth century and rejected the craze for Spanish-style mansions that was then sweeping Florida.

The name Vizcaya came from the early Spanish adventurers who sailed from Biscay, Spain, to the harbor in Florida which they named Biscayne Bay; they moored their craft off the shoreline Mr. Deering later bought. One of the ships had been the caravel *Vizcaya;* the spelling of the name is a Spanish variation of Biscay and Biscayne.

In his own yacht, the *Nepenthe,* Mr. Deering arrived at Vizcaya on Christmas Day, 1916, to open the mansion. As the craft was moored between the shore and a great stone barge that had been built as a breakwater, two antique Italian cannons were fired, liveried servants stood at attention and a celebration began.

Guests recall the mansion as an elegant home. Meals were served on gold plates, and Mr. Deering was shaved by a liveried valet in front of a gold-framed mirror. One of the frequent guests, John Singer Sargent, the noted painter, made a water color of Mr. Deering that still hangs in the home. Other guests included William Jennings Bryan, Alla Nazimova, Lillian and Dorothy Gish, and Paderewski.

The great Renaissance hall of Vizcaya has a large chimney piece and furnishings from French châteux. The table is inlaid with semiprecious stones.

On one occasion Florenz Ziegfeld attended a party there and put on a show with Follies girls, but it ended early in the evening.

Mr. Deering was born in South Paris, Maine, a descendant of Roger Deering, a shipwright from Dartmouth in Devonshire. When James Deering was a youth the family moved to Evanston, Illinois, and founded the Deering Harvester Company, which was merged in 1902 with a McCormick family concern to form the International Harvester Company.

After graduating from Northwestern University and attending M.I.T., Mr. Deering sold reapers, binders and tractors to farmers throughout the Middle West. He became vice-president of International, then switched most of his energies to the building of his castle.

He spoke French, Italian and German, which helped in his search for a site and for furnishings. France later enacted laws against the exporting of treasures on such a scale as Deering was doing, but it made him a chevalier and later on an officer of the Legion of Honor. His charitable gifts were numerous; those in the United States included $1,000,000 to the Wesley Memorial Hospital and $500,000 each to the Visiting Nurse Association and Children's Memorial Hospital, all of Chicago, and $500,000 to the Jackson Memorial Hospital of Miami.

6　*Deering*

As architects for Vizcaya Mr. Deering retained F. Burrall Hoffman, Jr., and Paul Chalfin. In answer to his demand for a type of seventeenth-century mansion, they produced something of a Venetian palazzo with Spanish and French Riviera overtones; the rooms, on three levels, are clustered around an inner court that provides light and air.

The big kitchens are on the third floor. A second-floor dining room favored by Mr. Deering has large doors and windows that provide a panoramic view for a quarter of a mile across the ten acres of formal gardens, pools, cascading stairs, ornate fountains and grottoes. The mansion now has a plot of 28 acres, the rest of the original 190 having been given or sold for hospital buildings, homes and other structures.

Mr. Deering and his architects reassembled in warehouses the rooms he had acquired overseas, then designed Vizcaya to accommodate them. The height of a tall gateway of marble and wrought iron, acquired from a palace of Niccolò and Vettor Pisani, adventurous Venetian admirals of the fourteenth century, determined the height of the second floor. Dictating some of the contours of the mansion also were the formal gardens, which were planned by Diego Suarez to rival those of the Villa d'Este in Tivoli and the Villa Albani in Rome. Suarez built twenty miles of driveways on the original acreage.

Espagnolette, a guest room in Vizcaya, is decorated in the Venetian style of 200 years ago. The bed can be enclosed by the silk curtains.

In the entrance loggia is a first-century Roman bath of yellow marble, with a seventeenth-century statue of Bacchus, the god of wine, above it. Flanking the bath are carved infants astride sea monsters. The combination seems incongruous until actually seen.

The tall entrance doors of Vizcaya are from the Hotel Beauharnais in Paris, once the palace of Napoleon's stepson. Two urns near the doors are of Egyptian granite, made during the craze for Egyptian art that followed Napoleon's African campaign.

The Adam-style library is typical of the best work of the Adam brothers of England, who developed a classic design that has strong Roman influences. The chairs in this room once belonged to Pauline, a sister of Napoleon, and their upholstery is French tapestry from the looms of Beauvais. A remarkable eighteenth-century rug is from a loom set up in Madrid by Bourbon kings to emulate those of La Savonnerie in Paris. The room has a great mahogany bookcase of Sheraton design and a portrait by John Singleton Copley.

The reception room is in the style of Louis XV, with lacquered paneling from a home in Palermo, Italy. The plaster ceiling is from the Palazzo Rossi, built in Venice in 1750. A telephone room has Venetian furniture, a Spanish chest and carved walnut Umbrian columns of the sixteenth century.

The great hall recalls the Italian High Renaissance. The lofty wood ceiling is in the style of Sansovino, whose buildings skirt two sides of the famous Piazza di San Marco in Venice. The chandeliers are from a Spanish cathedral. The huge French chimney piece is from a château near Paris. Lions appear in the carvings of the room, also in the rugs and tapestries. One of the tapestries, woven in 1550 for Duke Ercole II of Ferrara, shows Hercules killing a lion. The long rug of the great hall is one of the finest existing Spanish carpets of the fifteenth century. It was made for a grandfather of Christopher Columbus's patron.

The east loggia has doors and ornaments from the Palazzo Torlonia in Rome. A dolphin table is from the Sciarra Palace in Rome and large blue-and-white fish bowls are seventeenth-century Chinese. The music room, which has a pipe organ that can fill the entire mansion with vibrant tones, has walls and ceiling from a home in Milan and a spinet made in Italy in 1645. In the great banquet hall are furniture and tapestries dating back to 1500, along with two Deering family portraits.

Upstairs, Mr. Deering's bedroom and sitting room are of restrained classical design, comparatively simple. But the bathroom is something to ogle, with its gold fixtures, marble tub, silver urns and a tentlike fabric canopy as a ceiling.

A hidden door of one of the first-floor loggias opens onto stairs leading to an unusual swimming pool that is partly under the mansion and partly outdoors. On the ceiling are murals and embedded in the concrete walls are thousands of sea shells.

The outside of the house, made partly of native coral, blends harmoniously with the formal gardens. In an Italian manner, the gardens are like a vast room,

John Singer Sargent was a friend of James Deering and painted this water color of him at Vizcaya.

open to the skies, somewhat as Frank Lloyd Wright might have planned them if he had lived three centuries ago. Walls, masonry, clipped hedges, statues and splashing fountains provide a place for gracious living rather than just a background for flowering plants.

The gardens are on several levels. There is a secret one, completely enclosed in sculptured walls, with stairs leading to hidden grottoes. A theater garden has a raised stage. A tea garden is circular and a fountain garden has a seventeenth-century fountain from Bassano di Sutri, near Rome.

A peacock bridge, suggestive of the Orient, has twisted columns surmounted by peacocks, the sculpture of Gaston La Chaise. Another noted artist, A. Stirling Calder, did extensive sculpture for the estate, including the symbolic figures on the great stone barge at the waterfront.

A casino has a ceiling painted by Paul Thevanez, a Swiss artist, in the manner of early Venetian painters. The casino, on some of the highest ground of the gardens, provides views of colorful scenery in all directions.

Mr. Deering had enjoyed all this for just ten years when he died in 1926 at the age of sixty-six while returning from Europe on the liner *Paris.* The cause of death was pernicious anemia, which prompted someone to observe that he probably didn't get enough spinach and "should have had a wife to tell him what to eat."

Vizcaya was inherited by Mr. Deering's two nieces, Mrs. Marion Deering McCormick of Chicago and Mrs. Barbara Deering Danielson of Boston. A nephew, Deering Howe of Chicago, also received an interest but the two nieces soon bought it. The estate was appraised at $17,572,000.

The mansion generally was vacant after Mr. Deering's death, since the nieces had homes of their own in Florida. Dade County, which includes Miami, acquired the property in 1952. Mr. Deering's two nieces gave $1,500,000 worth of furnishings to the county and accepted as payment for the mansion and its twenty-eight remaining acres a $1,000,000 mortgage, to be paid from revenues derived from opening the mansion as the Dade County Art Museum.

Despite its 110,000 paid admissions a year the mansion has not produced much revenue beyond that needed to pay the salaries of the operating staff and to make essential repairs. There has been a continuing default on the interest and amortization charges of the mortgage.

However, Mrs. McCormick and Mrs. Danielson apparently do not intend to foreclose the mortgage and Dade County scarcely would dare to part with this great tourist attraction. The Vizcayans, an organization of society leaders, historians and other volunteers, have collected thousands of dollars to renovate the rooms and make other improvements at the mansion and perform yeoman work as volunteers in its operation.

The hurricane of 1926 flooded the cellars and wrecked the heating plant; consequently for years the mansion was dank in stormy weather and many of the costly fabrics on walls and furniture were ruined. The cost of replacing some was large but the volunteers raised the money. The heating plant now has been replaced and the furnishings are again protected from dampness.

❉ ❉ ❉ ❉ ❉ ❉ ❉

Vizcaya is on South Bayshore Drive, near U. S. Route 1 and the Rickenbacker Causeway. It is open from 10 A.M. to 5 P.M. every day except Christmas. The admission fee for the house and gardens is $1.25 for adults, 75 cents for military personnel and 50 cents for children. The gardens alone may be seen for 25 cents.

The Taj Mahal of North America

Henry Morrison Flagler's Marble Casa

PALM BEACH • FLORIDA

Juan Ponce de Leon, who discovered Florida in 1513, changed his mind about the healthful aspects of the subtropical peninsula when he was hit by an Indian's deadly poisoned arrow. General William Tecumseh Sherman took one look at the mosquito-ridden wilderness and summarily decided that "this state is not worth a damn." John James Audubon, the naturalist, visited it and found that "all is mud, mud, mud or sand, sand, sand."

Henry Morrison Flagler was more optimistic about Florida when he saw its wild jungles, mangrove swamps and great stretches of white sand beaches. One glimpse of the 500-mile finger of land pointing toward the Caribbean, and he was fascinated. In 1883, when he was fifty-three years old and on a honeymoon at St. Augustine with his second wife, he decided to make the Atlantic coastline of Florida an American Riviera. With several business careers and grown children behind him in the North, he embarked on the new venture.

He had become a multimillionaire as a partner of John D. Rockefeller in the oil business. He used $50,000,000 of his fortune to become the fiscal patron saint of Florida, now one of the fastest growing states in the nation and the largest winter playground in the world.

While building Gold Coast hotels, railroads, utilities, churches, schools, libraries, hospitals and citrus industries, Mr. Flagler constructed at Palm Beach his great marble home, Whitehall, in 1902. The mansion was something of a tribute to a comely bride, his third wife, who was less than half his age. He also wanted to show Europeans that palaces could be built by Americans and to stimulate the building of more big homes in the Sunshine State.

The mansion, at first pulsing with gay conversation and brilliant social events, became a place of tragedy for Mr. Flagler, who could not keep up with all the social activities his wife wanted to pursue. Pathetically lonely, the feeble old man fell down the marble steps of the sumptuous palace and was fatally injured.

Whitehall has been called by some architects and historians the Taj Mahal of North America, a marble palace furnished with art treasures from many parts of the world. One biographer asserts that Mr. Flagler had intended to reproduce the mansion of Dominquez Cerro, one of Havana's most imposing structures. But so many rooms were wanted that the plan could not be used, except for a general arrangement of rooms around a large interior courtyard.

In planning Whitehall, Mr. Flagler told his architects that he wanted the finest home conceivable. Their conception cost him $2,500,000 for construction, at 1902 prices, and several millions more for the furnishings and art treasures, including some of the largest Oriental rugs ever woven.

After the death of Mr. Flagler in 1913 the mansion was converted into a luxury hotel, with a ten-story addition of 300 bedrooms built atop part of it. In 1959 his granddaughter, Mrs. Jean Flagler Gonzales, and others bought it for $1,500,000, restored it with many of its original furnishings and in 1960 opened it to the public. Plans were drafted to raze the ugly and now useless ten-story hotel addition.

Mrs. Gonzales and 600 other people celebrated the reopening with a gay affair typical of the Palm Beach social whirl that Mr. Flagler created and Whitehall now memorializes as a museum. Whitehall's reopening included a dinner and ball with soft Victor Herbert music, gold-liveried footmen in powdered wigs and costumed servants with stockings of various colors to indicate the chores they performed. The mansion, which had become something of a tomb to Mr. Flagler, again vibrated with gaiety.

The Flagler achievements that inspired the reincarnation of Whitehall include the man's canny realization that great things were in store for Florida. This is the state with the oldest history and the newest population, where Spanish conquistadors landed long before the Pilgrims reached Massachusetts, but it re-

Whitehall's gold-and-white Louis XV ballroom is ninety-one feet long and has French chandeliers and panels painted by Boucher. The platform was for entertainers.

mained for one man with vision and money to start the area toward becoming a mecca for ten times more American tourists than go to Europe.

The saga that led to the building of Whitehall began with the birth of Henry Flagler in 1830 at Hopewell, New York. His father, the Reverend Isaac Flagler, was an impoverished Presbyterian clergyman and farmer. The family, whose name had been Flegler, had come to America in the eighteenth century from Franconia in the German Palatinate.

Henry, slim, clear-eyed and blond, was groomed by his father to become a farmer. At the age of fourteen, however, the youth went to work for the L. G. Harkness store in Republic, Ohio, at five dollars a month. Later he became manager of a Harkness distillery. Always a teetotaler, he had trouble reconciling the production of whisky with his Puritanical beliefs but he did reach a friendly understanding with Mary Harkness, and married her.

After gaining and losing fortunes in the salt business and other ventures at Saginaw, Michigan, and Cleveland, Ohio, Mr. Flagler met a contemporary who, like himself, neither drank nor smoked and who believed in tough, dynamic, imaginative, speculative business — John D. Rockefeller. In partnership they, with others, began building the Standard Oil empire. When the company became one of the largest in the world, John D., asked if he had originated the idea, replied: "No, sir! I wish I'd had the brains to think of it, but it was Henry M. Flagler!"

In 1877, after ten years in the oil business, Mr. Flagler moved to New York in search of new ideas. In 1878 he took his wife to Jacksonville for her health and had his first glimpse of Florida. Amazed by the lack of adequate rail and hotel facilities, he decided to withdraw from the oil business and take a close look at the Sunshine State.

The first Mrs. Flagler died in 1881, being survived by Mr. Flagler and three children, one of whom was Harry M. Flagler, a patron of the arts and former president of the New York Symphony Society. It was his daughter, Mrs. Gonzales, who spearheaded the reincarnation of Whitehall as the Henry Morrison Flagler Museum. She is now president of the nonprofit private group that manages it.

In 1883 Henry Flagler married Ida Alice Shourds and they went to St. Augustine for a honeymoon. They were captivated by the Old World charm of the city and the warm, yet invigorating, climate. They were not long captivated by each other, but Mr. Flagler retained his enthusiasm for the new frontier and built the huge Ponce de Leon Hotel at St. Augustine, still a classic resort for tourists.

The hotel's great size, ornateness and interesting embellishments earned for its designers, John M. Carrere and Thomas Hastings, top architectural rank. They later designed Whitehall, many Flagler hotels, the Senate and House Office Buildings in Washington, the memorial amphitheatre in Arlington National Cemetery, and New York City's Public Library and Metropolitan Opera House.

As Mr. Flagler built more hotels between St. Augustine and Palm Beach he extended his Florida East Coast Railway to serve them. He bought other lines and linked the rail system with steamer traffic on the Indian River. After the great freeze of 1894, Mr. Flagler was urged by Mrs. Julia D. Tuttle, who had 640 acres of wilderness on Biscayne Bay, to extend the railroad as far as Fort Dallas, now Miami. To convince him that Fort Dallas was much warmer than Palm Beach, she sent sprigs of orange blossoms to him. That did it, and the line was soon extended.

Later Mr. Flagler built the railroad another 156 miles along a necklace of coral islands to Key West at a cost of 700 workmen's lives and $20,000,000. He opened the railroad in 1912 but it was wrecked by a hurricane in 1936 and the right-of-way now is used by the Overseas Highway, part of U. S. Route 1.

Red-haired, blue-eyed Ida Alice was thirty-five and Mr. Flagler fifty-three when they were married. His first wife's nurse, she wanted to become an actress; she had a fiery temper and few cultural interests. She could not understand her husband's interest in books and felt that his greatest asset was his fortune. She often gave $1,000 tips to servants. While spending the summer at Mamaroneck, New York, in 1894, Ida Alice talked so much about Mr. Flagler's impending death and what she called his infidelity that they separated. Ida also talked about her own great love for the Czar of Russia, who, the ouija board had informed her, was madly in love with her and was sending a costly cat's-eye diamond ring as a gift. Friends put her in a mental sanitarium.

After trying vainly to get a divorce in New York State, Mr. Flagler returned to Florida and secured the adoption there of a law permitting divorce from a spouse who has been insane for at least four years. He gave the Florida Agricultural College $10,000 for a new gymnasium and promptly divorced his second wife. Some people considered him sharp, scheming and unscrupulous. Others considered him a dedicated humanitarian, typical of this country's titans of business. His gifts to philanthropies were numerous. He built several churches, both Protestant and Roman Catholic.

His divorced wife remained in a sanitarium and died there in 1930 but she fared well from the investments Mr. Flagler had made for her; the assets grew from $2,373,137 to $15,247,925. Seven days after his divorce in 1901 Mr. Flagler announced he would marry Mary Lily Kenan of North Carolina. He was seventy-one and she was thirty-four. A woman of beauty, grace and charm, she played the

The French salon of Whitehall has Louis XVI décor. The elaborately carved woodwork has overlays of gold and silver.

piano, sang and had other cultural interests. Mr. Flagler had met her at a party in 1891 and subsequently he lavished gifts on her, causing many tongues to wag.

Mary Lily had always wanted a marble palace, big parties and high social position. Mr. Flagler wanted her to have everything that money could buy. He had Whitehall built for her in the incredibly short time of eight months. He seemed to have no concern for the bills as they rolled in. His favorite exclamation was "Thunder!" and he said nothing stronger, even when confronted on the same day by a huge new bill for imported marble and an unexpected multimillion-dollar tax on Standard Oil investments.

Whitehall occupies a six-acre tract facing Lake Worth, which is part of the inland waterway separating islands such as Palm Beach from the mainland. The selection of this site rather than one facing the outer ocean set a new fashion, for which many Palm Beach home owners have been thankful when hurricanes and high seas lashed the outer shore.

Whitehall's grounds are rimmed by a high, ornate wrought-iron fence imported from England. On the grounds are royal palms, hibiscus, orange trees and other native Florida vegetation mingled with rare plants from other lands. Grant R. Bedford, the executive director of Whitehall, has called the orange trees mute reminders of Mr. Flagler's aid to the citrus growers after frost had ruined their fruit.

"The growers," Mr. Bedford said, "were inclined to think 'Holy cow, I've had it and I'm going back to Ohio.' Mr. Flagler gave them new courage and opportunity by sending agents with thousands of dollars to reimburse growers for losses in the big freezes. Mr. Flagler was always business and he wanted the citrus business to continue."

J. E. Ingraham, one of the agents, distributed $200,000 to growers after one of the freezes. He told the growers that Mr. Flagler would not let "one man, woman or child starve."

The architectural style of Whitehall reflects the influence of Spain, as does the pattern of many Palm Beach mansions. The front has tall marble columns and broad marble steps. Mr. Flagler avoided using this stately colonnaded portico, preferring for himself and his guests a small personal entrance on the side of the house.

The colonnaded entrance, which opens directly into the great marble hall, 110 feet wide and 40 feet deep, faces a marble staircase that divides into two parts as it rises to the second floor. A small elevator is near by.

There are seven varieties of marble in the hall's walls and floors. Among the decorations are rare cameo medallions, early French tapestries, a Persian rug forty-two by twenty-seven feet, symbolic statuary and chairs and tables from the royal domiciles of Europe and Asia. Mr. Flagler's fondness for symbolic art is shown in the hall ceiling. A painting molded into the twenty-foot dome represents the "Crowning of Knowledge," but nobody is sure who painted it. Painted panels on the walls symbolize prosperity and happiness.

The great hall is one of seventy-three rooms in the mansion, which had fifty-four servants in its heyday as a home. Old-timers recall that Mr. Flagler used many of the servants as guards; the house was so large, three of these servants always met a guest at the door, one of them accompanying him until he was met and recognized by a member of the family.

Adjacent to the marble hall is an Italian Renaissance library with carved panels, massive fireplace and rich red tapestries. Mr. Flagler often asked guests if they had "seen the lions in the library," meaning the unusual resemblance of lions in the grain of the wood.

A broad doorway connects the library with the music room, which is in Louis XIV style. The room has a pipe organ that was, when Mr. Flagler bought it, the largest ever made for a private home. The domed ceiling of the room has a painting of the Aurora, with great crystal chandeliers casting a soft glow on lounges.

Organ music relaxed Mr. Flagler and the organists were among his favorite employees. When one of them sought a pay increase one day, Mr. Flagler said he would do even better for the man — he would make investments for him. Shortly afterward he took a group of wealthy business men and the organist on his yacht to Miami Beach. Pointing to the vast expanses of vacant sand dunes he asked his guests if they would buy some of the property. All rejected the offer except the organist, who later lived a life of luxury as the owner of Miami Beach acreage.

Near the music room is a billiard room of Swiss design. The grand French salon, across the marble hall, is done in the décor of Louis XVI and has an elaborately carved marble fireplace, a domed ceiling and the finest paintings and sculpture in the mansion.

The dining room is finished in warmly glowing satinwood. A long satinwood table is surrounded by chairs covered with Aubusson tapestry. Carvings on the cabinets are among the finest, and the silverware and Louis Phillippe Limoges china are exceptional.

A ballroom ninety-one by thirty-seven feet, with glittering chandeliers, mirrored walls, soft Boucher panels and Louis XV gold-and-white decorations is a room of splendor. It opens onto an interior courtyard, which has in the center a marble fountain of Susanna and the Elders. Carved stone tablets on the walls of the courtyard were part of a Spanish fort near Tallahassee more than two centuries ago. One of the tablets is dated 1719, the year that Fort San Marcos was rebuilt there after destruction by pirates.

The bedrooms of Whitehall are on the second floor. Mr. and Mrs. Flagler's is so large and has such a small dressing room that reports recently circulated that Mrs. Flagler never had worn the same gown twice. The truth is that she merely liked a small room for dressing, with gowns kept elsewhere in the house. Sixteen guest bedrooms and baths attest to the frequency of the Flagler's entertaining. Nearly all the guest rooms are of distinctive design, ranging from early Oriental to late Colonial.

Henry M. Flagler's stern character was reflected in his photographs at Whitehall. (Below) The fireplace and mantel in Whitehall's dining room are of François I design. The painting is of a French cavalier.

Mr. Flagler's favorite part of the house was the "stone area" facing Lake Worth and his yachts. This part of the house, atop which the hotel annex was built, had an office, a great stone terrace and an enclosed solarium. The kitchens and servants' rooms adjoin it.

In his later years Mr. Flagler spoke of the vastness of the mansion and said, "I wish I could swap all this for a little shack," but he enjoyed being pushed in a wheelchair around the house and through the gardens by George Conway, his English valet and companion. Mr. Flagler's eyesight was failing and the valet often read to him.

In 1913 Mr. Flagler attended a tea party in the solarium of Whitehall and then left for a washroom off the marble hall. Pulling open the door, he started down four marble steps into the washroom when he slipped and fell. He received a broken hip and other injuries that led to his death four months later at the age of eighty-three..

His estate exceeded $100,000,000, some of which was inherited by his widow. She married Robert W. Bingham, a Louisville publisher. Upon her death much of her fortune went to Mr. Bingham, who was a generous contributor to Democrat Woodrow Wilson's campaign funds — an ironic development, considering that Flagler had been an arch-Republican.

When Mr. Flagler's widow left Whitehall, the mansion was deeded to the Florida East Coast Railway and in 1925 was sold to a syndicate that converted it into a luxury hotel, the Whitehall. The addition that was built provided 300 bedrooms and the mansion itself provided space for a lobby, restaurant, ballroom, salon, library, lounge and de luxe suites.

Mrs. Gonzales and others felt it a shame that Whitehall was not preserved as a monument to the pioneer developer of Florida and as a treasure house of the art he had collected. They bought the property and began reassembling the original contents. When the ten-story hotel addition is razed the original waterfront façade of the mansion will be restored.

Whitehall currently is lent to community organizations as a meeting place and it is the home of the Palm Beach Historical Society and the Palm Beach Round Table.

✧ ✧ ✧ ✧ ✧ ✧ ✧ ✧

Whitehall is on Whitehall Way, Palm Beach. It is open to the public from 10 A.M. to 5 P.M. every day except Monday and on Christmas. The fees are $1 for adults, 50 cents for children and 25 cents for students in groups.

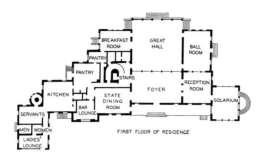

The main floor of Ca' d' Zan.

The second floor of the mansion.

John Ringling's mansion faces Sarasota Bay. The 200-foot terrace is marble, with different colors laid in a chevron pattern. (Opposite page) The inner court, or great hall, of Ca' d' Zan was the main living room. The floor has black marble from Belgium and white marble from Alabama. The chandelier was in the old Waldorf-Astoria Hotel in New York.

A Three-Ring Venetian Palazzo

John Ringling's Ca' d' Zan

SARASOTA · FLORIDA

JOHN RINGLING, the lusty, free-spending king of the American circus, fell in love with the West Coast of Florida. At Sarasota he built a Venetian palazzo that speeded the transformation of the cow-town of saloons and barnyards into a winter wonderland for tourists, much as Henry M. Flagler's *casa* had done at Palm Beach on the East Coast. Mr. Ringling called his home Ca' d' Zan — Venetian patois for House of John. At his death he left it as a legacy to Florida and now it is a star attraction of the state park system, visited by 250,000 persons a year.

While building his personal palace, Mr. Ringling dredged nearby bayous and built causeways, fond memories of Venice dominating his thoughts. He became something of a maharaja of the marshes as well as the king of the tanbark.

He established the winter headquarters of the circus at Sarasota, but his home, gardens and museum were remote from the race-track bugles and dance-floor trumpets of the East Coast. He gave to Sarasota the nucleus of what has become

Ringling 21

one of the finest centers of culture and most impressive assemblages of painters, writers and musicians in the Sunshine State.

But his home, like those of other titans, became a place of personal tragedy. While surrounded by $20,000,000 worth of art works, he heard the ominous knock of bill collectors at the front door of Ca' d' Zan and he wondered how the next grocery bill would be paid. He was stripped of control of the Ringling Brothers-Barnum and Bailey Combined Shows by friends he had trusted. His beloved first wife died and he became embroiled in an unfortunate second marriage which, however, gave him more thrills than the tanbark ever had.

John Ringling was born in McGregor, Iowa. His father, from Hanover, Germany, was a harness maker. The family name, Rungeling, remained so in this country until after a newspaper misspelled it "Ringling." When John and some of his brothers went into the circus business at Baraboo, Wisconsin, where the family finally settled, they adopted the newspaper's version of the name.

John's five older brothers, Albert, August, Otto, Alfred and Charles; his younger brother, Henry; and his younger sister, Ida, all appreciated Baraboo. They enjoyed fishing, reading, collecting violins, eating one-pound sirloin steaks for breakfast and building stark Midwest homes.

John wanted broader horizons. He roamed the world collecting acts for the circus, and he became the sport of the family — socially, financially, artistically and biologically. He told unabashedly of conning the strumpets in Chicago's sporting houses and after becoming a millionaire he devised ways to hoodwink hotel detectives who tried to prevent him from taking girls to his rooms. He shunned fraternizing with the girls in his shows, however; he felt such conduct would be undignified, bad for the shows and bad sportsmanship on his part. He was known as Mr. John in the show business and he wanted to keep it that way.

Traveling in Europe as a young man in the eighteen nineties, Ringling became interested in paintings. He began an intensive do-it-yourself education in art, visiting galleries, studying techniques and reading constantly. The knowledge he gained still amazes art connoisseurs.

The first picture he bought was one of a nude woman with a handful of cherries but his taste improved and he became one of the shrewdest buyers in the auction rooms of Europe. He assembled one of the largest and finest collections of paintings by Peter Paul Rubens. He also bought 500 works by Tintoretto, Rembrandt, Veronese, Reynolds, Gainsborough, Hals, El Greco, Velasquez and other masters. Admiring Michelangelo's statue of David in Italy, he had a copy almost twice as large made for himself. All the art objects now are part of the Ringling shrine.

Mr. Ringling also bought oil wells and railroads, sometimes while at the bar of the old Waldorf-Astoria Hotel in New York, which was on the site of the present Empire State Building. A deal made there one night with a new acquaintance from Oklahoma produced a quick $7,000,000 profit, and at one time Mr. Ringling's fortune was estimated at $100,000,000.

John and Mable Ringling were painted in water color at Ca' d' Zan by Savely Sorine.

In 1903, when he was thirty-seven years old, Mr. Ringling married Mable Burton, who had been a dancer in one of the circus acts. Eleven years his junior, she had a dark complexion and large laughing eyes in a piquant little face. John and Mable Ringling were constant and devoted admirers of each other throughout their marriage. When Mr. Ringling began buying land in Sarasota in 1912 he started to think about building a palace there for Mable and his art objects.

As he acquired culture, Mr. Ringling also gained polish. He shaved off his bushy mustachios, switched from store clothes to the latest fashions from Saville Row, filled his garages with Rolls Royces and Pierce-Arrows and stocked his cellar with vintage wines and Old Curio Scotch.

The thirty-seven acres of Ca' d' Zan, site of an earlier house before the present mansion was completed in 1926, are between the Tamiami Trail (U. S. Route 41) and Sarasota Bay. Across the bay is Longboat Key and, beyond that narrow spit of sand, the Gulf of Mexico.

Mr. Ringling also bought Bird, St. Armand, Coon and Otter Keys and several miles of Longboat, building a million-dollar causeway to link them. He also started a $2,000,000 Ritz Carlton hotel on Longboat; it was almost completed when the business slump of 1926 halted construction. Now it is an unsightly hulk among new homes, motels and the roaring bulldozers of Arthur Vining Davis, the Florida enthusiast who picked up the reins that Mr. Ringling and others dropped.

Several of the Ringling brothers ultimately moved to Sarasota, and intense jealousy developed between John and Charles. When John founded the Bank of Sarasota, Charles founded the Ringling Trust and Savings Bank. When John bought the big yacht *Zalophus,* Charles got a bigger one, the *Symphonia.* While John was planning Ca' d' Zan, Charles built near by a more orthodox mansion of classical Georgian design, which since has been converted into a college. But when John finally completed his home in 1926 it was, as it still is, the most grandiose showplace of the area.

Mable Ringling's bedroom has Louis XV furniture of inlaid sandalwood. Mrs. Ringling made the pillow covers of Venetian, Irish and Brussels laces she had collected.

A massive wrought-iron fence around Ca' d' Zan has a picturesque gateway of pink stucco and brown ashlar masonry, embellished with glazed tile and the name of the estate. Near the mansion are a Venetian museum that houses the bulk of Ringling's art works, a museum of circus relics, and the Asolo Theatre, which was built on a hill near Venice in 1798, brought to Florida in pieces in 1949 and reconstructed by the state on its present site in 1957.

When they enter the grounds of the mansion, visitors pass into a world of nostalgic homage to the Italy John and Mable Ringling adored. Hundreds of small statues from Venice line the walks and driveways, and more are interspersed among hibiscus, live oaks, bougainvillaea, poinsettias, oleanders, banyans and palms.

Mable Ringling had much to do with the designing of the mansion. She talked first with Thomas R. Martin, a Sarasota architect. Mr. Martin's son, Frank, made the preliminary drawings. Then Dwight James Baum of New York took over the final planning. The Ringlings, who had recently been in Italy, had a trunk full of brochures, drawings and photographs of the type of palace they wanted.

Mr. Ringling thought at first that "just a little palace" would suffice but his wife wanted something resembling the Doge's Palace in Venice and the old Madison Square Garden in New York, in which Mr. Ringling had an interest. Stanford White, the architect, was a close friend of Mr. Ringling and had incorporated in the Garden some of the Doge's ideas. As a crowning feature, Mrs. Ringling wanted a tower such as the old Garden had, but this plan had to be modified for reasons of cost, although the mansion now has a tower that dominates the skyline.

While the house was being built, the Ringlings induced Willy Pogany, the Hungarian artist and stage designer, to plan a ceiling for the third-floor game room that would show them in carnival attire, as they had seen the figures of owners on the ceilings of big Italian homes. Mr. Pogany later also painted figures of dancers on the ceiling of the first-floor ballroom.

Mr. Baum faced a special problem in finding materials suitable in colors and textures for the complex Venetian structure and still able to endure the intensity of the Florida sunshine. He chose for the exterior a rose-cream stucco accented by glazed terra-cotta medallions and moldings, with decorative corbels supporting the balconies and cornices. The adornments were painted at the kilns in soft red, yellow, green, blue and ivory tints, then glazed and baked to give the effect of fine faience.

Cast stone, marble with a subtle lavender cast and ashlar masonry of many tints also were used on the exterior of the building, its steps and terraces. The Venetian terrace on the waterfront, where Mrs. Ringling kept an authentic gondola until a hurricane wrecked it, is 200 feet long and paved with imported and domestic marbles of many colors, set in a spectacular chevron pattern.

From Barcelona, Mr. Ringling brought thousands of old red barrel tiles for the roof of Ca' d' Zan and related buildings. Ships were chartered to transport the tiles to Florida's ports of Tampa and Miami.

The house, 200 feet long, is topped by the tower, which rises 61 feet. Mr. Ringling always had a light shining as a beacon from it when he was at home.

John Ringling's bedroom is in French Empire style. On the ceiling is a large painting of a mythological subject.

The state dining room of the Ringling mansion has over the fireplace a tondo in the style of Della Robbia. The painting on the right wall is Granieri's "Crowded Marketplace."

Terra-cotta balustrades, columns veneered with Mexican onyx from Southern California and rounded arches add to the exterior something of the appearance of the Doge's palace.

A chief attraction currently is a bas-relief on the exterior of the house, near the front door, showing the easily recognizable life-size nude figures of John and Mable Ringling as Adam and Eve. Mr. Ringling blushed deeply when he first saw what the architects had done.

"Jesus!" he exclaimed. "Something has got to be done about that!"

So a workman added a fig leaf to the sculptured figure of Adam Ringling. However, when Florida took over the mansion, park officials would not endorse such prudery and the fig leaf was removed.

Ca' d' Zan cost Ringling $1,650,000 to build, and he spent about the same amount for the adjacent art museum. Art dealers estimate that he spent something over $3,000,000 for paintings and other art objects and that today they are worth over $20,000,000. A Frans Hals Mr. Ringling bought in Europe for $100,000 was sought by Andrew Mellon for $300,000 when it reached New York, but the offer was rejected and the picture went to Sarasota instead of to the National Gallery of Art in Washington.

Entertaining at Ca' d' Zan was on a grand scale. Visitors included Florenz Ziegfeld and his wife Billie Burke, James J. Walker, Alfred E. Smith, Will Rogers, Tex Rickard, Irvin S. Cobb and other prominent persons of politics and the entertainment world who could match Mr. Ringling's quick wit and storytelling skill. Adjacent to the dining room is a barroom — walls, bar, cabinets, windows and brass rail — that Mr. Ringling brought intact from the old Cicardi's Winter Garden Restaurant in St. Louis.

Many windows elsewhere in the mansion have panes of hand-blown Venetian glass, tinted in shades of rose, amethyst, purple, green, blue and straw. Some of the arched bronze frames of the windows were bought in Italy by the Ringlings. A two-and-one-half-story interior court served as a main living room for the Ringlings. As in many Italian palaces, this court is a central, unifying architectural feature for the entire building. Thirty main rooms and fourteen baths spread out from it. Kitchens and servants' quarters are in a wing.

Ca' d' Zan's interior court, or great hall, is remarkable for its coffered ceiling of Florida pecky cypress in Renaissance style, framing an inner skylight of colored glass. A large glittering chandelier is from the old Waldorf-Astoria and doors are from the old John Jacob Astor house in New York. The pillars are of Mexican onyx. The marble floor is laid in checkerboard squares; the black ones are from Belgium, and white from Alabama. A balcony at second-floor level reaches around three sides of the interior court and gives access to the principal bedrooms.

John Ringling liked Michelangelo's statue of David so much that he had it copied, nearly twice as large, for the garden of the museum he built beside his home.

Tapestries in the court and other rooms are seventeenth-century Flemish; there are many notable wood carvings, statues and other art objects. A collection of curios and jewelry was obtained by Mr. Ringling from Mrs. Oliver H. P. Belmont. A $50,000 Aeolian organ, played electrically as well as manually, can fill the entire mansion with rich and sonorous tones. Its hundreds of pipes are concealed behind tapestries in the court.

Much of Ca' d' Zan's furniture was acquired in New York from the Vincent Astor and Jay Gould collections. It reflects Renaissance influences and the styles of Louis XIV, XV and XVI. The ballroom has a golden splendor, with walls of yellow brocade blending with the Willy Pogany ceiling. In it is an Italian harpsichord made in 1652. Other rooms include a solarium and a breakfast room.

Mr. Ringling's bedroom on the second floor, which had a private elevator, is decorated in French Empire style, with gilded framework on doors and windows, a floor of black marble and a ceiling painting of a mythological subject. The circus king's wardrobe is on display in a closet.

Off the bedroom is an ornate bath, with walls of yellow Siena marble, a tub hewn from a solid block of the same stone and fixtures plated with gold. A modern barber's chair, where Mr. Ringling was shaved every morning by his valet, stands, an anachronism, near the tub.

Near Mr. Ringling's bedroom are the bedrooms of his first and second wives, each different. Mable's furniture is of inlaid sandalwood in the style of Louis XV, with pillow covers made by her from Venetian, Irish and Brussels laces she had collected. The second wife's furniture is made of gray lacquered wood, carved in a rococo style fashionable in American homes at the end of the nineteenth century. Mr. Ringling's office on the second floor has an oversize chair, portraits of his family, a revolving bookcase and an embossed silver telephone.

Ringling was a robust six-footer who would eat twelve oranges and five grapefruit at a sitting, wearing a bib and washing his hands in a basin that the butler provided. He liked all desserts, provided they were made of ice cream. His favorite dish was hash — any kind of hash. He would hire a servant merely because he was an experienced hash maker.

The end of a Florida land boom in the late nineteen twenties ushered in a dark period in John Ringling's life. Mable died in 1929 after only three years in Ca' d' Zan. She was younger than he, so he had never contemplated life without her. He said he could never feel gay again, but he saw Mrs. Emily Haag Buck, a widow, lose $32,000 one night at Monte Carlo and later that year he married her.

Just before the ceremony Mr. Ringling had Emily sign a waiver of rights to his estate, since he was determined to give Ca' d' Zan and the adjacent museum to the public as a memorial to Mable and himself. The ink of the marriage certificate was barely dry when Emily tore up the waiver. The two were soon in court, with sensational charges and countercharges flying back and forth.

Another crushing blow for Ringling was his loss of control of the family's circus. He refused to sell even one of his valuable paintings when hard-pressed for cash after the stock-market crash of 1929, believing that good times were just around the corner.

His financial troubles led to loss of a lease on the new Madison Square Garden in New York to a rival show, the American Circus Corporation. He turned the tables by buying the American Circus Corporation, but in the process he saddled himself with a $1,700,000 note that he later could not meet.

Ousted from his throne, Mr. Ringling saw a group headed by Sam Gumpertz and other persons he had once trusted take control of the circus. Years later, John Ringling North, a nephew, regained family control.

In his comparative poverty (although he had art treasures he could have sold), Mr. Ringling retired to Ca' d' Zan to live with a skeleton staff of servants. Shortly before his death he was driven in his Rolls Royce to Pensacola, to see the first big circus parade he had witnessed in fifteen years. He stared at it with a faraway look, tears cascading down his cheeks, then asked quietly to be driven back to Ca' d' Zan.

When he died in 1936 he had $311 in the bank, although his estate was later appraised at $23,500,000. Ca' d' Zan and related buildings were willed to the state. Emily was left one dollar. Their divorce suit was near completion when he died. There was long litigation over the estate but Florida obtained full possession of Ca' d' Zan and the other buildings in 1946.

✿　✿　✿　✿　✿　✿　✿　✿

The entrance to the Ringling residence and other buildings is from U. S. Route 41. The buildings are open from 9 A.M. to 4:30 P.M. Monday through Saturday and from 12:30 P.M. to 4:30 P.M. Sunday, except on Christmas and Thanksgiving. Guided tours of the residence are conducted. The admission fee at the residence is $1 and a combination ticket for all the buildings is $2. Children under twelve are admitted free.

John Ringling was aghast when he discovered that the architects had portrayed him and his wife as Adam and Eve on the front of the mansion.

Frank Lloyd Wright and his third wife, Olgivanna, received visitors in front of the living-room fireplace at Taliesin North.

Taliesin North is a low, rambling residence. Many of the walls are of native stone. Trees grow through some of the roofs, with special holes made for them.

The House of the Seven Murders

Taliesin North, the Home of Frank Lloyd Wright

SPRING GREEN · WISCONSIN

IT WILL BE many a day before people stop arguing as to whether Frank Lloyd Wright was the greatest architect in the modern world. There is little doubt, however, that of all the geniuses identified with the visual arts in America he has had a greater influence on the daily lives of more people than any contemporary.

There is something of the legacy of Mr. Wright's creative thinking in a ranch house that merges pleasantly into the greenery of a hillside, a low-ceilinged entrance hall that opens dramatically into a soaring cathedral-like living room, a clerestoried window that casts soft light on an inviting lounge, a massive fireplace that warms the heart as well as the hand, eaves that lack downspouts so that long icicles dangle from them like stalactites, rooms that flow freely together, a picture window that overlooks treetops, a living room that is closely integrated with outside terraces and walled gardens, a carport that supplants a garage, roofs that have trees growing through them, or a fascinating juxtaposition of organic materials that blend harmoniously with nature.

A revolutionist in architecture, Mr. Wright undertook to tear America away from its traditional square, rococo, ornate, painted and regimented housing, as well as from its conventional museums, office structures and schools. He also undertook to fight the common concepts of personal morality, although he had a set of ideals based in Wrightian logic and sincerity that he would stack up against any man's.

In these two great adventures his nonconformist activities merged to produce Taliesin North, his fifty-room home in the wooded hills of the dairy country at Spring Green, Wisconsin. Although not the most spectacular of the 700 structures that he built, it is considered by some experts to be his greatest and most interesting. It incorporates his basic concepts of architecture and it was steadily revised to meet his tastes throughout the forty-eight years that he lived there.

The revisions in his thinking at Taliesin were punctuated by two big fires. One of the fires was accompanied by seven murders, committed by a distraught employee. The other one found Mr. Wright on the roof with blistering feet, while lightning crackled around his head and he recalled the punishments of Isaiah. The changes in Taliesin also were punctuated by the arrival of the sheriff with foreclosure notices and accusations that Mr. Wright had violated the Mann Act, which concerns the transporting of women across state boundaries for immoral purposes. Consequently, Taliesin was one of the busiest mansions in America.

After bitter debate, the American Institute of Architects finally conferred its highest honor on Mr. Wright. But many persons still are annoyed by the architecture that Taliesin typifies and by Mr. Wright's acerbic pronouncements that Washington as a city should be razed and started anew; that the Air Force Academy in Colorado is a collection of factories; that the University of Mexico should be dynamited; and that New York City's Metropolitan Museum is a barn, the Seagram Building a whisky bottle on stilts, the United Nations Secretariat a gravestone, Rockefeller Center a crime against humanity and Wall Street the plague spot of America.

Mr. Wright was born near Taliesin, a son of William R. C. Wright, an Amherst College graduate, preacher, medical scholar, musician and teacher. The father taught his son to love Bach and Beethoven, and to be an independent thinker. When the boy was sixteen years old the father one night packed his suitcase, tucked his violin under his arm and left home, never to be seen again by his wife and three children.

The building of Taliesin stemmed from many influences. Important ones were those of Mr. Wright's mother and of three women he loved. His mother, Anna Lloyd-Jones Wright, was a schoolteacher and a descendant of Welsh preachers and farmers who had chosen the lush countryside of Wisconsin to settle in because it resembled Wales. Anna decided before Frank was born that he was to be a boy and an architect. To give force to the prenatal determination she hung pictures of the majestic cathedrals of England in the room the unborn child was to occupy.

The Lloyd-Jones clan, too, was proud of its independence. One of its mottoes was "Truth Against the World." Anna stimulated Frank's independent creativity by having him play with Froebel Blocks, designed by the Friedrich Froebel of educational fame. The blocks made him aware of color and form, and when he later was building Taliesin he commented that "those blocks seem to stay in my hands all my life."

Working for nineteen dollars a month on his Uncle James' farm, Mr. Wright learned another motto of the clan that is symbolized in Taliesin: "Add Tired to Tired." He later worked for a contractor in Madison, forty miles from Spring Green, and then in Chicago for Louis Sullivan, the noted architect. Shunning the traditional concepts of Richard Morris Hunt and Charles Follen McKim, who were building castles in the East, he made balanced compositions with plain bricks, concrete masses and unpainted timber.

In 1891 Mr. Wright built his first personal home. It still stands as a landmark at Forest and Chicago Avenues in the Oak Park area of metropolitan Chicago. He had just married Catherine Tobin, who was to give him four sons and two daughters but was not to become one of the influential women of Taliesin.

While other architects were thinking in terms of Gothic castles, Renaissance palaces and Romanesque strongholds, Mr. Wright broke completely with the past to design for his bride at Oak Park a horizontal "house of the prairies" in a style that became known as Usonian. The twenty-room structure has many of the continuing Wrightian devices — low lines, deep eaves, walled gardens, windows in rows, and bricks and timbers of earthy colors. It originally had a large willow tree growing through the roof.

In this house Mr. Wright experimented with a dramatic scheme, later used at Taliesin and in hundreds of other houses, of having a small entry open suddenly into a large, high room with a balcony and many points of interest. The effect of entering such a room is as exhilarating as drinking three Scotch highballs, some owners contend.

The high room at Oak Park was designed as a playroom and in it Mr. Wright, his wife and six children played classical music together, he at the piano and the others on drums, horns and string instruments. Wright was a good father and an energetic provider and the house was a joyous one.

It still is a joyous one. For the last twenty years it has been the home of Mr. and Mrs. C. W. Nooker, whose labor of love has been to maintain it in the colors and with the Oriental rugs and simple furnishings such as Mr. Wright had used. He visited the Nookers and was pleased. The Nookers are happy with their possession except when tourists annoy them for a view of the house. "You wouldn't lock up the Mona Lisa, would you?" one stranger said petulantly when told it was not convenient at the moment to admit him.

Frank Lloyd Wright's study at Taliesin North shows the organic design of the structure and the blending of indoors and outdoors.

Wright enthusiasts are that way. They have arrived at some Wright-designed houses with ladders to peek in windows, on horses to jump hedges and in buses to invade homes as though the properties were part of the public domain and the owners were caretakers. One woman told of leaving her bathroom with only a towel draped loosely around her to find a stranger with a yardstick in the living room measuring the floor size.

Having broken with the architectural past, Mr. Wright interrupted his personal life spectacularly in 1909. Selling his Japanese prints and other valuable possessions to get quick cash, he eloped to Europe with Mamah Borthwick Cheney. She was the comely wife of one of his best clients. Edward H. Cheney, a manufacturer of electrical equipment, and the mother of two young children.

When her husband was on the high seas, Mrs. Wright said her heart was still with him. Mr. Cheney took a dimmer view of the event. So did the preachers of the nation, who dealt in sermons on the errors of "affinity fools" and "soul mates."

From this crisis in the life of Frank Lloyd Wright, Taliesin began to grow. When he and Mrs. Cheney returned from Italy, the adverse publicity and the loss of contracts from husbands with pretty wives convinced him that Oak Park was not the place to live. His mother then gave him the 200 acres of family farms at Spring Green, later increased by Mr. Wright to 4,000 acres.

So he planned a mansion for himself and the woman who was being discussed from pulpits as a creation of dressmakers, dancing academies, hairdressers and the devil. When the first part of the house was finished he invited newspapermen to come and see it for themselves. He was in a purple robe and Mrs. Cheney in an Oriental gown as they met the reporters. He intended to be Mrs. Cheney's protector the rest of his life, he said, and she was his loyal comrade. Mr. Cheney divorced his wife, but Mrs. Wright balked at a divorce, so there was no marriage at Taliesin.

Taliesin was the name of a Welsh bard who sang the glories of the fine arts. The name means "Shining Brow" and Mr. Wright thought it was especially appropriate for his home. No house, he said, should be on top of a hill but just on the brow, where he built Taliesin. A mansion of fifty rooms, a score of baths and a dozen fireplaces, it so harmonizes with the landscape that it seems to have grown there.

As Taliesin rose he spoke of the modeling of the house merging with the modeling of the hills, becoming woven into a fabric that included the greenery of summer, the snows of winter and the glorious blaze of autumn. Architecture should be in league with the land so that each could be happier because of the other.

Rock outcroppings on the brow of the hill were exploited to produce a "natural house" among the birches, the pines and the cedars. A stone quarry a mile from the house provided a sandstone of the yellowish, earthy color that Mr. Wright favored using inside and outside his houses. Local workmen, most of them novices in construction, were taught how to build the house walls and the gardens so they harmonized with the natural ledges of rock.

Taliesin became a home and a workshop inside a garden, with a mass of apple blossoms behind the house in the spring and perfume of the orchard drifting down the valley. The exterior wood trim of the house and the shingles were treated with preparations so that they blend with the silver-gray trees in the violet light at sunset.

The chimneys of the great stone fireplaces rise heavily through the house wherever the rooms have gathering places for people. Outside, they are quiet rock masses bespeaking strength. Mr. Wright soon had the country masons setting a few stones in place, then stepping back to view the effect as a sculptor might look critically at his creation. The virtuoso cussing of Ben Davis, commander of the crew, stimulated the workmen and amused Mr. Wright.

One of the master carpenters was William Weston, whose dexterity, intelligence and co-operative attitude so impressed Mr. Wright that he was appointed superintendent of the estate. He remained at Taliesin fourteen years.

No gutters or downspouts were permitted on the house. Mr. Wright wanted it to be a frosted palace in winter, with six-foot icicles hanging from the roof and glistening with prismatic colors as the sun struck them. Persons outside the large windows could look over banks of snow and through the icicles to see the bright reflections of wood fires.

Each of the rooms was designed so that the sun would stream in at some hour of the day, the windows of every room opening onto treetops to admit the fragrance of foliage and the singing of birds in summer. The rooms have built-in bookcases, nooks and other places of interest, all in woods of natural color, but they have little provision for paintings and etchings. "Pictures," Mr. Wright said, "deface walls oftener than they decorate them."

He moved seven grand pianos into Taliesin, however, and on one occasion said: "What I call integral ornament is founded upon the same organic simplicities as Beethoven's Fifth Symphony — that amazing revolution in tumult and splendor of sound. Architecture is like music."

One of the organic simplicities at Taliesin is the Wrightian device of trees growing through roofs. Others are floors paved with slabs of stone or made of broad cypress planks, and plaster mixed with raw sienna to give the walls a tone of natural tawny gold. The outside walls have the same tone.

The furnishings of Taliesin generally are simple and occasionally Oriental. Thin tan-colored flax rugs were used at first by Mr. Wright but later he removed them to expose the severe simplicity of the floors of stone and wide planks. The lack of elegant furnishings is not apparent in the living room because of its many points of interest, including a high and irregular ceiling, clerestoried windows, built-in bookcases, an inviting fireplace, lounges, picture windows and furniture made by Taliesin craftsmen.

As Mr. Wright expressed it, Taliesin is not a flamboyant display of extravagance but a pleasant house of the North, low, wide and snug in seeking fellowship with its surroundings. In the summer, he said, it should be open like a camp, with the rain beating rhythmically on the roof and the wide eaves permitting the door and windows to be left open even during the severest storms.

For his extraordinary library and collection of Japanese prints that he was again assembling, Mr. Wright installed in Taliesin a huge fireproof stone vault. The table silver and other valuables, however, did not have the protection that items vital to Mr. Wright's profession received.

The halls and the stairs bear another Wrightian trademark. Trimmed to his size, which was five-feet-eight-inches tall and not very wide, they are not intended for the comfortable passage of taller and bulkier persons. Some visitors in Wright houses say the rapid changes of heights and widths are oppressive. Others find them delightful. The variations and the points of interest they emphasized were an encouragement to relaxation for Mr. Wright.

All seemed to be serene and settled at Taliesin in the summer of 1914. Then a horrendous event occurred on a sultry afternoon in mid-August. Mr. Wright had gone to Chicago on business. Mrs. Cheney's two children, John, ten, and Martha, twelve, were visiting her at Taliesin.

She and the children were sitting at a luncheon table on a screened terrace. They were served soup by a thin-lipped Barbadian Negro named Julian Carleton, who worked in the kitchen with his wife, Gertrude. He had been complaining about the hardship of working in the isolation of the Wisconsin countryside and had induced his wife to give notice that they would soon quit their jobs. After serving the soup to the three Cheneys and to six Taliesin employees in a service dining room he sloshed gasoline on the kitchen floor and tossed a lighted match into it.

Screaming maniacally and brandishing a hatchet, Carleton ran to the terrace and killed Mrs. Cheney and her son, John. Pursuing the little girl to a lower terrace he slew her there. Mr. Weston, the estate superintendent, ran from the service dining room and tried to overpower Carleton but was knocked down by a blow of the hatchet and then saw his son, Ernest, thirteen, killed. David Lindblom, a workman, tried to put out the fire in the house, then ran to the yard with his clothes afire, and there he was killed by the raving Barbadian. Emil Brodelle, a draftsman, also was slain but Herbert Fritz, another draftsman, received only a broken arm and rolled down an embankment to save his life. Thomas Brunker, a workman, fleeing with his clothes afire, was overtaken and killed. Soon most of the house burst into flames, although some of it ultimately was saved by farmers who rushed to Taliesin with pumps and hoses.

Mr. Wright received some of the tragic news in Chicago by telephone and the rest from newspaper headlines as he rode by train toward Spring Green. For a person of less stamina the disaster would have been overwhelming. In a matter of minutes the things dearest to his heart had been wiped out. That night he spent on a cot in a house near the ruins of Taliesin, rising many times before dawn to pace the floor and ponder the future.

The next day some of the neighbors spat tobacco juice on the ruins of Taliesin and muttered that Mr. Wright finally had received what was coming to him. But they joined him in organizing armed posses to search for the killer, who had vanished. One of the searchers finally found Carleton inside the huge furnace of Taliesin, his lips and throat burned by muriatic acid that he had swallowed. He muttered something about wanting to die, and his wish was fulfilled a few hours later in jail.

Taliesin North was built in 1911 and rebuilt after fires in 1914 and 1925. The main residence is on the right. Studios and estate buildings are to the left.

Feeling that a funeral ceremony for Mamah would be a mockery, Mr. Wright decided to bury her with his own hands in utmost simplicity in the family cemetery at Taliesin. He had the Taliesin carpenters make a simple pine box of unfinished boards, cut flowers from her favorite garden and put them in the box. His son John helping, he lifted Mamah into the box and put more flowers on top. In a spring-wagon drawn by his favorite horses, he took the box to the cemetery. He lowered it into the grave and asked everyone to leave before he covered it with earth and flowers. He stood there until after sunset, then he walked slowly up the hill to the charred walls of Taliesin — and to his plans for reconstruction of the house.

Thousands of letters, most of them sympathetic, were received by Mr. Wright. One that especially impressed him was from Mrs. Miriam Noel, a sculptress who was divorced and had three grown children. He answered it, and less than six months after the fire, Mrs. Noel moved into the rebuilt Taliesin as its new mistress.

All was not blissful at Taliesin, however, as Mr. Wright continued to work on it with Mrs. Noel. He declared that she made his life there "a perfect hell." Hoping that it would restore happiness, he finally married her when his wife consented to a divorce. The ceremony took place in the middle of a bridge spanning the Wisconsin River, supposedly to symbolize the bridging of the differences of the bridal couple. Miriam later moved to California and started a series of lawsuits that were to pester Mr. Wright for many years.

One pleasant experience for him in this period was a meeting with Albert M. Johnson, president of the National Life Insurance Company of America and the financial backer of Death Valley Scotty's Castle in California. Mr. Johnson wanted Mr. Wright to build in Chicago a "virgin skyscraper," different from any ever before built. The two men journeyed to California to visit the desert castle but the skyscraper was not built.

At a performance of Russian dancing in Chicago, Mr. Wright met Olga Iovanova Lazovich Hinzenberg, a vivacious Montenegrin divorceé who had come to the United States with her daughter, Svetlana. He was fascinated. For the next thirty-two years, Olgivanna, as she called herself, was his constant and devoted companion. Miriam charged that Mr. Wright's new alliance violated the public order of Wisconsin but the sheriff could not locate him at Taliesin — or did not want to locate him. Later, however, the sheriff of Hennepin County, Minnesota, found Mr. Wright, Olgivanna and Svetlana at a resort cottage. Also present was Mr. Wright's and Olgivanna's infant daughter, Iovanna. The sheriff took them all to jail and there was talk of prosecution under the Mann Act but good sense intervened and the case was dropped. In 1927 Miriam at last consented to a divorce and one year later Mr. Wright and Olgivanna were married.

The second big fire at Taliesin, in 1925, was believed to have been started by defective wiring in Mr. Wright's bedroom. He joined with others in fighting the flames as a high wind fanned them. Trying to spur the firefighters to greater

Relaxing at Taliesin North, Frank Lloyd Wright is sitting beside a stone lion from China, one of his Oriental treasures 4,000 to 5,000 years old.

efforts to save the house, he climbed to the roof with a hose. His feet were burned, his lungs seered, his hair and eyebrows scorched. Suddenly the wind changed, lightning flashed, thunder rumbled and a torrent of rain put out the flames. Salvaging charred marble heads, Ming pottery and other relics from the ashes, Mr. Wright began weaving plans for another reconstruction of Taliesin.

Meanwhile, his financial difficulties threatened to destroy Taliesin more effectively than fire ever had. He borrowed $20,000 at a time to drive the sheriff from the door but besides paying his bills he would also use the money for new pianos, fur-lined coats and costly Oriental curios. In 1929 he needed $75,000 to save Taliesin from the bankers and his friends helped him get the money. In 1955 the Wisconsin Supreme Court ruled that Taliesin, although used partly for training architects, was not an educational institution within the meaning of the law and was subject to normal taxes, of which Mr. Wright owed $18,000. His reply to the people of Wisconsin was: "Very well. I'll tear down Taliesin and leave the land idle. Let the tax people collect on that."

Friends organized a banquet, at which $10,000 was raised to save Taliesin and the people gave Mr. Wright a standing ovation. Deeply touched, he continued living and working at Taliesin. When he died in 1959, he was buried in the family cemetery at the foot of the hill. The simple grave is marked by a slab of the native stone like that used in Taliesin.

In 1932 Mr. Wright set up the Taliesin Fellowship, which his widow now heads, for the training of apprentices in "essential architecture." As part of the training the apprentices also study philosophy, sculpture, painting, music and the industrial arts. School buildings are apart from the residence. Small Wrightian varieties of homes for the students also have been built, and visitors staring into the picture windows often find young bearded scholars from many nations staring back at them.

In the nineteen thirties Mr. Wright bought large acreage on the desert at Scottsdale, Arizona. He built a winter home, Taliesin West, as a sprawling structure that merged with the desert just as the other home merges with the Wisconsin countryside. He called the desert architecture "pole and Gothic." The Taliesin Fellowship now holds winter sessions at the Arizona house.

At Taliesin North, Mr. and Mrs. Wright perfected a system under which students perform all the chores of operating the establishment. They wait on table, cook, garden and build. The work is supposed to be healthful and character-building, thus making the students "complete human beings" fit to become great architects.

The construction and reconstruction never ceased at Taliesin. Mr. Wright had a constant flow of ideas for changes, and the noise of saws and hammers was music to his ears.

Most of the students approve the manual labor and everything else Mr. Wright stood for. Occasionally there have been revolts. An Italian prince studying at Taliesin balked at serving a visiting compatriot who was only a marquis. On another occasion an Oriental who, after sawing wood for three months, demanded, "When do I start on organic architecture?" and was told that he had been doing it for three months, packed his bags and departed.

Young persons at Taliesin most likely to develop a "creative conscience," according to Mr. Wright, quickly learned to "pile tired on tired" and to demonstrate possession of: an honest ego in a healthy body; a love of truth and nature; courage and sincerity; ability to act decisively; fertility of imagination; a capacity for faith and rebellion; a disregard of commonplace elegance; and instinctive co-operation.

"And always remember," Mr. Wright cautioned his apprentices, "that the physician can bury his mistakes but the architect can only advise his clients to plant vines."

Not many owners of Wright houses have planted vines to conceal errors, and there are none at Taliesin. But quite a few owners have built high fences and acquired watchdogs to gain privacy from Mr. Wright's legion of enthusiastic disciples armed with cameras and yardsticks.

✦   ✦   ✦   ✦   ✦   ✦   ✦   ✦

Taliesin is near State Route 23 at Spring Green, Wisconsin. It is the personal home of Mrs. Wright in the summer but most of the grounds and the buildings may be seen by visitors from early May to late November. A custom is to charge $1 a person for conducted tours on Saturdays and Sundays.

The Miles Brewton house, a military headquarters in the Revolutionary and Civil wars, was the birthplace of the Historic Charleston Foundation. (Right) The Waterford crystal chandelier of the Miles Brewton house is one of the most remarkable in America.

It Happened Here . . .

A Galaxy Under the Guns of Sumter

CHARLESTON · SOUTH CAROLINA

"JUST NAME IT and they have got it here, whether it's architecture, history, gardens, plantations, romance or just plain drama," a world-traveler declared as he reviewed the distinctions of houses in South Carolina's low country at Charleston.

The mansions in this galaxy are not enormous in size, nor do they reflect much of the modern architectural thinking about housekeeping comforts, single-floor efficiency and the integration of indoor-outdoor living. Despite touches of modernization here and there, they are a constellation of another era — and the people of Charleston are exceptionally proud of it. The houses memorialize the quality of early American designs and the spectacular events that occurred within the walls.

Along the crooked streets on the city's peninsula, where the Ashley and Cooper Rivers converge to flow into the Inland Waterway and the Atlantic, there are houses with cannon balls of the Revolutionary and Civil wars embedded in roofs, walls and gardens. There are houses that are grim reminders of financial panics, slavery, political bloodshed and offenses against the morals of mankind. And there are houses held together by iron rods and emergency underpinnings because of the ravages of hurricanes, floods, earthquakes and the cannonading from Fort Sumter.

Asked to pinpoint one mansion that would have the most to tell if it could talk, an officer of the Historic Charleston Foundation replied quickly and positively, "The Miles Brewton house at 27 King Street. Its walls could tell the story of Charleston right down to the present moment. Six generations of one family have lived in the house and every generation has contributed something different to it."

Miles Brewton, born at Charleston in 1731, became a merchant prince with $500,000 in the bank early in life. While operating a mercantile business and shipping lines to Europe he became a member of the Commons House of the colony and was repeatedly re-elected. In 1759 he married Mary Izard, herself the inheritor of a fortune large by the standards of that era.

The Brewtons went to Europe to plan the King Street house and to buy furnishings for it. They chose Georgian architecture, and in 1765 the construction was begun. The chief planner was Ezra Waite, a London builder and wood carver brought to Charleston by the Brewtons. Also from England came red bricks, gray stone, red tile, colored flagstones, hardware and other items. The cost of the building was £8,000, or about $40,000.

European furniture, paintings, silver and china were put in the mansion and some of these items are still there. Among them is a large silver tankard engraved with the Brewton insignia and the date 1769. A portrait of Mr. Brewton, painted by Sir Joshua Reynolds, still hangs in the drawing room. This room also has a six-foot Waterford crystal chandelier that is one of the most magnificent in America.

The chandelier, along with the pilastered doors, pedimented windows and cornices of ornately carved wood rather than cast plaster, make the Brewton house a focal point for architectural scholars.

Like many of the Charleston residences, the Brewton house is on a plot narrow for the size of the house. The plot is 150 feet wide and a block deep. There are two main floors and a large attic, all set on a foundation so high that it provides another floor of rooms at ground level.

In the rear of the house are gardens, walks and pools. On the rim of the property are brick buildings for thirty slaves and a large carriage house now used for automobiles. The separate kitchen building was discontinued when employees became scarce; a kitchen was built in the basement and recently a modern one, complete with wall ovens, was installed on the first floor adjacent to the dining room.

The house has four main rooms on each of the four floors, plus such things as hallways fifty-four feet long and eleven feet wide. Among the shortcomings are attic steps so narrow and winding no modern builder would construct them. Such stairways, along with occasional doorways so low six-foot persons bump their heads, are found in many of the Charleston houses.

But the Brewton house has a broad and gracious stairway linking the two main floors, with a triple-arched window casting soft light on polished mahogany balustrades and doors.

At the rear, facing the gardens, are projections known as Charleston piazzas, partly enclosed with brick arches. Steps lead down to the gardens. The roofs of some of the balconies were covered with sheets of lead until the Confederate troops used the metal for bullets. Two cannon balls fired in the war plunged through the main roof of the house.

The Waterford crystal chandelier is suspended in the center of the twenty-eight-foot drawing room, on the second of the two main floors. For nearly two centuries family weddings have taken place under the sprawling arms of crystal and brass, which have crystal pendants and festoons and twenty-four glass windshields.

Here is how Miss Mary Pringle Frost, one of the Miles Brewton descendants, felt about it:

"The chandelier is a work of science and art. It is beautiful in its simplicity, yet intricate in its adornment of crystals. To understand this chandelier requires a knowledge of glass, an understanding of mathematics and physics, and a combining of these into a form of symmetry and beauty.

"With every hour of the day, with every season of the year, the prisms refract the rays of light, varying with the sunlight. The refractions are never the same, for the combination of earth and sun and atmosphere vary, though the variations be undiscernible to human sense.

"There are times when no colors are seen. The chandelier is then the hue of a pearl and is beautiful only for quiescence and form. There are times of many small jewels of all colors and times of large and brilliant jewels.

"In the early morning the western wall of the drawing room is covered with the colors of the rainbow in the oval form of the pendants, only larger. One can appreciate this only by seeing it. My sister Susan called my brother, my sister and myself into the room to behold these lights. We who had been brought up in the traditions of the house, together beheld this work of God."

In 1775, ten years after the house had been built and elegantly furnished, Miles Brewton's wife and children were lost at sea while traveling between Charleston and Philadelphia. Mr. Brewtons' will would have given the house to his wife, along with "one yellow girl" named Luca to serve her as long as she remained a widow, but all this now was changed.

Lord William Campbell married Sarah Izard, a cousin of Mrs. Brewton, and the couple moved into the Brewton house, from which Lord William, as governor, ruled the colony. When Mr. Brewton died the house was inherited by his sisters, Mrs. Charles Pinckney and Mrs. Jacob Motte.

Mrs. Motte was living there with her three attractive daughters when British army officers moved in, without invitation, to use the house as their Charleston headquarters in the Revolutionary War. A fine Axminster carpet was cut up for saddle cloths. On the marble mantel of the front parlor an officer scratched a profile of Sir Henry Clinton, their commander, which is still clearly visible.

In the parlor of the house the women of Charleston pleaded with British commanders, in vain, to spare the life of Isaac Hayne, a martyr of the Revolution. Mrs. Motte also pleaded with the British officers to stop making advances to her three daughters. Still fearful that the girls would be molested, she moved them into the attic and kept them locked there for months. Only Mrs. Motte herself navigated the precipitous steps to the attic — steps so steep and narrow, fortunately, that one of the girls could stand at the top with a club and beat off an army of men when the mother was absent.

The Brewton chandelier survived the war, and so did the Motte girls, who finally were married under it to American army officers — William Alston, John Middleton and Thomas Pinckney. Later, Mrs. Middleton became the second wife of Mr. Pinckney, who was minister to the Court of St. James and a candidate for President of the United States. The Alstons moved into the Brewton house and in 1791 George Washington visited them there. Mr. Alston was a wealthy rice planter and kept a stable of race horses and several yachts.

The next occupants of the house were Mrs. William Bull Pringle, a daughter of the Alstons, and her family. The Pringles had many children and some were married under the chandelier. Two of the sons were killed while serving the Confederate Army in the Civil War. One of them, Major Robert Pringle, died on the front steps of the house while being carried home from battle. When Charleston was evacuated by the Confederates in 1865, the Union Army moved in and again the Brewton house was chosen as the best place for a military headquarters.

In the era of poverty in the South after the war, the descendants of Miles Brewton neglected the maintenance of the mansion and took in boarders to help pay the taxes. Miss Susan Pringle succeeded her parents as the owner. Three of her nieces, the Misses Susan Pringle Frost, Mary Pringle Frost and Rebecca Motte Frost, occupied the house after 1917.

Susan, widely known as Miss Sue, called herself a "fighter" and she constantly demonstrated that she was one. While campaigning for woman suffrage, she picketed the White House in Washington, D. C. Miss Sue became the first court stenographer in Charleston, then invaded the financial marts and founded the Charleston Society for the Preservation of Old Dwellings. President of the society for many years, she started the city on the house-preservation path that is still being followed.

The Roper house at 9 East Battery in Charleston overlooks the harbor. It was a sumptuous home for ante-bellum entertaining. (Right) Molded rope around the door of the Roper house was a symbol of the family name. The cast-iron lions' heads are the ends of earthquake bolts.

While living for forty-three years in the Brewton house she fully restored it and also salvaged scores of other houses. She saved shrines from becoming gasoline stations and kept the bulldozers away from Cabbage Row and St. Michael's Alley.

Miss Sue welcomed visitors to the Brewton house, serving them sherry on the piazzas. She also was a famous host to birds, stray dogs, homeless cats and former servants in need of lodgings. She died in the house in 1960 at the age of eighty-seven.

Mr. and Mrs. Edward Manigault are the current occupants of the Brewton house. Mr. Manigault is the board chairman of Charleston's daily papers, the *News and Courier* and the *Evening Post.* Mrs. Manigault, the former Mary Pringle Hamilton, is a cousin of Miss Sue and a descendant of Miles Brewton on both sides of her family.

"The house is not too big for modern living," Mrs. Manigault said. "But heavens, I'll be lucky if I can keep two servants where thirty once worked. It is very discouraging to read in old letters in trunks about Robert being the servant just for the front steps and the brass, George just for the chandelier and others just for other special jobs."

Another mansion typical of old Charleston is the Robert William Roper house at 9 East Battery, near the tip of the peninsula. Overlooking the harbor, it was built in 1838 at about the time the Battery's sea wall was constructed to protect the lower part of the city from flood tides.

Mr. Roper was a wealthy planter and merchant, and he wanted a sumptuous home for the relaxed entertaining that distinguished Charleston in the ante-bellum days. To achieve grandeur he chose the Greek Revival style of architecture, with a two-story portico facing the side yard — as was the vogue at the time. The house of three stories and an attic is of red brick, with immense white columns topped by white balustrades that give the structure a theatrical appearance.

The house has twenty rooms, some of them twelve feet high, and fifteen baths. The architect was Edward B. Bryan, who later married Mr. Roper's sister Julia, whom he met during the construction. In the trim of the portal near the street is a molded rope, indicating the identity of the first owner — as a coat of arms might do.

Rudolph Siegling, former editor of the *Evening Post*, later lived in the house. From 1929 to 1955 it was the winter home of Solomon R. Guggenheim of New York, the copper millionaire and donor of the Guggenheim Museum in New York. Despite his taste for modern art and new architecture, Mr. Guggenheim enjoyed the old-fashioned Roper mansion's atmosphere. He spent $75,000 to renovate the structure and install an elevator.

In the rafters of the attic Mr. Guggenheim found embedded the thousand-pound tail of a cannon, lodged there when the weapon exploded at the Battery during the bombardment of Fort Sumter and sent the piece flying through the air. The attic stairs, like those at the Brewton house, are too narrow to permit removal of the huge chunk of iron, so it is still there.

Earthquake shocks have wracked the Roper house so severely that long bolts have been extended through it from wall to wall to save the building from collapsing. Many of the old Charleston houses have been similarly preserved. The ends of the bolts on the outside of the Roper house are decorated with cast-iron lions' heads, except where they have been knocked off recently by the explosive impact of jet planes breaking the sound barrier.

J. Drayton Hastie, head of television and real-estate concerns throughout the nation, now is the owner of the Roper house. He spent $40,000 redeveloping the interior into four comfortable apartments, one of which he and his family occupy. He also added air conditioning, the big old windows being too difficult to open on hot days. The Hastie family has owned Magnolia Gardens, a 350-acre horticultural spectacle near Charleston, since 1671. Some of the antiques from the old mansion at the gardens now are in the Roper house.

Tides, especially during September hurricanes, sometimes sweep across the sea wall and flood the mansions at the Battery. Sewers also back up and add to the havoc. In the Roper house, the water rises three feet up the living-room walls. When storm warnings are sounded the families on the first floor carry all their possessions to the upper floors.

The old Nathaniel Russell house at 51 Meeting Street, an 1809 residence of Adam architecture, now is the headquarters of the Historic Charleston Foundation.

One of the sights just outside the city is Boone Hall Plantation and Gardens in Christ Church Parish, on U. S. Route 17 eight miles north of the city line. Open to visitors, the plantation of 738 acres has become popular with motorists on the New York-to-Florida journey.

Boone Hall is approached on magnificent Oak Avenue. Ninety-one live oaks festooned with eerie Spanish moss provide a canopy across the road. Some parts of the motion picture *Gone With the Wind* were filmed there and occasionally directors return to make other films.

Close to Oak Avenue is a well-preserved "street," as the old slave quarters were known. The quarters include nine brick cabins, still roofed with the original red tiles. The original ginhouse, built in 1750 when cotton was the chief crop of the plantation, also is still intact.

The original Boone mansion, however, was destroyed long ago. It was built by Major John Boone, who received a royal grant of the acreage in 1697. He was a member of the Governor's Council until he was caught trading with pirates at the plantation, which borders a small river leading to the ocean. His daughter Sarah grew up at the plantation and became the mother of Edward Rutledge, a signer of the Declaration of Independence.

(Left) A flying staircase in the Russell house spirals from floor to floor without side supports or steel frame. (Right) The Russell house, of classic Adam design, was built in 1809 by Nathaniel Russell, a wealthy merchant.

Boone Hall Plantation has a mansion built of old materials in an ante-bellum design.

In 1817 Boone Hall was bought by John Horlbeck, an architect and builder responsible for some of the fine mansions of old Charleston. He planted 15,000 pecan trees on the plantation and they are still flourishing.

Thomas A. Stone, a retired diplomat from Canada, became the owner of Boone Hall Plantation in 1935 and built the present mansion. He used old materials and tried to build a house that would be typical of those of ante-bellum days but some historians disapprove his conception. The house has seventeen rooms, a dozen baths and a ballroom that now has been converted into extra bedrooms.

Prince Dimitri Djordjadze, of a royal European family, and his wife, the former Audrey Amory of Cincinnati, Ohio, bought the plantation in 1940 and set up a famous stable of race horses and an equally famous cycle of parties. Five years later Dr. Henry Deas, a Charleston physician, moved into the mansion.

In 1955 the plantation was bought by Harris M. McRae of Ellerbee, North Carolina, a produce broker and peach grower. He and his wife Nancy and their two children now spend part of every year there. With its lacy iron gates, pecan groves, prize cattle and quaint buildings, the plantation is a magnificent memento of the pre-Civil War era when horses clip-clopped through the low country and slaves drowsed under the trees.

✿　✿　✿　✿　✿　✿　✿　✿

The exteriors of the Brewton house at 17 King Street and the Roper house at 9 East Battery may be seen any time, but the interiors only by invitation. The Russell house at 51 Meeting Street, like others of the Historic Charleston Foundation, may be visited from 10 A.M. to 5 P.M. on week-days and from 2 to 5 P.M. on Sundays all year for $1. Boone Hall, eight miles north of Charleston on U. S. Route 17, is open from 9 to 5 P.M. on week-days and from 1 to 5 P.M. on Sundays all year except between Christmas and New Year's Day; the fee is $1.25.

Boone Hall Plantation's slave quarters are still standing just as they were before the Civil War.

Tarheel Elegance

Tryon Palace

NEW BERN · NORTH CAROLINA

WILLIAM TRYON, the royal governor of the North Carolina Colony under the British two centuries ago, was aristocratic, handsome, debonair and wealthy. Critics said he had a superiority complex; he was proud of himself, proud of his job and especially proud of King George III. He decided to build a splendid monumental residence that would be a credit to his monarch and also would impress the settlers and the Indians.

He was forty years old. His wife, Margaret Wake Tryon, was wealthy and cultured and had been educated in England, as he had been. Their daughter, Margaret, was nine years old.

Governor Tryon obtained from the Colonial Assembly of North Carolina a grant of £15,000, or about $75,000, to begin building the palace in 1767. He told objectors that besides being his home the palace would be a government house. The site that he chose was beside the Trent River in New Bern. The river was part of the all-important water route to Europe.

John Hawks, an English architect, was brought from England to design a typical "London vicinity house" of the Georgian style then in vogue. The design was similar to those of many houses that wealthy persons were then building in the prosperous suburbs of London, but it was unusual in America. Materials and skilled workmen were brought from Europe for the construction.

North Carolina property owners grew to detest Governor Tryon as they saw the building and their tax bills rise together. They rebelled at public meetings, and some historians contend that this was a factor leading to the Revolutionary War.

The Tryons moved into the palace in 1770 but in the following year Governor Tryon was transferred to New York. Josiah Martin, the new royal governor, immediately moved into Tryon Palace and also retained Mr. Hawks to add rooms and auxiliary buildings to it.

Tryon Palace became a home with forty-five rooms, twenty-seven fireplaces, broad gardens, a kitchen house, smokehouse, garden house, poultry house and washhouse. This did not endear Governor Martin to the people of the colony; in 1775 he and his family had to flee for their lives and the rebels moved in.

The meetings held by American patriots in the palace were among the earliest on the continent in defiance of British orders. The first provincial convention

The ballroom of Tryon Palace was used for council meetings before the Revolutionary War and later for meetings of North Carolina's highest officials.

Mrs. Maude Moore Latham played in the ruins of Tryon Palace in childhood and resolved to rebuild if she became rich, which she did. (Right) A musical clock in Tryon Palace was made by Charles Clay in London in 1736 and is from the J. P. Morgan home. Its chimes and bells play operatic tunes.

of North Carolina was held there before the Revolutionary War, and later the first state officials were inaugurated at ceremonies in the rooms and on the lawns. After the Revolution, the general assemblies met in the palace and four governors were inaugurated there before the seat of the state government was transferred in 1794 to Raleigh.

George Washington never slept in Tryon Palace but he did dance there. In 1791 he attended a ball in the building and later on frequently spoke about the charm and the beauty of the young women he had met on the dance floor. He also referred to the inadequate maintenance of the old mansion. Some residents of New Bern still gloat over its decay. They say the dilapidation was a suitable symbol of George III, "who lost the colonies, lost his mind and lost the respect of noblemen."

On the bleak, winter night of February 27, 1798, fire swept through Tryon Palace. A clergyman was living in part of the house. A small school was in another part. A Masonic Lodge occupied some of the larger rooms and men had been at a meeting there just before the fire. A poultry farmer kept chickens in the basement and had heat in incubators for the hatching of eggs. There are many theories about the origin of the fire.

Tryon Palace's library has 200-year-old books and furnishings. The mantel and paintings are English, the rug is Spanish and the chair is Chippendale. (Below) The upstairs supper room of Tryon Palace has Chippendale furniture. Huge English taxes on mirrors made popular this use of a picture with a small mirror.

The only wing of Tryon Palace which survived the fire was converted into an apartment house. George Street was built across the site of the main part of the mansion and a bridge was constructed to carry the street across the Trent River. Thirty-five small houses were built on the remainder of the grounds.

Maude Moore lived two blocks from the redevelopment area as a little girl. She and her playmates were fascinated by stories about the old palace. When Maude Moore grew up and became the wife of James E. Latham, a prosperous business man in Greensboro, she recalled those stories and decided to redevelop the grounds and buildings exactly as they had been when royal governors lived there.

From 1944 until her death in 1951 Mrs. Latham gave $3,000,000 for the restoration, and the North Carolina Legislature contributed $227,000 toward the purchase of the eight-acre site. The property had become part of an expensive downtown area of New Bern. Mrs. Latham died when the physical redevelopment was barely started and the project was completed by a state commission headed by her daughter, Mrs. John A. Kellenberger.

Intensive research had resulted in the discovery of copies of the original plans drawn by Mr. Hawks and also of inventories of all the furnishings. Some documents were found in England and others in archives of the New York Historical Society.

The walls of the wing that survived the 1798 fire were found to be 90 per cent intact, with the bricks Governor Tryon had used, but the roofs had to be revised to comply with the original design and all the rooms had to be rearranged. Gradually the palace was reconstructed, with walls three feet thick, doors of mahogany and the shutters and other details exactly the same as those of the original palace.

Typically British cornices were installed and Italian marble mantels of monstrous size were used where the old plans called for them. Woods painted to resemble marble also were used; they had been fashionable in the eighteenth century although they are now referred to as "the deceits of the day."

The great kitchen fireplace has a rotisserie spit actuated by weights. Many of the fireplaces have andirons and screens of polished steel, which had been more fashionable than brass before the Revolution. A men's recreation room near the front door, reserved for gambling, smoking and storytelling, has an ancient "Shove Ha' Penny Board," used much as a shuffleboard court would be used today except that coins are knocked with knuckles toward the scoring circles.

The rebuilt palace has eight original red sandstone steps that were found among artifacts when new foundations were built. Stones to match were obtained from a quarry at St. Bee in Cumberland County, England. Chunks of the old plaster provided for decorators at least two of the original wall colors that Governor Tryon had used. Wrought-iron gates that had been installed in 1741 in front of a London mansion were obtained for the rebuilt palace.

Virtually all the furnishings in the house date back to 1770 or earlier. They include a thirty-five-foot Isfahan rug reaching the entire length of the ballroom, English cut-glass chandeliers, a walnut spinet made in 1720 in London by Thomas I. Hitchcock and a tall clock made in 1736 in London by Charles Clay. The clock, which formerly belonged to J. P. Morgan in New York, has chimes and bells that play operatic tunes; it also records the day, the month and the position of the moon.

Tryon Palace is something of a North Carolina counterpart of Historic Williamsburg, Virginia. Women in colorful costumes of the colonial era conduct guided tours. Its rooms have become a mecca for connoisseurs of early furniture, paintings, silver, pewter, porcelain and rugs.

Since it was reopened in 1959 it has been more comfortable than it ever was in colonial days. It now has central heat and air conditioning. The uniform temperature and humidity were needed especially to preserve its decorations and perishable furnishings.

The mansion, its gardens and auxiliary buildings on eight acres are owned by North Carolina and are managed by the Tryon Palace Commission. Members of the commission, besides Mrs. Kellenberger, include the governor of the state, the mayor of New Bern, other public officials and a number of prominent citizens such as Mrs. Henry F. du Pont of Winterthur in Delaware, who is a direct descendant of John Hawks and a historian and restorer in her own right. Miss Gertrude S. Carraway, the director of Tryon Palace, is a former president-general of the Daughters of the American Revolution.

✿ ✿ ✿ ✿ ✿ ✿ ✿ ✿

Tryon Palace is on U.S. Routes 17 and 70 and State Route 55 in downtown New Bern. It is open from 9:30 A. M. to 4 P. M. Tuesday through Saturday and from 1:30 P. M. to 4 P. M. on Sunday, except on New Year's Day, Easter, Thanksgiving and Dec. 24, 25 and 26. The fees are $2 for adults and $1 for children.

A Blue Ridge Château

George W. Vanderbilt's Biltmore

ASHEVILLE · NORTH CAROLINA

THE FRENCH RENAISSANCE château of 250 rooms in the Blue Ridge Mountains at Asheville, North Carolina, was built by George Washington Vanderbilt when he was a twenty-six-year-old bachelor. He had grounds of 146,000 acres for his home, although the family now has disposed of all except a mere 12,000 acres. The shortest drive from the massive front gates to the residence still is more than three miles long, circling through a carefully landscaped wonderland of majestic conifers, hardwoods, rhododendrons and 40,000 azaleas of 500 different varieties.

Mr. Vanderbilt developed a feudal realm, American style, and he named it Biltmore. Visitors there today are finding it a fairyland principality with a strange Graustarkian flavor of grandeur, romance and adventure.

In any statistical listing of American mansions, Biltmore is a place of superlatives. All the rooms are furnished with antiques and art treasures from many nations. Some of the rooms are large enough to accommodate a modern ranch house with double garage, yet the furnishings have been arranged in a manner to produce a feeling of intimacy along with elegance.

A New York interior decorator, planning a visit to Biltmore, wrote to the superintendent that "it certainly must be propaganda" that the banquet hall was seventy-five feet high. "My God, it's true!" he exclaimed later when he stepped into it. He was equally amazed to find in the room a cathedral pipe organ taller than a three-story building, three large fireplaces in a row, two thrones from European palaces and seventy-six matching antique Italian chairs around the dinner table.

Mr. Vanderbilt had been rocking on the front porch of Asheville's old Battery Park Hotel and gazing at the spectacular mountain views in the late eighteen eighties when he suddenly decided that of all the places in the world he had seen this was the one that appealed to him the most for permanent residence. He had a lively imagination and millions of dollars to implement his wishes. All the Vanderbilts were builders; but George, in addition, was the scholar and the only non-businessman of the clan. The nucleus of the family fortune had been gained from transportation by George's grandfather, Commodore Cornelius Vanderbilt. It had

The gardens of Biltmore were designed by Frederick Law Olmstead, who planned New York City's Central Park and several university campuses.

The library at Biltmore has 20,000 books, which George W. Vanderbilt really read. A spiral staircase leads to the gallery.

been increased many-fold by the varied enterprises of William Vanderbilt, a son of the Commodore and the father of George.

Forsaking New York and Newport society, George Vanderbilt assembled the Biltmore acreage. It reached forty miles in one direction and Mr. Vanderbilt and his overseers occasionally spent a week riding around it on horseback. Unlike his friends and relatives in Newport, Mr. Vanderbilt was not an early convert to automobiles. He clung to the use of spirited horses and elegant carriages until he found himself outnumbered and outdistanced on the highways after the turn of the century.

As conceived by Mr. Vanderbilt, his new principality was typical of those developed by royal families in Europe hundreds of years earlier. The "palace" and gardens were developed atop a high plateau, with dependent farmers, craftsmen, artisans and laborers living in clusters around the rim.

Biltmore derived its name from Bildt, the town in the Netherlands whence the van der Bildts had come, and from "more," an English word for rolling, upland country. On emigrating to America the family had changed its name to Vanderbilt. The village that Mr. Vanderbilt built for his employees now has been absorbed by Asheville. The estate is in adjacent Buncombe County — the source of the slang "bunk."

Mr. Vanderbilt spoke and wrote in eight languages, traveled extensively throughout the world and was a student of architecture. When he decided to have the mansion in French Renaissance design he hired as the architect his friend, Richard Morris Hunt, who had studied at the École des Beaux Arts in Paris and had been a founder and president of the American Institute of Architects. He had built several fine mansions at Newport, office buildings in New York and university structures for Yale and Princeton.

Frederick Law Olmsted, a master of natural landscape architecture, was hired to lay out the grounds of the estate; he had designed New York's Central Park, other public parks and several university campuses. Chauncey Delos Beadle was superintendent of Biltmore for sixty years and developed the gardens. Gifford Pinchot, later governor of Pennsylvania, directed the preservations of woodlands.

On the Biltmore tract was the old hamlet of Shiloh, populated largely by Negroes. Mr. Vanderbilt relocated the homes and gave jobs to most of the men, whose descendants still work on the estate, and built new schools, churches and a railroad station for the families. He developed two reservoirs and a filtration plant that still serve the estate, with water piped six miles from the Busbee Mountains.

To transport construction materials to the mansion, a three-mile railroad spur was built. Hundreds of craftsmen, including many from Europe, moved to the area to carve stone and wood for the mansion. For five years 1,000 workers were steadily engaged.

The French châteaux of Chambord, Chenonceaux and Blois inspired the architecture of Biltmore but many of Mr. Vanderbilt's own ideas also were incorporated in the structure. While the walls were rising he traveled widely in Europe to buy paintings, tapestries, statues, porcelains, woodwork, and an entire palace ceiling, thrones and other objects. The rooms at Biltmore were quickly redesigned to accommodate them.

In 1895 Biltmore was formally opened with a big Christmas party at which Mr. Vanderbilt's mother presided. When, later, he was married, he brought his bride, the former Edith Stuyvesant Dresser of New York, to the mansion. When their only child, Cornelia, married John Francis Amherst Cecil of London, Biltmore became the Cecils' residence.

After Mr. Vanderbilt's death in 1914, part of the estate was given to the national government for the Pisgah National Forest. Other parts were converted into modern home sites and a long stretch was used for the Blue Ridge Parkway. In 1926, Mrs. Vanderbilt married Senator Peter G. Gerry of Rhode Island and moved to that state; and in 1930, Mr. and Mrs. Cecil opened the estate to the public.

Mr. Cecil, a son of Baroness Amherst of Hackney and Lord William Cecil, had been the First Secretary of the British embassy in Washington and was eleven years his wife's senior. At Asheville he became so integrated in the local life that he convinced the mountaineers that he preferred moonshine to Scotch but he did not convince his wife that Biltmore was a matrimonial Shangri La.

Biltmore's spiral staircase is a copy of the one in the Château de Blois, except that it turns in the opposite direction. The chandelier, three stories high, hangs from one pin. (Right) The banquet hall of Biltmore has three fireplaces and a ceiling seventy-five feet high.

Mrs. Cecil went to London in 1932, taking her two sons, George and Bill, and leaving Mr. Cecil at Biltmore. The sons served in the British Royal Navy in World War II. Biltmore also served in the war: its huge cellars were used as a secret storage vault for paintings and sculpture from the bomb-threatened National Gallery of Art in Washington.

In her childhood Cornelia Vanderbilt had been known as a "shy little farm girl" who was shielded from the realities of life and did not mix with many other children.

On arriving in London, Mrs. Cecil, no longer shy, dyed her hair pink and cut a swath in Mayfair. She obtained a Paris divorce in 1934 and in the same year, according to a divorce complaint in Switzerland, began an intimate life with Guy Baer, an artist. Fifteen years later she married a British bank clerk and began living unpretentiously in staid Kensington Square in London. Friends report that in recent years she and her husband have spent much of their time working in a small garden that would have been lost on the Biltmore grounds.

Her father, who left her $50,000,000, asked that she spend at least one-half of every year in the mansion, but Mrs. Cecil relinquished her interest in Biltmore

Biltmore, as seen from the lagoon of a lake on the estate, is closer to structural per-fection than the French châteaux from which it was copied.

after she had chosen England as her home. The estate now is managed by a board of trustees in which George and Bill Cecil have a strong voice. When Bill, the younger of the two, becomes thirty-five years old in 1964 the brothers will become the full owners of Biltmore.

"It's a rather remarkable collection in the mansion and we intend to keep it together permanently so that people who cannot afford to travel in Europe can always come here and see such treasures," George Cecil has said.

The cost of maintaining the mansion is offset partly by a dairy that the brothers operate on 4,000 acres of the estate. It has 1,400 head of registered cattle and it also is a distribution center for 300 independent farmers. The estate has 800 employees, many of them working on the 17 miles of paved roads, 120 miles of gravel highways, uncounted miles of trails and dirt road, and in the gardens. Long terraces have canopies of wisteria and trumpet creeper. An Italian garden has three pools, sacred lotus of Egypt and aquatic plants. The rose garden has 5,000 bushes and vines, and an English garden has ivy from Kenilworth Castle. Mr. Vanderbilt, who reputedly started the nation's first forestry school at Biltmore, also started a perpetual reforestation program that his heirs are expanding.

The rose garden, in front of the conservatory at Biltmore, has 5,000 rose bushes and vines.

George Cecil and his brother live on the estate in houses that are Lilliputian, compared to the mansion, which is 780 feet long and not only has innumerable stairs but passenger and freight elevators. The grand staircase is a copy of the famous one in the Château de Blois, except that it spirals in the opposite direction from the original. It has no side supports as it winds around a gigantic wrought-iron chandelier that is three stories high and is said to be the largest one in the world suspended from a single iron pin.

The Palm Court is a sunken area of marble near the entrance hall; in all seasons it is filled with palms and bright flowers from Biltmore's own greenhouses. Like other rooms, it has fountains and plaques by Karl Bitter, the now-famous Viennese sculptor and carver who had just arrived in this country at the time Biltmore was started.

Paintings by Landseer, Reynolds, Whistler, Renoir, Sargent, Zorn and Zuloaga are among the pictures. Chessman that Napoleon Bonaparte used while imprisoned on St. Helena are displayed; a letter from his doctor authenticating them "walked off" with a tourist one day. The furnishings include an 800 B.C. Chou Dynasty sacrificial vessel, lamps of the Chien Lung Dynasty, rare Persian rugs, exquisite Wedgwood china, Dürer prints, Spanish and Italian chests, sixteenth-century tapestries and Circassian walnut library panels.

On the shelves of the library are 20,000 books, many of them with costly leather bindings and some containing original documents. A circular staircase in the library leads to an attractive gallery, and adjacent to the library is a private room to which Mr. Vanderbilt retreated for study and meditation.

The ceiling of the library was acquired from an Italian palace; part of the arrangement was that Mr. Vanderbilt would never reveal which royal family degraded itself by exchanging this art legacy for American cash. The ceiling painting is allegorical and is attributed to Giovanni Antonio Pellegrini (1675-1741). It closely resembles a ceiling still in the Palazzo Labia of Venice.

Mr. Vanderbilt left no record of what Biltmore had cost. A popular estimate is $7,000,000. Today it probably would cost $50,000,000 to $60,000,000. It is likely that Mr. Vanderbilt spent $3,000,000 for construction, $4,000,000 for furnishings and $1,000,000 for land.

❈   ❈   ❈   ❈   ❈   ❈   ❈   ❈

Biltmore is open to the public from 9 A.M. to 6 P.M. every day in the year except Thanksgiving, two days at Christmas and on New Year's Day. It is on the edge of Asheville, just east of the Great Smokies National Park. The gates of the estate are on U. S. Route 25. Admission fees are $2.40 for adults and $1.40 for children under sixteen.

The Idea-Man Cometh

Thomas Jefferson's Monticello

CHARLOTTESVILLE • VIRGINIA

THOMAS JEFFERSON'S mind, like his heart, contained two pumps. One circulated ideas about such things as the innate freedom and equality of all men — a theme he crystallized so effectively in the Declaration of Independence that he became the Father of American Democracy. The other circulated ingenious ideas for new buildings — ideas so appealing that he became the Father of American Architecture.

One of the brightest stars in the constellation of Jeffersonian buildings is Monticello, his home for fifty-four years. It is a thirty-five-room structure on a 658-acre tract atop a lofty plateau in the Blue Ridge Mountains of Virginia near Charlottesville.

Containing his architectural ideas and also many of his inventions, the mansion bears a plaque that says the structure more truly represents the genius and industry of one man than any other house ever built. There is a degree of truth in the claim. . . .

Jefferson began building Monticello in 1769, when he was twenty-six years old; and he continued the job for forty years, interlacing the task with his work as a lawyer, revolutionist, diplomat, governor of Virginia, Secretary of State and President of the United States. As his own architect, he intuitively developed a Greco-Roman-Colonial style that had many of the benefits later evident in the modern ranch house. Most of the living quarters, including bedrooms, are on the first floor of Monticello. Auxiliary rooms are on the second floor. Servants' quarters are in long wings projecting from the rear of the building on a lower level, with "breezeways" linking the various rooms.

Jefferson was as much of an avant-gardist in his day as Frank Lloyd Wright was to become generations later. Monticello was his timber-and-brick "declaration of independence." Its dome inspired those built later on the United States Capitol and the Jefferson Memorial in Washington. In addition to his work on Monticello, he went on to design the University of Virginia, the State Capitol and many private homes.

Jefferson's inventiveness is evident even at the entrance of Monticello. A weather vane atop the house turns a large arrow on the ceiling of the porch, where it can be viewed through the windows of five rooms.

Over the front door of the entrance hall is Jefferson's clock, the winding of which requires a ladder and fifteen minutes of a houseman's time once a week. The clock has long cables extending to each side of the hall, with Revolutionary War cannon balls on the ends. The weight of the cannon balls, when raised by the winding of the clock, powers the time-keeping mechanism.

As the cannon balls creep lower on the walls each day they indicate the day of the week as marked on the walls. However, Jefferson miscalculated so that "Friday" is at floor level and the cannon balls have to pass through holes in the floor to reach "Saturday" on the wall of a recreation room below.

For 150 years persons had been mystified by the manner in which a pair of doors in the entrance hall, separately hung and apparently free swinging, opened and closed in automatic harmony. Most observers figured that Jefferson had built a series of levers in the ceiling to make the doors operate in unison. In 1953 the mystery was solved when the floor had to be repaired. Under the boards was found an intricate mechanism of hand-wrought chains and sprockets that controlled the mysterious action.

Other Jeffersonian creations in the house include a revolving chair as modern as a TV chair, a rotating pantry door, a campeachy chair resembling a modern posture chair, octagonal tables, octagonal rooms and a music stand for quartets to gather around. Jefferson, who was freckled and had red hair, was six-feet-two-inches tall and when he played the violin, which he frequently did at Monticello, he needed a music stand of extra height.

When Tom Jefferson went to college, architecture was not included in the curriculum. Deciding to teach himself, he assembled an extensive collection of books on the subject. He soon rebelled against Georgian architecture as much as he did against Georgian tyranny. His favorite design for houses became a Classical Revival style with Roman domes, Greek columns, red-brick walls and white trim.

That was the style he used for Monticello. He carefully followed the Greco-Roman rules of harmonious proportions when he returned from a trip to France with some major revisions in the plans for the house. Special attention was given to the works of the Venetian architect Palladio. In a handbook of Robert Morris, a British architect, he found plans for octagonal rooms, along with illustrations of brick-and-wood adaptations of Palladio's style.

Disregarding structural difficulties, Jefferson designed rooms of beauty and then decided how to build them. Some of the structural problems concerned Monticello's dome, of a design borrowed from a temple of Vesta; also a Corinthian frieze borrowed from a temple of Jupiter.

Floor plans were drawn to exact scale by Jefferson. Using ink that permitted no erasures, he calculated all proportions in advance. So precise was he that he did not translate 26/63 of an inch to one-half an inch, or even five-twelfths, but made it .4127 of an inch.

He brought artisans from New York, Philadelphia and Europe to work on the mansion, besides teaching slaves how to work as masons and carpenters. All intricate work was so closely supervised by him that he once commented that the

Monticello's entrance hall has a seven-day calendar clock. The weight of cannon balls on cables on each side of the doorway provide the power.

The bed in which Thomas Jefferson died at Monticello is in an alcove, open on both sides for ventilation. The stairs, like all others in the house, are narrow.

workmen "could not proceed for more than one hour without me." When the workmen inadvertently made an architrave in the dining room one and one-half inches smaller than he had specified, he redesigned an entire cornice and frieze for the room.

On the first floor Jefferson made the important rooms two stories high to provide a gracious atmosphere for entertaining. He provided alcoves for beds. Some furniture was built into the walls. Every room had a fireplace for heating purposes. Dumb waiters, air shafts and twelve skylights are other features of the house. In the rows of rooms in lower-level wings are kitchens, a smokehouse, stables, servants' rooms, the Honeymoon Cottage and a law office.

One thing that Monticello lacks is a grand staircase to guest rooms and the Sky Room over the main living quarters. Instead, there are stairs so dark and narrow that persons who are feeble or heavy have difficulty navigating them. This is strange, the Sky Room having been a billiard room until Virginia outlawed such games and also having been used by Jefferson as a ballroom for big parties.

"He loved to tear down and then build anew," a guide once commented, as she stepped cautiously down the stairs. "He was happiest when he discovered a better way to build something in the house. I can't understand why he didn't think of a better kind of stairs to build."

The planning of Monticello began to take shape in Jefferson's mind when he was a boy. His father, Peter, had received a royal grant of land on the mountain and Jefferson roamed the grassy hillsides to dream of building a mansion. Before the first stone was turned he decided to call it Monticello, "Little Mountain," in Italian.

Virtually all the materials for the house were obtained on the property. Stones for the foundation were quarried from the side of the mountain. The red bricks were baked in a kiln that Jefferson built. The timbers were cut from his forests. Nails were made in his own nailery. He had to buy some of the intricate parts for locks, glass for the windows and items such as porcelain inlays for the dining-room mantel.

Although unfinished, Monticello was sufficiently habitable in 1772 for Jefferson to take his bride to it. She had been Mrs. Martha Wayles Skelton, a twenty-two-year-old widow whom he had met while practicing law in Williamsburg. The life of the couple together at Monticello was happy but brief. They had six children, then Mrs. Jefferson died in 1782. Jefferson never remarried; his daughter Martha, the only child who lived as long as he did, became his hostess at the mansion.

Just before Mrs. Jefferson's death British troops marched on Monticello. Jefferson had been warned that they intended to imprison him and he fled successfully as they were swarming across the lawns and into the mansion.

Thomas Jefferson's library at Monticello has many rare books on law and architecture, also a leather chair he used in Washington, D. C.

Retiring to Monticello in 1809, Jefferson had a continuous stream of visitors from many parts of the world. Some guests who had "just come for dinner" stayed for weeks. People considered Monticello one of the most interesting houses in America and their host one of the most gracious statesmen.

The entertaining, with the cost of fifty servants and foods, placed a heavy burden on Jefferson. As a lawyer he seldom earned more than $5,000 a year and his $25,000 annual government pay was a thing of the past. As his plight worsened, Jefferson sold his library of 13,000 books for $23,950 in 1814. Still the sheriff kept knocking on his door; small donations from thousands of citizens just before his death provided $16,500 for creditors.

He died in his bedroom at Monticello on July 4, 1826, on the fiftieth anniversary of the Declaration of Independence that he had drafted. He was buried near the house. Monticello had to be sold to pay his debts, as did the remaining furnishings that had been his choicest possessions.

James T. Barclay bought the house and acreage for $7,000 and began planting mulberry trees with the idea of growing silkworms for an American silk industry. The venture failed and Monticello again was posted for sale. It was bought in 1834 by Commodore Uriah Phillips Levy of New York, a retired Navy officer. He paid only $2,500, just about what the place was worth, with its sagging roofs, rotted timbers, mutilated walls and neglected gardens.

Mr. Levy, an admirer of Jefferson, undertook to restore the property and retrieve some of the furnishings. When he died, he willed Monticello "to all the people of the United States" but his executors felt it should remain in the family and they upset the will. During the long litigation the mansion again became dilapidated and farmers even stabled cattle in it. Jefferson M. Levy finally became the owner of the property.

Historical and patriotic associations ultimately became interested in buying and restoring Monticello as a public shrine. In 1923 the Thomas Jefferson Memorial Foundation was organized and with funds contributed throughout the United States it bought Monticello for $500,000.

An additional million dollars was spent later to repair the building, restore the gardens and retrieve the furnishings. In patriotic zeal, many persons stripped their homes of Jeffersonian treasures so that Monticello could have them.

In 1938 termites in Monticello's timbers, along with natural decay, required a beginning of major reconstruction. The original bricks, which Jefferson had waterproofed with pine oil, were in good condition but new mortar was required between them.

Another factor that caused the mansion to sag was the 100 tons of nogging — consisting of bricks, mud and straw — that Jefferson had used between floor joists and in the walls as insulation against fire, cold, heat and sound. The dead weight alone, according to Robert E. Lee, Jr., head of a contracting firm on the restoration job, was enough to make the old mansion sag.

In 1953 major structural repairs under the supervision of Milton L. Grigg, architect for the Jefferson foundation, included complete removal of the nogging and the installation of eighty structural-steel beams at a cost of $200,000. Rooms long neglected, including the beer, wine, rum and cider cellars, were restored. Added to the mansion for the first time were modern oil-fired heating and air-conditioning systems.

The mansion, its gardens and its 360-degree views across the valleys of the Blue Ridge Mountains now are seen by 250,000 visitors a year.

✿　✿　✿　✿　✿　✿　✿　✿

Monticello is on State Route 53, three miles southeast of downtown Charlottesville. Roadside signs mark the route. The mansion is open from 8 A.M. to 5 P.M. daily from March 1 to November 30 and from 8 A.M. to 4:30 P.M. daily from December 1 to February 28. The single admission charge is $1. Adults in groups of fifteen or more pay 60 cents and children in such groups pay 30 cents.

All living quarters at Monticello are largely on one floor. Long wings contain kitchens, stables, servants' quarters and, at one end, a law office.

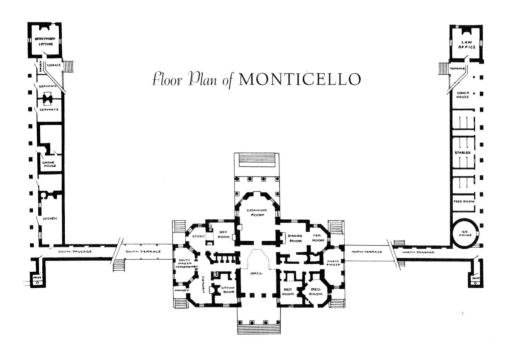

Floor Plan of MONTICELLO

Stratford Hall has thick walls of red brick made on the property. The two towers

A House of Heroes, Politics and Lust

Stratford Hall, the Birthplace of Robert E. Lee

WESTMORELAND COUNTY · VIRGINIA

IF HOUSES COULD TALK, few could have more to say than Stratford Hall. It could even tell about the birth of a nation. . . .

For the last 235 years the massive brick structure has stood on a plantation overlooking the broad reaches of the Potomac River ninety-six miles south of Washington. With its auxiliary buildings, broad fields, formal gardens, boxwood hedges and schoolhouse, it is mute evidence of how a master and 500 slaves once lived in self-sufficient unity; and today it still is in operation as a plantation, although with considerably different labor policies.

Stratford Hall has led as many lives as an apple has seeds. They have been dramatic lives, any one of which could furnish the basis for an exciting novel of love, hatred, loyalty and intrigue. It has witnessed such events as:

. . . campaigns in the wilderness against Indians, pirates and convicts.

. . . the boyhood romping of George Washington, who was born just down the road.

. . . the evolution of the American colonies.

70   *Stratford Hall*

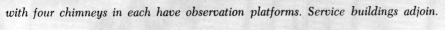

... the personal lives of the only two brothers who signed the Declaration of Independence.

... the personal life of Henry (Light Horse Harry) Lee when he was a brilliant officer of Washington's military staff in the Revolutionary War, followed by his incarceration in a debtors' prison for not paying the bills of Stratford Hall.

... the birth and the boyhood of General Robert E. Lee, commander of the Confederate Army in the Civil War and later the revered president of Washington College, now Washington and Lee University.

... the philanderings of Henry (Black Horse Harry) Lee and the birth of an illegitimate child to his young and attractive sister-in-law.

... the sister-in-law's ultimate marriage to a man of wealth, followed by her return to Stratford Hall for fifty years of strange but contented life.

... the formation of the Robert E. Lee Memorial Foundation, with enthusiastic members in virtually every state, to buy Stratford Hall and 1,204 of its acres for perpetuation as a memorial to the Lees.

How important a goal that was to attain is reflected in a letter President John Adams once wrote: "The complaint against the family of Lees is a very extraordinary thing indeed. I am no idolater of that family or any other, but I believe that their greatest fault is having more men of merit in it than any other family."

How well the goal of the foundation has been achieved is indicated by a recent comment of the director of a historic restoration in New York State: "Stratford Hall is my favorite house in all the world!"

Not many visitors at the plantation are inclined to share this enthusiasm when they get their first glimpse of the stark, harsh and rather monotonous exterior of the house. However, they soon find that it has a dual personality; the interior is warm, inviting and spacious, with architectural features and antique furnishings of exceptional interest. The adjacent buildings, including the kitchen, slave quarters, schoolhouse, smokehouse, counting house, law office, wash house and stables, as well as the gardens, boxwood hedges and brick patios, add to that interest.

The plantation once consisted of 6,500 acres, many of them planted with barley, oats, corn and tobacco. Only the tobacco is gone today; it robbed the soil of nitrogen. Prize cattle and thoroughbred horses still roam the pastures.

The construction of Stratford Hall was begun in 1725 and completed four years later. The original owner was Thomas Lee, whose English grandfather had settled in Virginia in 1641. Thomas Lee was a judge, president of His Majesty's Council and commander of the Virginia Colony. Rascals had burned an earlier home of his, causing the death of a servant and forcing Lee's pregnant wife to leap from a window. England gave him a bounty with which he started Stratford Hall.

The dining room of Stratford Hall has colonial paneling. In the alcove is a portrait of Queen Caroline of England, who gave a bounty to start the mansion.

Negro slaves and indentured white servants made the bricks for Stratford Hall from clays found on the property. They obtained lime for the mortar by burning sea shells from the mouth of the Potomac.

The site chosen for the house is a mile back from the river. Steep cliffs, deep ravines and woodland separate it from the water. This combination of natural fortifications protected the Lee family from attacks by Indians, pirates, convicts and sailors from the river. However, the site was moderately close to the main highway — the river — for travel to other parts of the colonies and to Europe.

The house was built in the form of an *H*, using a style of architecture that was popular in Tudor England. In America it had been used only for Virginia's capitol at Williamsburg. Thomas had seen the capitol in 1716, and many of the measurements of Stratford Hall are similar to those of the Williamsburg structure. The house and grounds also are similar to those of the Ashdown House estate of the Earl of Craven, in Berks, England.

Stratford Hall has eighteen main rooms, sixteen of them on corners of the building because of the *H* design. On the lower floor, at ground level, are most

The Mother's Room at Stratford Hall was the birthplace of two signers of the Declaration of Independence, and of General Robert E. Lee and other famous Lees.

of the bedrooms; this made heating with large wood-burning fireplaces easier in winter, and the high ceilings helped to cool the chambers in summer. Twelve outside doors aided ventilation.

The second, or main, floor is approached by one inside staircase or by stairs on the front of the house and others elsewhere on the exterior. The great hall of the main floor is thirty-five feet long and has a vaulted ceiling like those of English castles. This floor also has a library, bedrooms, and dining room and the most famous room in the house — the Mother's Room. It was here that many of the Lees were born, including General Lee.

All the meals were cooked in the adjacent kitchen building, which has a fireplace large enough to roast an ox, and then were carried up the steps by slaves to the dining room.

Turkey carpets, better known now as Oriental rugs, are used in the house and there is a collection of 3,000 books, manuscripts, letters and other items identified with the Lees. Gradually, furniture that was used by the Lees, or is of the same period, is being acquired through gifts and purchases.

At the edge of the lawn in front of the house is a Ha-Ha wall. The lawn is on the same level as the top of the wall, which permits an unobstructed panoramic view of the countryside from the house. On the far side of the wall there is a four-foot drop to the level of the fields and pastures; thus, the farm animals are prevented from approaching the house.

A number of Lees of several generations served in high governmental posts under the British Crown. Then two brothers, Richard H. and Francis L. Lee, rebelled. Richard, working with Patrick Henry, helped to inspire the break with England. Francis was associated with Benjamin Franklin in the cause.

Matilda Lee, their niece, inherited Stratford Hall. She married her cousin, Light Horse Harry, and their son was Henry Lee, called Black Horse Harry by some. Light Horse Harry married again later and Robert E. Lee was a son by the second marriage. Unable to pay his bills at Stratford Hall, Light Horse Harry was jailed for two years.

Although he left Stratford when he was four years old, Robert E. Lee often returned to visit his half-brother, who became the owner. In 1861, on the eve of the Civil War, General Lee wrote that he hoped some day to buy Stratford Hall because it "inspires me with feelings of pleasure and love." He told his wife it would be a poor place to earn a living but they could have cornbread and bacon and their clothes could be made in the weaving house.

Henry (Black Horse Harry) was twenty-one years old when he inherited Stratford Hall in 1808. He was not as handsome as his half-brother but he was a storyteller par excellence and a bon vivant of Washington and Philadelphia. He amused men and held women spellbound. Three times elected to the Virginia House of Delegates, he later became an infantry major.

Next door to Stratford Hall was the 2,000-acre plantation of the McCartys, a wealthy family from Ireland. Anne and Elizabeth McCarty, sisters, were among the wealthiest girls in Westmoreland; they had attended finishing schools and traveled extensively. Henry married Anne in 1817 and the union meant new wealth for his impoverished home. Anne brought servants and table silver made in 1620 with the McCarty coat-of-arms. She also brought to Stratford Hall her sister Elizabeth, who was sixteen years old — three years younger than Anne. Elizabeth had Henry appointed her guardian and turned over her legacies to him to manage.

In 1818 Anne gave birth to a daughter, Margaret, who when a child of two plunged down the steep front steps of Stratford Hall and was killed — exactly as another child of the Lee clan had done a few years earlier. In the gloom that settled over the house, Anne began using morphine and Henry spent money so fast that he dissipated Elizabeth's wealth as well as his own.

Friends said that Henry developed "a predilection for the flesh pots of Egypt." They also reported that he developed a deep affection for Elizabeth, and he himself wrote that they were "thrown into a state of the most unguarded intimacy." Elizabeth bore Henry a child, who died at birth.

Tongues wagged in Westmoreland. Henry was blamed for "seduction" and "crime of the blackest dye." Anne never again spoke to Elizabeth, whose stepfather, Richard Stuart, took her to his home. Elizabeth cut off her hair and became a recluse. A nine-year fight ensued over a settlement of her financial claims against Henry.

Grim times settled on Stratford Hall. Anne went to Tennessee to live. Parts of the old house decayed and crumbled. Broken fences remained unmended and slaves ran away. Wolves devoured the livestock; on bleak winter nights Henry was awakened by shrieks of death from the barns.

In desperation, Henry sold Stratford Hall in 1822 to an old military friend, William C. Somerville, an author and diplomat. The sale, for $25,000, was subject

On the steep front steps of Stratford Hall two Lee children were killed in accidents. In front is a Ha-Ha wall that kept cattle from approaching the house.

to a mortgage that had been given to Elizabeth. Henry went to Fredericksburg, but former friends slammed doors in his face. He took a menial job with the Post Office Department in Washington and then met President Andrew Jackson, who hired him to write speeches and edit personal papers.

Accompanying President Jackson to the Hermitage, the Jackson home near Nashville, Henry met Anne and they had a brief reunion. Anne later went to Paris, where she died in poverty, with a dog as her only companion. A plea to Elizabeth for help might have brought money, for the younger sister was wealthy.

Elizabeth married Henry Storke in 1826 and three years later gained the ownership of Stratford Hall though foreclosure of the mortgage. Elizabeth lived in the house for the next fifty years. Still in penitence, she rarely left the plantation. She studied the medicinal properties of herbs and developed an herb garden that can still be seen. She made balms, ointments and teas, especially for children. Very religious, she taught the catechism to slaves on Sunday mornings. She died in 1879 and is buried in a corner of the garden, near the Lees. The ownership of Stratford Hall went by inheritance to Charles E. and Richard H. Stuart, great-nephews of Elizabeth, then to Charles E. Stuart, Jr.

In 1929 the Robert E. Lee Memorial Foundation was set up to buy Stratford Hall and the remaining 1,204 acres for $240,000. Many persons throughout the United States contributed to the fund. Directors of the foundation are from most states; its president is Mrs. Randolph C. Harrison of Greenwich, Connecticut. Vice Admiral Irving T. Duke, who retired from the Navy after commanding the battleship "Big Mo" of World War II fame, became the superintendent of Stratford Hall.

Extensive repairs have been made to the buildings in recent years, including the removal of termite-infested timbers. Fortunately, drawings and other records of the buildings and furnishings were found, making possible a truly authentic restoration.

President Franklin D. Roosevelt said he had "stumbled upon" Stratford Hall late in life and had been thrilled. He felt, he said, like Balboa when he sighted Darien. He spoke of the "amazing dignity" of Stratford Hall and declared that the shrine was a memorial to "a brave young civilization for which modern America will always be grateful."

❋ ❋ ❋ ❋ ❋ ❋ ❋ ❋

Stratford Hall is near State Route 3, east of U. S. Route 301. It is open from 9 A.M. to 5 P.M. all year. The admission fees are $1 for adults and 25 cents for children. On the night of every January 16, General Lee's birthday, admission is free for a celebration by candlelight. Admission also is free on the Fourth of July, in recognition of the signing of the Declaration of Independence by two Lees; on October 12, the day of General Lee's death, and on the first Sunday in May, in observation of the day Light Horse Harry brought his first bride to the house.

The Most Revered Home in America

George Washington's Mansion House Farm

MOUNT VERNON · VIRGINIA

GEORGE WASHINGTON was described in Congress by Henry (Light Horse Harry) Lee as the man who was "first in war, first in peace and first in the hearts of his countrymen." His home beside the Potomac River in the upper neck of Virginia became a decrepit and unwanted shambles fifty years later but after a dramatic rescue it has assumed first place in the hearts of Americans who like to visit mansions.

More than a million visitors a year roam the house, gardens and lawns to enjoy the panoramic views and to learn things about the Father of His Country that they never before took time to understand. Along with the American tourists are increasing numbers of visiting foreign dignitaries, both secular and religious leaders; Mount Vernon is as much a symbol of America as the Statue of Liberty.

One oft-made discovery at Mount Vernon, a surprise and a shock to many visitors, is the record showing that Washington was born not on February 22, the

Mount Vernon's banquet hall has a Palladian window. The wall decorations resemble Wedgwood pottery. The furniture was Washington's.

day that is celebrated, but on February 11. The Washington family Bible at Mount Vernon bears the proof, in handwriting showing that George arrived at 10 A.M. on February 11. After seeing the Bible many a visitor can scarcely wait to get back home to tell people what a blunder they have been committing in recognizing February 22 as the birthday of the man who could not tell a lie.

They really have not been blundering, however, nor is the family Bible misleading as to the February 11 birthday. The archives in Mount Vernon explain that a switch from the old Julian calendar to the new Gregorian calendar in 1752, when George was twenty years old, permitted the youth to add eleven days to the date of his birth.

Similarly, not many of the visitors are aware at first that the magnificently maintained estate had been in ruins until one person who cared decided to shame the nation into doing something about it. The mansion had sagging roofs, rotted pillars, peeling paint, shattered windows and broken fences as it nestled forlornly among tall weeds and untrimmed shrubs.

Congressmen of the United States and legislators of Virginia refused to accept Mount Vernon even as a gift. The estate had become a costly white elephant, and the era of mansion-preservation had not yet arrived. Steamboats wending their way up and down the Potomac blew whistles and rang bells as they passed Mount Vernon, actually in honor of the Father of His Country but seemingly, to some persons, in derision at the unsightly wreckage of the mansion.

One of the women passengers in 1853 who sensed this derision wrote home to her daughter about the sad plight of Mount Vernon. The daughter, Miss Ann Pamela Cunningham, was shocked. She lived on a South Carolina plantation and she had been a semi-invalid for many years because of injuries received in a fall from a horse. The custom of the day was for young ladies to remain aloof from worldly affairs, even such virtuous ones as saving old mansions.

Miss Cunningham, however, organized a campaign that reached into every state of the nation. Two of her most effective aides were the Reverend Dr. Edward Everett, a silver-tongued orator from Massachusetts, and Miss Sarah C. Tracy of New York State, who had the courage years later to face bullets, army generals, politicians and President Abraham Lincoln to save Mount Vernon from destruction when it was caught between Confederate and Union forces in the Civil War.

Miss Cunningham organized the Mount Vernon Ladies Association of the Union and its barnstorming orators were as successful in awakening the people as Paul Revere's ride had been. In 1858, $200,000 had been collected to buy the estate from John A. Washington, Jr., a descendant of George Washington. Then the dark days of the Civil War arrived, along with the heroism of Miss Tracy.

In Washington's bedroom is the bed in which he died — a specially made bed six feet six inches long, since he was six feet two inches tall.

All the cooking at Mount Vernon was done in the kitchen house, near the mansion. An oven is on the right of the fireplace.

The Association first bought only 200 acres of the 8,000 that George Washington had assembled during his forty-five years of ownership. Gradually, more were acquired by the women until the present 500 were assembled; these compose Washington's Mansion House Farm.

Now, as when Washington was there, the estate consists of the mansion, which has eighteen main rooms, and fourteen auxiliary buildings, including the kitchen, washhouse and other dependencies. The exact evolution of the buildings is something of a mystery. It is known that John Washington, great-grandfather of George, acquired some of the property in 1674. It is believed that in 1698 someone was living on the property and that in 1735, when George's father, Augustine, built a four-room house there he incorporated some of the earlier building in it.

That simple four-room, one-story structure kept growing in size, as George Washington did in physical and political stature. He lived there as a child; also later, as a young man when it was owned by his elder half-brother, Lawrence. The house was one-and-one-half stories high when George acquired it in 1754, after Lawrence's death.

In 1759 Mount Vernon received a mistress when Washington married Martha Dandridge Custis, a widow with two children. The house was enlarged by the addition of another floor, porches and wings. There also were added formal gardens, a kitchen garden, a smokehouse, stables, a greenhouse and other structures.

Mount Vernon became — and it still is — one of the most distinguished examples of Colonial architecture. Its charm and importance are not due so much to component parts and details of woodwork as to the total harmony of the composition of mansion, gardens, lawns and dependencies.

Efforts to identify the architects have failed, but the indications are that Washington himself was largely responsible for the basic design as now presented. Architecture was not a common profession in his day and the property owner often did his own planning. Washington apparently was influenced in his planning by the Governor's Palace at Williamsburg, as shown by the design of wings of the house, the bowling green and the gardens and by references in his writings.

He had access to English books on the architecture of country homes, and the windows, cornices and doors of Mount Vernon bear striking resemblances to pictures in some of those early volumes. Tools, hardware and some of the trim used in building the mansion were imported from England.

One of the dominant features of the mansion — and perhaps the most copied feature in new houses of Colonial design — is the high-columned piazza that extends across the front, overlooking the Potomac. This piazza was something of an innovation when first built and it entitles Washington to a niche in the architectural world.

The banquet hall was built during the Revolution by Lund Washington, a distant kinsman of George. Detailed directions for its construction were written by the General while he was entrenched at Harlem Heights in New York. Later, while in Philadelphia, he sent instructions to Lund for decorating it. The fireplace mantel in this room was a gift from Samuel Vaughan of England. The pastoral scenes of its sculptured panels harmonize with the agricultural implements in the stucco ceiling and doorway friezes.

On the first floor also are a center hall, a little parlor, a west parlor, a library, a dining room and a downstairs bedroom. About 65 per cent of the present furnishings were Washington's and the percentage steadily increases. Few of the original items were there when the Association acquired the property, but by gift and by purchase the originals have gradually been reassembled. Washington's swords, paintings by Charles Wilson Peale, a key to the Bastille given by Lafayette and hundreds of other items are displayed.

Five bedrooms on the second floor include Washington's which contains the bed in which he died in 1799. It appears to be unusually short because of its exceptional width and height, but actually it is six feet six inches long. Washington was six feet two inches tall and at the age of fifty-four weighed 190 pounds.

The founders of the nation sat on this piazza at Mount Vernon to look upon the Potomac River and discuss the perplexing affairs of state.

One of the treasures at the estate is a clay bust made of Washington in 1785 by Jean Antoine Houdon. The portrait painters of that time often endowed their subjects with bon-bon facial expressions. Many of the portraits of Washington were no exceptions, but the Houdon bust presents Washington as a real man, supervising an estate with 215 slaves and vast fields of grain. The bust is on a pedestal at the exact height of Washington.

Despite Washington's affection for his home, he had been ready to sacrifice it in the Revolution. While Lund was in charge, a British warship anchored off shore and demanded provisions, in return for which the sailors agreed not to destroy the buildings. Lund complied, and besides taking provisions the sailors carried away twenty servants. When Washington heard of this, he wrote to Lund:

"I am very sorry to hear of your loss. I am a little sorry to hear of my own; but that which gives me the most concern is that you should go aboard the enemy's vessel and furnish them with refreshments. It would have been a less painful circumstance to me to have heard that in consequence of your noncompliance with their request, they had burnt my house and laid the plantation in ruins."

One of the owners of Mount Vernon after Washington's death was Bushrod Washington, a nephew who became an Associate Justice of the United States Supreme Court. Bushrod added a decorative railing to the roof of the piazza to dress it up, and he also added porches. When research proved in 1936 that these had not been there during George Washington's ownership, they were removed.

Nothing is necessarily static at Mount Vernon, either in correcting or preserving the buildings or adding to the authentic furnishings. Donations have included Washington's harpsichord from Nelly Custis, a relative of his wife, and Washington's bed from Custis Lee, another kinsman. Martha Washington had a habit of giving a cup and saucer to any guest she liked; cups and saucers are still finding their way back to Mount Vernon from all parts of the nation.

Phoebe Hearst, mother of William Randolph Hearst, sent $15,000 from California for a retaining wall to halt erosion on the estate. She was a vice-regent of the Mount Vernon Ladies' Association. Mrs. Justine Van Rensselaer Townsend of New York gave a burglar-alarm system.

The rear of Mount Vernon has the commonly-used entrances opening onto carriage roads. Servants' buildings are on either side.

For $20,000, J. P. Morgan of New York bought, and then contributed, the dress sword Washington had worn when he retired as commander of the Army after the Revolution. Later Mr. Morgan's son donated a sash that had been worn with the sword. Henry Ford gave motor-driven fire apparatus to the estate. Thomas A. Edison designed a power system for all the buildings. Others contributed to the redevelopment of the greenhouse, which had burned.

Cash donations were used to restore the exterior of the mansion, which has an unusual form of "rustication" that Washington developed. The yellow-pine siding is grooved so that it appears to be blocks of granite. It has several coats of white paint, with sand embedded in it so that the final texture is rough like that of stone. In contrast to the white sides of the house, the roof of thick colonial shingles is reddish brown. The doors also are reddish brown, and the shutters are green.

Members of the Association agree with the description Washington gave of the property: "No estate in America is more pleasantly situated than this. It lies in a high, dry and healthy country 300 miles by water from the sea, on one of the finest rivers in the world. It is situated in a latitude between the extremes of heat and cold."

In a farewell address to the Association, Miss Cunningham said: "Ladies, the home of Washington is in your charge. See to it that you keep it the home of Washington. Upon you rests this duty."

How well the duty has been performed is shown by the attendance, which now has reached 1,128,000 a year. The revenue provides for maintenance, but financially the estate is not well off. The governor of Virginia and a Board of Examiners visit the property periodically, since the state would obtain title to it if the Association did not fulfill its responsibility. There is every indication that both are determined to perpetuate the shrine and that Congress never again would shun an opportunity to preserve it.

❀   ❀   ❀   ❀   ❀   ❀   ❀   ❀

Mount Vernon is on Memorial Highway in Fairfax County, sixteen miles south of Washington, D. C., and near U. S. Route 1. It is open every day in the year, from 9 A. M. to 5 P. M. from March 1 to October 1 and from 9 A. M. to 4 P. M. the rest of the year. The admission is 75 cents for adults and 40 cents for children over twelve. Other children, military personnel and foreign dignitaries are admitted without charge.

Every President Added Something

The White House — a Montage

WASHINGTON · DISTRICT OF COLUMBIA

OF ALL THE MANSIONS in America, the White House is known to the most people. Visitors are streaming through it at a rate of 1,300,000 a year. Its stately portals and new interior elegance are familiar to millions of others who read the papers and watch television. Contemporary views are had of diplomats at rocking-chair conferences with President John F. Kennedy and of guards adding chicken wire to massive wrought-iron fences to keep Caroline's pets from roaming.

But there is a dramatic behind-the-scenes saga of the evolution of the White House that is generally overlooked . . . it is a mansion of memories.

The individual imprint of every President is indelibly ledgered in the walls, the adornments, the gardens and the customs of the fifty-four-room structure. Although the imprints overlap and blend into a unit for the modern home life of First Families, they provide mute evidence that every President had strong personal tastes and did not hesitate to exercise them.

Begun in 1792, the White House is the oldest public building in Washington. It was originally a gray sandstone residence of twenty rooms, without baths, running water, electricity, gas, elevator or even a service bell. It was a simple residence on the edge of a swamp, in the new Federal City that was excessively hot in summer, cold in winter and dank most of the time. But its site was the only one geographically acceptable to the northern and southern segments of the new nation.

George Washington, the only President who never lived in the White House, shared in choosing James Hoban, an immigrant Irishman of Charleston, South Carolina, as the winner of a $500 prize for the best design for the residence. The plan was Georgian, inspired by the Duke of Leinster's Palace in Dublin and pictures of English gentlemen's houses in an architectural book of James Gibbs, a disciple of Sir Christopher Wren. A plan by Thomas Jefferson for a Greco-Roman classical structure was rejected.

Washington, who died before the building was completed, limited the construction costs to $400,000. The house was first known as the President's Palace and it did not get its first coat of white paint until after the British had set fire to it in 1814.

The State Dining Room is one of the most elegant rooms in the White House and is the scene of important social and political events.

Weddings, funerals, plays, recitals, entertainments and big receptions have taken place in the East Room of the White House.

President John Adams became the first occupant of the residence in 1800 and set a custom, followed by some of his successors, of donning a bathing suit and sauntering down to the Potomac River for a swim. Life at the mansion was that informal.

Although Jefferson had lost the contest for designing the mansion, he had a fling at planning revisions of the structure when he moved in as President in 1801. He hired Benjamin Latrobe to design the stately north and south porticos, which were built several years later. He also converted the drawing rooms into informal reception centers and built terraces and colonnades resembling those of Monticello, his home in Virginia. He added rotating clothes closets and built cabinets that held official documents and his carpenters' tools in adjacent drawers.

When President James Madison took office, his wife Dolley, a famous hostess, got rid of the carpenters' tools and restored the drawing rooms. Dolley was unprepared, however, for the British soldiers who arrived without invitation in 1814 while her husband was absent. She fled for her life as the mansion was set afire. Under her dress she carried a Gilbert Stuart portrait of Washington, which she had cut from its frame. Today the portrait is the only remaining item of the original furnishings.

Lincoln's bedroom in the White House had been his cabinet room. Here he signed the Emancipation Proclamation. All Presidents since Lincoln have occasionally slept in this bed.

Moving into the restored mansion in 1817, President James Monroe installed huge chandeliers, rich brocades, French Empire furniture and Hannibal and Minerva clocks. He also built the south portico designed by Latrobe. But the gardens of the White House became spectacular only when President John Quincy Adams arrived.

Then the north portico, providing the imposing entrance on Pennsylvania Avenue, was added by President Andrew Jackson. He planted the famous magnolia trees on the grounds and piped the first water into the mansion. Martin Van Buren added gold table service and lavish decorations. His successors also spent heavily until James K. Polk arrived to end extravagances and also to bar drinking, card playing, dancing and profanity. He did, however, pipe the first gas into the house.

Millard Fillmore could not find a dictionary when he assumed the Presidency. He added not only a dictionary but a $2,000 library of rare books. Franklin Pierce installed the first central heating system.

During the Civil War, Union soldiers camped on the grounds and slept on the floors of rooms and corridors. President and Mrs. Lincoln bickered over what he considered excessive "flubdub" decorations. After his assassination, most of the valuable furnishings vanished. Some historians say Mrs. Lincoln sold them; others assert that vandals stole them. The missing items still are being returned to the White House through gifts and purchases.

Andrew Johnson, the one-time tailor from Tennessee, added the high wrought-iron fences of the grounds and Ulysses S. Grant installed elaborate false timbers and cut-glass chandeliers in the East Room. Other Presidents made changes but it remained for James A. Garfield to install an elevator and discard twenty-four van loads of "Mississippi riverboat" furniture he considered objectionable.

Weddings and funeral took place in the East Room. The six lively children of Theodore Roosevelt used the room for jujitsu, also for some of their guinea pigs, dogs, cats, birds and snakes, and even a pony once was smuggled into the building. Roosevelt decorated the family dining room with stuffed heads of animals. On a marble mantel he inscribed the following quotation of President John Adams that visitors still can see:

"I pray heaven to bestow the best of blessings on this house and on all that shall hereafter inhabit it. May none but honest and wise men ever rule under this roof."

Bathtubs large enough for four people were installed by William Howard Taft, a man of imposing girth. He also added Oriental art objects along with Japanese cherry trees on the lawn.

Most of Grant's ugly decorations gradually vanished, and Roosevelt's stuffed animal heads were so distasteful to Woodrow Wilson that he had them removed. Wilson's first wife, an artist, set up a studio in the mansion.

The White House's Blue Room is an oval drawing room. The parquet floor is uncovered. On the walls is blue-and-gold damask.

In the Red Room of the White House is an Aubusson carpet and Dolley Madison's sofa. The walls are covered with red silk; borders have gold scrolls.

All the Presidents kept adding more pipes, wiring and conduits until the honeycombed timbers sagged dangerously and the foundations, on soft clay, settled several feet. Franklin D. Roosevelt strengthened the walls, added a swimming pool, enlarged the office space and built a bomb shelter but real trouble developed after Harry S. Truman moved in and added the controversial balcony to the south portico — controversial on the ground of symmetry.

At a reception in the Blue Room in 1948, Mr. Truman heard strange creakings and cracklings. Overhead he saw a heavy chandelier sag and vibrate; he felt as though the sword of Damocles were hanging over his head, he said.

Lorenzo S. Winslow, the White House architect, and other officials reported that the White House was standing upright "just through force of habit." While broken timbers and sagging stairs were still being examined, the East Room's ceiling dropped six inches and a leg of a grand piano plunged through a floor.

Most experts thought the least costly thing to do would be to tear down the mansion and build anew, but the public demanded that the old White House be preserved. A total reconstruction of the interior, with modern steel and concrete, marbles and fine woods, was undertaken at a cost exceeding $6,000,000.

Moving into the rebuilt White House in 1952, Truman converted Lincoln's old cabinet room into the Lincoln Room. In it is much of Lincoln's furniture, including an oversize bed made for his long frame. Mrs. Kennedy reports that all recent Presidents "have loved to sleep in the Lincoln bed." She feels that if "any room in the White House has ghosts, it is the Lincoln Room."

Mrs. Kennedy has made a personal project of improving and preserving the decorations and furnishings of the White House. Thousands of items that had wandered from the residence are gradually being retrieved, to join the Eisenhower gold china, the Madison sofa, the Van Buren chest, the Daniel Webster lounge, Franklin Roosevelt's golden eagle piano, chandeliers made 200 years ago in France and other historic objects.

"This house will always grow," Mrs. Kennedy has commented.

A White House committee headed by Henry F. du Pont, owner of the Winterthur mansion in Delaware, has been set up to seek more original items for the mansion. Presidents in the past had the privilege of disposing of White House furnishings but under a 1961 law all furnishings now are part of a permanent collection. If any First Family ever wants to dispose of an object, it must be given to the Smithsonian Institution.

Formerly the dining room, the Green Room of the White House is a Federal-style parlor. The classical chandelier and furniture are eighteenth century.

The mansion is becoming "a stronger panorama of our great history," President Kennedy has said. "What is particularly interesting is that two-thirds of the visitors now are boys and girls. I have always felt that American history is sometimes dull. But if the people come here and see this building alive and in a sense touch the Presidents who have been here, they'll go home better Americans."

* * * * * * * *

The White House is at 1600 Pennsylvania N. W. but the tourists' entrance is around the corner on East Executive Avenue. The East, Red, Blue, Green and State Dining Rooms are open from 10 A. M. to noon Tuesday through Friday and from 10 A. M. to 2 P. M. Saturdays, except on holidays. Admission is free.

A main entrance of the White House is at the north portico, where a driveway circles in front of the doors.

A Wonderland of Americana

Henry F. du Pont's Winterthur

NEW CASTLE COUNTY · DELAWARE

NESTLED IN THE WOODED HILLS of Christiana Hundred near Wilmington is the foremost mansion of the du Pont family, developed while the members of this clan were the money kings of America. The mansion is Winterthur, a 110-room private house that now has been converted into a museum of Americana. Each of the rooms is different, representing in its design a specific period of early architecture and in its furnishings a definite era of artistic taste — or lack thereof.

The years represented by the rooms span the two centuries from 1640 to 1840. The woodwork, the ceilings, the walls, the windows, the fireplaces and the floors of entire rooms of old houses from New Hampshire to North Carolina have been bought with du Pont money and carted to Winterthur to be re-established in the mansion, which actually is just a big shell to hold them. When a 1775 room from Wernersville, Pennsylvania, recently failed to fit into an allotted space, the walls of Winterthur were pushed out twelve inches.

Winterthur 93

The antique furnishings have been so painstakingly collected and sorted that all objects and decorations in each room harmonize. Collectors and architects generally agree that the result is probably the largest assemblage of bona fide fine old chests, sconces, chairs, tables, rugs, prints, silver, china, pottery, decorative arts and other objects in this country.

The patriarch of the du Pont family in America was Pierre Samuel du Pont de Nemours, a noted French political economist, publicist and statesman. He was one of the constitutional monarchists forced into hiding during the French Revolution. Captured and sentenced to death on the guillotine, he was saved by the fall of Robespierre at the end of the Reign of Terror. He faced, however, such a perilously uncertain future in France that he came to America to re-establish his family and start a new career with the help of his old friends, Marquis de Lafayette, Thomas Jefferson and George Washington.

The du Pont family arrived at Newport, Rhode Island, in 1800, soon settled at Bergen Point, New Jersey, and in 1802 moved to Wilmington, where Pierre's son, Eleuthere Irénée du Pont, built a powder mill on Brandywine Creek. Each successive war and its demands for gunpowder added to the family fortune, which

The Chinese Parlor at Winterthur has wallpaper painted in 1770 and Oriental art treasures that first reached Europe in Marco Polo's time.

ultimately exceeded $5,000,000,000. Expanding their investments, the du Ponts became major owners of General Motors, United States Rubber and companies that produced rayon, cellophane, "fabrikoid," "pyralin," shatterproof glass, paints, dyes, photographic film, artificial rubber, cutlery and pharmaceuticals. Some of the profits helped to develop Winterthur.

The family has always been closely knit. The father of Irénée made his sons pledge with drawn swords, a salute and an embrace to "promise each other to be always firmly united, to comfort each other in every sorrow, to help each other in all efforts, to stand by each other in all difficulty and danger." That was in 1784 and through the generations the members of the family generally complied with the pledge and retained tight control of the du Pont dynasty and all its assets.

Henry Francis du Pont, who converted the old family home of Winterthur into the museum that it is today, is a great grandson of Irénée, the founder of the du Pont company. Born in 1880 at Winterthur, which then was the estate of his father, Colonel Henry A. du Pont, a United States Senator and du Pont executive, he has been a director and a member of the bonus, salary and finance com-

Specially designed for furniture by the New York cabinetmaker Duncan Phyfe, the Phyfe Room at Winterthur is elegantly simple.

The imposing Readbourne Stair Hall at Winterthur is from a mansion built in 1733 near Centreville, Md., by Colonel James Hollyday.

mittees of the company for most of his adult life but he has not been active in the company as a full-time executive. Instead, his interests have been in raising cattle, in collecting antiques and in the arts — especially in perpetuating the culture that in his view Winterthur exemplifies.

"Individuals and nations take their greatest inspiration through the continued remembrance of a glorious past," Mr. du Pont gave as the Winterthur creed. "My purpose is to show Americans the way early Americans lived and to preserve our country's rich tradition of craftsmanship in architecture and household arts."

He began the extensive collection of old rooms and furnishings in 1927 and deeded the estate in 1951 to the Winterthur Corporation, a philanthropic, educational, endowed foundation. He lived in the mansion until 1951, when he moved into a new house next door. His wife, an ardent collaborator in collecting the art treasures, was the former Ruth Wales of Hyde Park, New York. They have two daughters, who are married and live elsewhere.

The first owner of Winterthur was James Antoine Bidermann, who came to America from Winterthur, Switzerland, in 1814 to study the du Pont powder mills. In 1816 he married Evelina Gabrielle du Pont, a daughter of Irénée. Their

A graceful spiral staircase at Winterthur is from Montmorenci, a show place built in 1822 near Warrenton, N. C., by General William Williams.

son, James, was born in 1817. After acquiring 445 acres in Christiana Hundred, the Bidermanns built in 1839 a large house that was the beginning of what is now the Winterthur Museum. It has been enlarged and remodeled more times than anyone can remember. The building is largely of concrete and it has shutters, many chimneys, dormers and pillared façades. The exterior architecture is baffling but it has a strong French flavor.

James Bidermann became the owner of Winterthur at his father's death in 1865. Two years later he sold the estate to his mother's brother, Henry du Pont, who doubled the size of the tract by acquiring adjacent farms. In 1889 the estate was inherited by Henry's son, Colonel Henry A. du Pont, who had won a Congressional Medal of Honor in the Civil War and later became a senator. At the Colonel's death in 1926 the estate went to his son, Henry Francis du Pont, founder of the museum.

Many of the art objects in Winterthur today are priceless but general valuations of the estate and its contents range from $3,000,000 to more than $10,000,000. Millionaires, artists and clerks rub elbows in touring its wonders. The president of General Motors dropped in one day and soon was chatting about antiques with a factory worker from a near-by plant. He who regards antiques as outmoded and as uninteresting as yesterday's newspaper cannot escape the impact here of the soundness of American craftsmanship, its functionalism and its enduring common sense. Here are two centuries of domestic architecture, furniture, metal work, textiles, ceramics, paintings and prints chosen with meticulous regard for quality and fitness of location. The scope of the mansion and the workmanship displayed give a new understanding and respect for the integrity of American craftsmen. And every known material used in early American houses, whether it is Italian marble, Spanish brass, French plasterwork or English carved wood, is shown in Winterthur as it was originally used.

There is signed furniture by famous cabinetmakers of Salem, Boston, Newport, New York and Philadelphia. There are textiles of the colonial era. Blue-and-white checked linen draperies from old Pennsylvania mills in one room contrast with an adjacent room's pastel satins designed by Phillipe de Lassalle, the textile genius employed by Louis XVI. Walls of some rooms are covered with rare flock paper and decorated canvas. Neighboring rooms have hand-painted Chinese papers and block-printed French scenic papers.

Paul Revere made some of the silver tankards and pitchers in Winterthur. Paintings include several by John Singleton Copley, Benjamin West and Gilbert Stuart. On the floors are carpets from Persia and Asia Minor, famous weaves of Isfahan, Ushak and the Caucasus. They were the so-called "Turkey carpets" imported before the Revolutionary War. Of later date are the tapestry-weave Aubusson carpets, imported in the early nineteenth century, and colorful American woven strip carpets.

Typical room installations in the mansion include such items as the Port Royal Entrance Hall from a house built in 1762 on Frankford Creek north of Philadelphia by Edward Stiles, a wealthy planter and merchant from Bermuda. In this hallway the Doric entablature follows the severe pattern of classical architecture. The arched fanlights crowning the doors suggest the pierced shells seen in Chippendale ornamentation. A paneled dado skirts the lower walls; above it is eighteenth-century Chinese wallpaper painted with tree peonies, bamboo, birds and butterflies in muted colors.

The Readbourne Stair Hall was taken from a house built in 1733 near Centreville, Maryland, for Colonel James Hollyday. The halls, as well as the rooms, of plantation houses were exceptionally large for coolness in summer.

The Latimeria Room was originally part of a house built in 1815 by William Warner in Wilmington from plans drawn by his friend, Eleuthere Irénée du Pont. The Stamper-Blackwell Porch and Parlor were formerly in a Philadelphia house built in 1764 for John Stamper, a prosperous English-born merchant and mayor of Philadelphia. It later was the home of the Reverend Dr. Robert Blackwell, a leading clergyman.

The du Pont Dining Room has paneling from the Readbourne house near Centreville. The mantelpiece and overmantel are from Willow Brook, built in 1800 near Kernstown, Virginia. Over the mantel is a Stuart painting of Washington. The Candlestick Room has cupboards and shelves, from an 1800 store in Chelsea, Pennsylvania, which have been adapted to display the wide variety of candlesticks used in American homes from 1750 to 1850.

The Baltimore Rooms from eighteenth-century houses have decorations reminiscent of the Roman Republic. Inspired by the art objects found in excavations at Pompeii and Herculaneum, the classical ornamentations were extremely popular in the Federal period in this country.

A graceful spiral staircase dominates the broad Montmorenci Stair Hall, formerly the outstanding feature of a mansion near Warrenton, North Carolina. Built in 1822 by General William Williams, known to everyone as Pretty Billy Williams, the mansion was his gift to his third wife. Many gay parties were held there. One of the guests at the Williams mansion was Lafayette.

The Marlboro Room was taken from a plantation house known as Patuxent Manor, built in 1744 for Charles Grahame in Calvert County, Maryland. A superb collection of furniture by the New York cabinetmaker Duncan Phyfe graces the Phyfe Room, illustrating the elegant simplicity of the Federal period and the American adaptations of the styles of Thomas Sheraton, French Directoire and English Regency.

Other rooms portray the Queen Anne, Chippendale, Classical, Empire and other periods. Among the ones generally shown to everyone are the Hart Room (Massachusetts, 1640), the Oyster Bay Room (Long Island, 1667), the Wentworth Room (New Hampshire, 1673), the Vauxhall Room (New Jersey, 1725), the Queen Anne Dining Room (New Hampshire, 1760), the Flock Room (Virginia, 1714), the Chestertown Room (Maryland, 1762), the Chinese Parlor (China, 1770) and the Empire Parlor (Albany, 1830).

Noted for their colorful azaleas, dogwoods, broad lawns and winding paths, the gardens of Winterthur were described by a Delaware newspaper in 1852 in the following words, still appropriate today:

"The visitor is astonished and delighted at the romantic appearance — first at the beautiful fields as he wends his way on the serpentine road, next at passing through the beautiful forest which is decked in various directions with gravelled walks until he arrives in the valley where the stupendous tenant house, large barns and outbuildings attract his attention, surrounded by timber. A short distance to the east on the summit of the hill stands the splendid mansion of the proprietor. It is enclosed with big oaks and other trees, overlooking the valley and other points, which render it a perfect palace."

Winterthur is not the only attraction of the du Pont family in this area. Longwood Gardens at near-by Kennett Square are among the most spectacular displays in the country. There are formal flower gardens, an ensemble of fountains with colored lights playing on geysers of water, and a glass-enclosed arboretum covering the equivalent of three city blocks.

Longwood was the estate of Pierre Samuel du Pont, who died in 1954. After opening the gardens to the public in 1921, he endowed a foundation in 1931 to operate them in perpetuity. They are open to the public, without charge, from 11 A. M. to 5 P. M., daily, also occasionally at night from May to October for the illuminated display of dancing geysers. The residence is not open to the public.

Just one minute off U. S. Route 13 at Odessa, Maryland, is another du Pont shrine. It is the restored Georgian residence of William Corbit, a wealthy Quaker and tanner from Philadelphia. It was built in 1774 and was restored recently by the Winterthur Corporation.

        ✿ ✿ ✿ ✿ ✿ ✿ ✿ ✿

Winterthur is on Kennett Pike (State Route 52), ten minutes by automobile from Wilmington. During most of the year only sixty visitors a day are admitted to all the 100 rooms that are on display, and advance reservations by mail are advisable. In May, twenty of the more important rooms and the gardens may be seen without reservations. The rates are $2.50 for full-day tours, $1.50 for half-day tours and 25 cents for students in groups. The hours for tours are from 9:30 A. M. to 4:30 P. M. every day except Sunday, Monday, New Year's Day, Washington's Birthday, Memorial Day, Thanksgiving and Christmas. It also is closed the first two weeks in July.

The Five-and-Dime Babel

Hubert T. Parson's Shadow Lawn

WEST LONG BRANCH · NEW JERSEY

WHAT KIND of a Shangri La would a five-and-dime store clerk dream of building some day, just so his wife and he could live it up in a manner that seemed wildly impossible while he was behind a counter ten hours a day selling ribbons and goldfish?

Hubert T. Parson, who rose from a lowly clerkship to the presidency of the F. W. Woolworth Company during forty years with the concern, gave the answer when he spent $9,500,000 to build and furnish a 128-room mansion on 108 acres in the heart of America's oldest seaside resort area.

He chose a location on West Long Branch's millionaires' row, near estates made famous by Solomon R. Guggenheim, Ulysses S. Grant, Jim Fisk and James A. Hearn, in an area of gambling houses, block-long hotels and steeplechase parks. He built his home, Shadow Lawn, on the exact site of a previous Shadow Lawn mansion that had been the famous summer White House of former President Woodrow Wilson.

Mr. Parson put the Wilson house, a fifty-two-room colonial structure, to shame by constructing a three-story limestone extravaganza with a penthouse and two basements. In decorating the rooms he used forty-six varieties of marble and petrified woods, with 1,500 mirrors to provide multiple reflections of himself. Even in the ornate Pompeian swimming pool he could not avoid seeing himself on the ceiling and on all the walls — unless he closed his eyes.

The mansion has a great hall three stories high, on the ceiling of which Mr. Parson installed a leaded-glass skylight 100 feet long with thousands of electric bulbs. He installed a pipe organ he could play electrically from many parts of the house, and built an Aztec solarium on the roof. There were seventeen master suites of Chinese, Japanese, French, English, Spanish, Italian and other national designs, with nineteen harmonizing baths. The house included a theater for 300 persons, a gymnasium, two bowling alleys and a billiard room.

For the servants, he built a wing with thirty-five bedrooms and twelve baths, plus a $100,000 cottage.

He rimmed the acreage with a wrought-iron fence suitable for a Buckingham Palace, and inside it he had constructed a nine-hole golf course, pools, patios, gardens and a spectacular fountain that tosses geysers of water into the air while orchestrated colored lights play upon them.

Shadow Lawn has been called the Versailles of America, the same label that a number of chambers of commerce have given their best tourist attractions. While Shadow Lawn is not the size of the palace at Seine-et-Oise in France, it does have some of the grandeur and significance of it, including the affiliation with Woodrow Wilson, one of the makers of the Versailles Treaty.

The original Shadow Lawn mansion attracted considerable interest when it was built, in 1903, by John A. McCall, president of the New York Life Insurance Company and a former Superintendent of Insurance of New York State. Mr. McCall made it an elaborate place, with gold-plated fixtures and king-size rooms. He had a hankering for many bathtubs and kept revising the plans to add more; when the house was completed there still were extra bathtubs on the lawns.

Mr. McCall was soon deprived of enjoying the luxuries. Devoted to promoting the insurance business, he believed that company money should be contributed to political organizations and lobbyists so new legislation would benefit the companies. Some persons said his spending "united the solid integrity of the bankers with the cold realism of the politicians." Legislative investigators and the directors of his own company had other opinions. Besides losing his job, Mr. McCall lost Shadow Lawn.

The estate then had a succession of owners, including the colorful John A. White — known as "Postage Stamp" White after his successful purchase of a $15,000,000 bond issue with a sole investment of two cents for a stamp to mail his bid. Captain J. B. Greenhut, a wealthy New York merchant, was the owner in 1916 when President Woodrow Wilson decided to return to his home state of New Jersey to campaign for re-election. The Captain lent the estate to the President, who contributed $2,500 to charities in appreciation.

From the front porch of the old mansion the President gave speeches, on one occasion talking to 3,000 persons on the lawn. He went to bed at Shadow Lawn on election night believing he had been defeated, since the old *New York World* had erroneously reported a victory for Charles Evans Hughes. While shaving the next morning he heard of his victory.

In 1918 the neighbors of Shadow Lawn contributed $25,000 toward buying the estate as a permanent summer White House. A bill authorizing the government's acceptance of it was filed in Congress. In 1919, however, Mr. Parson, who had just become president of the Woolworth chain, bought the property for $1,000,000.

Mr. Parson, tall, dark-haired and handsome, had been born in Toronto, Canada, and migrated to Brooklyn. While a young man he had put a five-cent job-wanted advertisement in a New York newspaper and Frank W. Woolworth had hired him for twelve dollars a week.

When he became an executive, Mr. Parson expanded the chain until it had 2,430 stores in many parts of the world. He also experimented with adding merchandise that sold for as much as twenty cents, quite a daring experiment for a Woolworth store in those days.

Mr. Parson took his wife, the former Maysie Gasque of Brooklyn, on some of his travels. Together they collected choir stalls, French tapestries, paintings and other art treasures of past centuries that would fit into the new mansion that had long been in Mr. Parson's dreams.

In 1927 a fire at Shadow Lawn burned the old house to the ground. Many of the treasures Mr. and Mrs. Parson had collected were lost, including costly silver, jewelry and precious stones. Guards were stationed on the property to prevent the looting of an estimated $100,000 worth of melted silver and gold.

Plans for a new mansion of modified French design then were drafted and the ground was broken in 1928. The work continued for two and one-half years, running into the worst part of the depression and into a financial setback and a loss of health for Mr. Parson. The ninety tons of coal a month that the new mansion needed for heat was one of his financial troubles.

The architect of the mansion was Horace Trumbauer of Philadelphia. One of the first things that Mr. Parson directed him to do was to plan a fireproof building. Indiana limestone was used for the exterior and much of the interior was built of stone.

The exterior has wrought-copper balconies and pillared entrances. Sphinxes flank wide steps to a terrace, and on the roof are cupids and dolphins. The fountains are part of the formal gardens. Avenues of trees line the walks and roads to the edges of the estate.

The great hall of Shadow Lawn is three stories high. The walls are marble. A leaded glass skylight is 100 feet long.

(Left) From a bedroom at Shadow Lawn the formal gardens are a winter wonderland after a snowfall. (Right) The Aztec solarium of Shadow Lawn has murals and a fountain of glazed tiles.

The staircase from the grand hall to the second floor has a landing large enough for a piano, an organ console and enough furniture to fill the living room of a modern home. Mrs. Parson had electricians install hidden buttons at convenient places in the mansion so she could play the organ electrically at will, the pipes reverberating in crescendo or singing in a muted whisper, according to her mood at the moment.

Elevators and fireplaces are at each end of the great hall, the leaded-glass windows of which are typical of those in other rooms. Some of the windows were obtained from a sixteenth-century English abbey. All the mantels in the mansion are different. The ornate ceiling of the dining room was reported to have cost $75,000. The kitchen has two walk-in safes for table silver and silver dishes, and most of the bedrooms have wall safes.

The bedrooms and baths on the second floor are arranged in a chain so that if all the doors are open a person can walk from one room to another without going into the hall. One bath is twenty feet wide. There also are convenient rooms for arranging flowers; the Parsons kept bouquets throughout the mansion.

A bath with walls of petrified wood is of special interest. This paneling from Arizona is a variety of quartz in which minerals have replaced the wood. Shadow Lawn has one of the best displays of this petrified wood in America.

The mansion has a built-in electronic communications system. Master switches at the bedsides in the two largest suites, which Mr. and Mrs. Parson occupied, permit the immediate illumination of every room in the mansion if intruders are detected.

The large suites having living rooms and ornate baths with built-in scales so delicate that they can register a heart beat. Besides gold-plated fixtures, the baths have mirrors on all sides; as noted, some rooms even have mirrors on the ceilings. Closets of a few master bedrooms are double deckers, with narrow stairs to the upper levels.

The Parsons had only a few years in the mansion. As the depression deepened, the cost of illuminating the great hall for one evening about equalled the weekly wage of a Woolworth clerk. Taxes of $24,000 a year became so onerous that the Parsons stopped paying them and moved back to New York.

Shadow Lawn was known as a white elephant from almost every point of view. When the back taxes reached $132,000, the borough of West Long Branch foreclosed and bought the property for $100. Mrs. Parson rescued the furnishings still in it by paying a $30,592 tax lien that had been levied against them. The borough tried to set up a jockey club in the mansion but this failed.

The place had been vacant for many years when Dr. Eugene H. Lehman, an educator and former mayor of Tarrytown, New York, took a look at it. He had moved his Highland Manor College from Tarrytown to West Long Branch, later converting it into Monmouth College, and was looking for a new campus.

Dr. Lehman, who even at the age of eighty enjoyed throwing the hammer on the Shadow Lawn grounds and running around the lawns in shorts, decided to offer $150,000 for the mansion and eighty acres. He met with the borough officials but, suddenly feeling that he really could not afford more than $100,000, offered that amount.

The borough officials looked doubtful and reserved decision. When Dr. Lehman returned home his wife scolded him, believing that the deal had collapsed because the offer had been too small, but a few days later it was accepted.

Monmouth College moved to Shadow Lawn in 1956. The mansion was converted into a delightful main building for administrative offices, classrooms, study halls, theater, bookstore, lounges and recreation rooms. The co-educational college has 2,000 students. Near-by estates, outmoded as homes by rising taxes and a scarcity of servants, have been added to the campus.

❀　❀　❀　❀　❀　❀　❀　❀

Shadow Lawn is at Cedar and Norwood Avenues in West Long Branch. It is open for college business from 9 A.M. to 8 P.M. Monday through Friday, except during college holidays. The grounds and the exterior of the mansion can be seen at any time and the rooms may be visited by special arrangement.

Coke, Bloodshed and Grandeur

Henry Clay Frick's Sanctuary

NEW YORK CITY · NEW YORK

HENRY CLAY FRICK, who lit the coke ovens of Pennsylvania for the age of steel, came out of the murky smoke and bloody labor strife of mill towns to build one of the finest private homes on New York City's fashionable Fifth Avenue. It is one of the few in the metropolis that will remain indefinitely as evidence of an era when millionaires did not have to share much of their wealth with the government and could spend $5,000,000 for a town house and an equal amount to furnish it.

Such spending was just what Mr. Frick did on a plot of land between Seventieth and Seventy-first Streets on Fifth Avenue, across the avenue from Central Park. To assure perpetuity of his block-long creation he bequeathed it to the public for the display of fine arts and set up a $15,000,000 trust fund to pay the bills.

Visitors commonly refer to the building as a "mansion" being used as a "museum." Those two words are shunned by the Frick family and associates, who speak of the building as a "former residence" that now is the home of "The Frick Collection." This terminology seems appropriate for a legacy from the cool, taciturn and strong-willed Mr. Frick, who spent money freely but spoke modestly.

The first floor of the house is open to visitors. Several of the rooms — including a gallery 100 feet long — are arranged much as Mr. Frick had left them. In forty years of collecting he brought together 160 works of art, which he arranged not by rigid classification but so as to create an intimate atmosphere of a private home.

The number of rooms in the entire house, which has two floors above and two below the main floor, is not publicly discussed. The structure is larger in some respects than the Georgian mansion that Andrew Carnegie built twenty blocks farther north on the avenue, which has sixty-four rooms and its own miniature railroad in the basement to move supplies.

Mr. Frick built his residence in 1913-14 but he would never have got around to it if the marksmanship of a Russian assassin had been better in 1892. The building bears no evidence, however, of the violent life he once led. As it stands today the big stone structure typifies a man of culture and generosity — which Mr. Frick was — and not a tough manufacturer and unrelenting labor-union smasher — which he also was.

He was born in Pennsylvania's Westmoreland County in 1849, the year of the California gold rush. His father, of Swiss ancestry, was a farmer. His mother, of a Mennonite family, inherited an interest in the profitable Old Overholt whisky distillery.

With only thirty months of formal schooling, Mr. Frick went to work at the age of seventeen in an uncle's store and later became a bookkeeper for Old Overholt at $1,000 a year. In the financial debacle of 1873 he bought coke ovens and coal mines at panic prices. Becoming the King of Coke, he was a millionaire when Andrew Carnegie later made him a manager and partner in the Carnegie Steel Corporation.

In 1892 Mr. Carnegie posted notices in the factories that wages would be reduced and jobs would no longer be given to members of the Amalgamated Association of Iron and Steel Workers. Then he departed on a luxury liner for his castle in Scotland for a long vacation, leaving Mr. Frick to fight what was to become the bloody Battle of Homestead, Pennsylvania, on July 6, 1892.

Mr. Frick, married at the age of thirty-two to Adelaide Howard Childs, had traveled in Europe to begin his art collection and had begun dreaming of building a millionaire's castle, while developing an intense dislike of labor unions. "We have reached the point at Homestead where the men are dictators of our business," he commented. "An employee cannot be promoted without their permission. If expensive machinery is installed, they will not permit it to be fully worked."

A living room of the Frick residence has intricate cornices, El Greco and Hol-bein paintings and Giovanni Bologna sculpture.

He notified the Homestead mill workers that the reduced wages had to be accepted. The workers not only refused but some of them fortified themselves behind fences that Mr. Frick had installed to protect the mills. He hired 300 Pinkerton detectives, who tried to enter the river-front plant secretly on two great armored scows pulled by tugs.

When the workers detected the Trojan horses on the river they opened fire with rifles. The Pinkertons returned the fire, and a savage battle ensued. At the end of the day 14 men had been killed and 163 had been seriously injured. As federal troops moved in to restore order, Mr. Frick's business future and his dreams of a castle seemed to be in eclipse.

Seventeen days later the eclipse almost became a total blackout when Alexander Berkman, a Russian who worked in the mills, entered Mr. Frick's office in downtown Pittsburgh, shot him twice with a revolver and stabbed him several times with a knife.

Public sentiment, which had been violently against Mr. Frick, turned strongly in his favor. Editorials, sermons and political speeches lauded his "courageous fight." The union left Homestead, and Mr. Frick resumed his art collecting and the planning of a residence to house it.

A bitter quarrel between him and Mr. Carnegie over business policies later occurred but was settled after long litigation. Although both built large homes on Fifth Avenue, they never spoke to each other after the quarrel — even when they mixed with the same business leaders and searched for treasures in the same art galleries.

Mr. Frick had seen some of the Vanderbilt mansions in New York City and had estimated that the upkeep of one of them was about $300,000 a year, or nearly $1,000 a day. That, he thought, would be just about right for him. He bought the old Lenox Library in the block above Seventieth Street, tore it down and picked the brains of architects and friends to determine what style of house he should build.

Georgian mansions, Tudor castles, Venetian palazzi and Spanish villas were rising wherever millionaires lived. Mr. Frick decided on a style reminiscent externally of a French town house of the eighteenth century and internally of an English home of later vintage.

Carrere and Hastings were the architects, with Tom Hastings doing most of the planning. The firm also designed the New York Public Library on Fifth Avenue and the partners considered the Frick home and the library their masterpieces. At any rate, the Frick building is a sculptured masterpiece, with every cornice, balustrade and wrought-iron fence designed carefully to harmonize with all other parts of the home.

The exterior is of Indiana limestone. The adornments, which visitors are immediately aware of in the fences and walled gardens, were produced by Piccirilli Brothers. Ceilings and woodwork of some of the rooms are of walnut

(Above) In the dining room of the Frick residence are tables expandable for fifty guests, Gainsborough paintings and a carved-wood chandelier. (Below) The Fragonard room of the Frick residence has art, furniture and a fireplace from France.

Built of five varieties of imported and domestic marble, the grand staircase of the Frick residence has a large landing for an organ.

and mahogany, and many of the walls, even in upper-floor corridors, are of marble. Among the marbles used in harmonious contrasts are three from France — Tavernelle Fleuri, Tavernelle Rose and Rouge de Rance. Others include a veined red Italian marble and the St. Genevieve Rose marble from Missouri.

The grand staircase of five marbles has a landing, midway between floors, on which there is an organ, with pipes that reach through the upper floors. Mr. Frick loved simple music and he often would sit in the gardens or living rooms while a professional organist filled the building with the penetrating melodies of "The Rosary" and "Silver Threads Among the Gold." One of Mr. Frick's biographers pictured him seated under a Bagdad baldachin with a copy of *The Saturday Evening Post* in his hands.

Near the dining and living rooms and the gardens Mr. Frick built a west gallery that is 100 feet long. In this today are many of the 160 paintings and statues that Mr. Frick collected, as they were when he was alive. Among them is his favorite, one of the finest pieces of art in the collection, a self-portrait by Rembrandt made late in the artist's life.

In the rooms also are paintings by Ingres, Goya, Van Dyck, Velazquez, Turner, Whistler, Gainsborough, El Greco, Renoir, Vermeer, Holbein and Constable, as well as statues by Houdon and others. Some of the Persian carpets are 300-year-old treasures.

The Boucher Room has eight panels painted by Boucher for Madame de Pompadour. The Fragonard Room has fourteen panels by Fragonard, bought by Mr. Frick from the J. P. Morgan family for $1,250,000. The panels were installed in the Frick home under the supervision of Sir Charles Carrick Allom, a British decorative expert. In the Enamel Room are forty Limoges, also bought from the Morgans, for $1,500,000.

Some of the art works in the house have figured in history. A Holbein portrait of Sir Thomas More was reported to have been thrown in anger from a palace window by Anne Boleyn. The painting was found in the street by a servant and taken to Rome, where it was exhibited for many years before reaching the Frick home.

Ironically, portraits of Mr. Frick were circulated in Europe — perhaps because of all the money he was spending there for art treasures. An American traveler stopping at a roadside tavern in Ireland's County Galway in the Black and Tan period was astounded to see a fine life-size portrait of Mr. Frick on the dining-room wall.

A garden fountain of the Frick home was carved from a ten-ton block of marble. Records show that eighteen blocks of marble were quarried and carefully examined before one was found with the exact tonalities desired.

Special velvets of changing colors were woven as wall coverings for some rooms. As visitors shift positions, the colors of the velvets vary. One room has a concealed motion-picture projector in a wall.

Mr. and Mrs. Frick had three children, two of whom survived to live in the Fifth Avenue home. A picture of his deceased daughter, Martha, appeared on many of the checks that Mr. Frick gave to children's charities. He contributed to hospitals for children and when the Christmas Club savings of 5,000 children were wiped out by a bank failure, he paid the accounts in full.

Mr. Frick died in 1919 and left the Fifth Avenue home to his wife for her lifetime. After she died, in 1931, the house became a public shrine for display of The Frick Collection. A self-perpetuating Board of Trustees includes the Fricks' surviving son, Childs Frick.

Following the death of Mrs. Frick, John Russell Pope, retained as architect to alter the residence for public use, added an entrance hall, cloakrooms, a courtyard, lecture rooms and galleries. The numerous bedrooms were converted into administration offices, study rooms and galleries for future use.

The public opening of the collection in 1935 was attended by 1,600 leading citizens, with 35 special detectives supplementing regular guards to make certain none of the art objects would disappear. The attendance now averages 700 a day but occasionally reaches 2,400. The administrators are elated but note that "the more business we do the more money we lose," Mr. Frick having stipulated that admission to the collection was to be free.

Miss Helen Frick, the surviving daughter, built a reference library as an adjunct of the collection but resigned as a trustee in 1961 because she felt "inferior works of art" were being admitted to the galleries. Her resignation followed the board's acceptance of two marble busts and a Piero della Francesca portrait bequeathed to the collection by John D. Rockefeller, Jr.

"Having known my father's wishes at first hand, whereas most of the trustees had never even met him," Miss Frick said, "I could not accede to the resolution passed by the majority. It was never Mr. Frick's plan to have other persons give or bequeath their works of art to his collection, which he had formed with love and understanding throughout a long period of years."

Despite the Rockefeller gifts, however, the collection typifies Mr. Frick. Illustrated lectures are given from October through May, and frequent organ and chamber-music recitals are given just as he would have had them.

❖ ❖ ❖ ❖ ❖ ❖ ❖ ❖

The entrance to The Frick Collection is at 1 East Seventieth Street, just off Fifth Avenue. The collection is open from 10 A.M. to 5 P.M. Tuesday through Saturday and from 1 P.M. to 5 P.M. on Sundays and holidays. It is closed on Mondays, January 1, May 30, July 4, Thanksgiving, Christmas and throughout August.

The Stone Mansion of a Midas

Andrew W. Mellon's Home

PITTSBURGH · PENNSYLVANIA

ANDREW W. MELLON was one of the three richest men in America although the public seldom realized the magnitude of his wealth. People never even saw his photograph in the major newspapers until he was suddenly catapulted at the age of sixty-six into the limelight by appointment to the post of Secretary of the Treasury.

When the great depression of the nineteen thirties was at its depth his income still was $13,480,000 a year because of his continuous successes in banking and the operation of companies such as Gulf Oil, Koppers Coke and the Aluminum Corporation of America. He once had major interests in 300 corporations and was a director of 51.

Mr. Mellon finally acquired a magnificent Tudor mansion of forty rooms and fifteen baths, but the great stone house came late in his life, after his marriage had gone on the rocks. His attractive wife had left him to return to England and

Ireland, where she had spent most of her early life. She had found the smoke and the dinginess of Pittsburgh's industrialized countryside too harsh a contrast to the lush greenery and slow, friendly tempo of the neighborhoods where she had lived as a girl.

Despite his business acumen, Mr. Mellon impressed some persons as a Casper Milquetoast with a college education. He was quiet, courteous and genteel. He advocated prohibition although he had a large financial stake in the Old Overholt Distillery. Like Henry Ford and John D. Rockefeller, Sr., he was lean and angular and could have posed in costume for the posters that portray Uncle Sam. He did not concentrate on a diet of graham crackers and goats' milk, as Mr. Rockefeller did, but acquaintances recall that "he looked like a skinny bookkeeper afraid of losing his job."

As one of the wealthy men of Pittsburgh, Mr. Mellon shared in entertaining the McMullens of London, part of the Guinness brewery clan, when the family visited the steel center in 1900. He was forty-five years old and Nora McMullen was eighteen. She caught his eye and he fell so deeply in love with her that he followed her back to England and married her in a castle there.

It was no castle that Mr. Mellon took his bride to live in at Pittsburgh but she tried to endure it. She bore him two children, Ailsa and Paul, while the clouds of smoke from factory chimneys and the grimy industrial workers of the crowded city increasingly depressed her. After making several trips to Ireland, England and the French Riviera, she decided in 1909 not to return to Pittsburgh.

Mr. Mellon obtained a divorce on grounds of desertion in 1912. He received the custody of the two children and Mrs. Mellon got $30,000 a year for support. Although he withdrew even farther into private life, Mr. Mellon occasionally played golf, bought paintings, rode horses and finally decided to buy a mansion that would be gay, luxurious and in keeping with his wealth.

In 1897 the Laughlins of the Jones and Laughlin Steel Corporation had built a home in one of the fine old residential neighborhoods on Woodland Road, twenty minutes from the center of the city. It was this house that Mr. Mellon bought in 1917 for himself and his two children.

The house has a basement and three floors. With an exterior of red brick, stone and massive timbers, the structure has gables, leaded-glass windows, many chimneys, stone birds on roof projections and other details popular in the country homes of the English countryside in the late nineteenth century. Ivy now covers many of the exterior walls.

Mr. Mellon renovated and enlarged the mansion. Tennis courts, two bowling alleys and a sixty-foot indoor swimming pool were built. Fish pools, elaborate gardens and pleasant walks beneath tall willows, oaks and maples were developed, and the property was expanded to twenty-seven acres. Illuminated by old-fashioned gas lamps, the grounds still are much the same as Mr. Mellon left them and are pleasant places in which to stroll.

Masterful Italian carving over a fireplace is one of the many eye-catching details inside the Mellon mansion.

When Mr. Mellon was appointed Secretary of the Treasury in 1921 by President Warren G. Harding he turned the mansion over to Paul and Paul's wife. He often returned for visits while planning such far-reaching federal programs as the reduction in the physical size of paper money — which saved the government $552,000 in paper and $120,000 in ink a year — and while gaining a reputation as "the greatest Secretary of the Treasury since Alexander Hamilton." When he became Ambassador to the Court of St. James, his daughter, then Mrs. David K. E. Bruce, became his hostess and practiced some of the social graces she had learned in the Tudor mansion in Pittsburgh.

Paul and his wife lived in the mansion until 1940, three years after the death of Andrew Mellon. Then they gave it to the Pennsylvania College for Women. The gift, valued at the time at $750,000, included not only the mansion but a ten-car garage, stables and gardens. Across a picket fence was the main campus of the college. In 1955 the institution changed its name to Chatham College.

The mansion now is a luxurious dormitory for thirty-six students of the college, which has an enrollment of 475. Only seniors are eligible to live in Mellon Hall, and those who win rooms in the mansion feel they "have really made it" on the social and academic ladder. The swimming pool, with dressing rooms and vaulted ceiling, is one of the largest in Pittsburgh, and the ballroom near it has a raised platform for musicals and shows presented by the students.

Almost every room has a marble or elaborately carved-oak fireplace mantel — even a dressing room has one. The dining room, lounges and marble solarium are king-size, and in the paneling are such interesting things as a secret door to a hidden closet — which the college women did not discover for two years.

Some of the original Mellon furnishings are still in the mansion, especially several large chests and oversize rugs. Some of the Mellon employees also are still there. They recall the elder Mellon's constant smoking of small after-dinner cigars, which he bought for two cents apiece.

They also recall the distinguished night watchman who was there for years; he had a white beard and wore a dinner jacket as he patrolled the grounds and admitted Mr. Mellon's friends. Then, too, there was the Mellon automobile, which had cost $40,000 to assemble from aluminum parts, and other items made in factories of the family.

Some of the old-timers recall the day that Andrew Mellon made a telephone call to a local newspaper to complain about an inaccurate story it had printed. In his restrained voice he told the city editor that "This is A. W. Mellon," and the dubious city editor, believing that he was being ribbed, replied: "Yeah? Well, you old sonofabitch, how about lending me five dollars?"

Nick Mancuso, a caretaker and gardener who had been with the Mellons for thirty-two years, remained at the mansion when the college received ownership. He recalls that Andrew and Paul Mellon frequently shook hands with him, using both hands, as they inquired: "How are you feeling?" He says the old mansion is "heaven" to him; he works seven days a week there by choice.

Nick noted that the old Mellon stables, where six horses, a carriage, two automobiles and a motorcycle had been kept, now are an art studio for the young women of the college. On the first floor of the mansion he called attention especially to a carved Italian mantel and, behind carved panels, an elevator to the upper floors. A breakfast room paneled in Norwegian pine also attracts most visitors.

The present library of the students had been Mellon's library. On the second floor is a den where he did much of his business planning; it is paneled in pine, with butterfly pegs, and has a maroon fabric on the walls. This floor formerly had a cedar closet thirty feet long and a dressing room made of aluminum.

Large mirrors have been used abundantly on the walls of the second floor, and a radio system that Mr. Mellon installed there can be tuned into any room in the house. On the third floor are eight bedrooms that formerly were for family servants.

Chatham College notes in a bulletin that Ralph Waldo Emerson said that "An institution is the lengthened shadow of one man." The shadow of Andrew Mellon is on the campuses of several colleges, because of his great benevolences, although this man was personally so shy and withdrawing that he once skipped a college commencement because he might be introduced and have to say a few words.

His generosity, as well as his desire for anonymity, emerged when he donated the National Gallery and its paintings and sculpture in Washington, which were valued at $65,000,000. It was the largest gift of its kind in history, and Mr. Mellon ordered that his name not be attached to the gallery.

✿　✿　✿　✿　✿　✿　✿　✿

Chatham College and its Mellon Hall are on Woodland Road, off Fifth Avenue between Negley and Pennsylvania Avenues. The exterior of the mansion and the surrounding gardens may be seen any time and some of the rooms occasionally may be seen by appointment.

At his feudal barony of 245,000 acres, William Randolph Hearst built La Cuesta Encantada as a personal home.

The Shelter of the Publisher and the Show Girl

William Randolph Hearst's La Cuesta Encantada

SAN SIMEON · CALIFORNIA

WHEN THEY ARE BURIED and their final scores are tallied, few men leave more than a ripple on the waters of life. William Randolph Hearst left waves — big waves that rolled and tossed temporarily in journalism, politics and finance. A Hearstian wave that is still cresting, with an influence that may endure for centuries, stems from the architectural pile of rock, mortar and timber that he spent twenty-eight years assembling atop a hill in California's Santa Lucia Mountains overlooking the Pacific Ocean, midway between Los Angeles and San Francisco.

The incredible castle, on which the hedonistic Mr. Hearst lavished $35,000,000 to demonstrate his command of men and his love of the ornate and the Baroque, attained lasting life after he had died. This perpetuity of the castle is the result of public ownership made possible by the generosity of Mr. Hearst's heirs, who wanted to shed the economic white elephant and also comply with a desire of Mr. Hearst that it be dedicated as a memorial to his mother, Mrs. Phoebe Apperson

Hearst. So the grandiose estate, which is a combination palace and museum un-equalled since the days of the Medicis, now is the stellar tourist attraction of the California Department of Parks and Recreation.

For many years the motorists traveling on serpentine California State High-way 1, which clings to precipitous cliffs along the ocean front, had looked five miles up into the hills and seen the twin-towered Spanish Renaissance castle with its white alabaster walls and red tile roofs glistening in the sun. On bright days some motorists stopped at roadside telescopes for closer views; armed guards and iron gates prevented them from entering the castle's enclave. Fog sometimes clothed the foothills in the foreground, leaving the silhouetted castle rising above the fog as though it were floating in air like the pictorial fantasies of Maxfield Parrish.

Now anyone may travel to the top of La Cuesta Encantada, tour the 146-room castle, and see many of the bedrooms and baths. In doing so, he discovers that the spectacle seen from afar was neither a hallucination nor a flimsy movie setting but one of America's few real castles with medieval allurements and twentieth-century vitality.

Mr. Hearst called the estate a ranch but it really was a feudal barony. It sprawled across 245,000 acres of mountains and valleys. It was one-third the size of Rhode Island, although the publicly owned property now has been whittled down to 132 acres surrounding the castle, plus 30 acres for parking and a tourist reception center beside the highway. The state also has a permanent right-of-way for tourist buses and official cars across the five miles of ranch between Route 1 and the castle.

By telephone from his upper-floor Celestial Suite and Gothic Study, the king of the domain, whose pip-squeak voice belied his large and powerful physique, ruled a far vaster business empire than La Cuesta Encantada. His newspapers, magazines and radio stations played a part in war and peace, and he influenced millions of people, although he did not win many personal friends.

One close friend and guiding hand in the development of the principality at San Simeon, however, was his princess, Miss Marion Davies, the Cinderella show girl from Brooklyn. She was his constant personal companion while the castle was being built from 1919 to 1947 and she toured Europe with him to collect many of the art treasures now in the castle.

Mr. Hearst's wife, Mrs. Millicent Willson Hearst, who had been a dancer in Broadway shows before marrying him in 1903, and their five sons lived in a palatial New York City apartment and in another Hearst castle, on Long Island, that had once belonged to Mrs. Oliver H. P. Belmont. While feverishly developing La Cuesta Encantada, Mr. Hearst talked to his wife by telephone almost every day and she sometimes visited there. So did the sons, who addressed Miss Davies as "Aunty Marion." ("What else could we have called her?" one of them said.)

To comprehend the motivations of Mr. Hearst in building his fantastic castle, one must understand his family background, personality, boundless vitality, wild imagination, thirst for power, longing for conquest and determination to build, build and build, coupled with his frequent disregard of common concepts of propriety, manners, morals and good taste.

Mr. Hearst — "Willie" to his wife, "Pops" to Miss Davies and "The Chief" to his editors — was of Scotch, English and Irish ancestry. He was born in a San Francisco hotel room, near the Barbary Coast's brothels and gambling emporiums. His father, George Hearst, had struck it rich in mining and was a millionaire who became a United States Senator through political maneuvering. An uncouth murderer of syntax who played poker for $5,000 stakes, George Hearst swore like a trooper, loved bourbon and chewed tobacco until the juice stained his gray beard and white shirt.

Ironically, Mr. Hearst's mother, the former Phoebe Apperson of Missouri, was gentle, cultured and aristocratic. She was a nineteen-year-old schoolteacher when George, then forty-one, met her while he was in Missouri burying his mother. Phoebe's parents considered him a roughneck and disapproved of their daughter marrying him, so the couple eloped. Later, in San Francisco, Phoebe held musicales and teas in the Hearst home; George considered the events almost subversive but he gave her a free hand and sent her and Willie on tours of the cultural centers of Europe. On those junkets, Willie saw the great museums and castles for the first time; they ignited in him the spark of collecting that was to become a conflagration.

When he saw the Louvre in Paris, he exclaimed: "Buy it for me, Mom! We can afford it." She did not buy it, but when Willie grew up he came close to buying the equivalent. The records of his purchases show that he spent $50,000,000 in fifty years buying interior panels, iron gates, tile floors, tapestries, paintings and other objects — largely from castles, monasteries, churches and palaces in Europe. Many of the objects now are at La Cuesta Encantada.

As a student at Harvard University, Willie learned to drink beer, fall in love and spell words his father could not even pronounce. After a few romances, he took over the care and maintenance of an expelled classmate's mistress, Tessie Powers, who worked in a Cambridge restaurant. He was soon expelled himself after his professors had received gift packages containing chamber pots with their names inscribed inside.

The youth returned to the West Coast, to choose a career in journalism, which he was to follow enthusiastically for sixty-six years. His father, in some of his manipulations, had become the owner of the *San Francisco Examiner* and gave it to his son.

It was at the *Examiner* that Hearst developed his explosive brand of journalism, with no issue of the paper meeting his approval unless it would theoretically make readers leap to their feet and shout: "Great God, it can't be!" His passion for the dramatic figured later in the development of his castle.

(Left) The Neptune Pool is beside Hearst's home. On the pediment of the Greco-Roman temple are statues of Neptune and Nereids. (Right) Marion Davies and William Randolph Hearst are shown together at a California military ball.

Resuming his friendship with Tessie Powers, a few years before his marriage and long before meeting Miss Davies, Hearst toured Europe with her. They returned with curios, statues, paintings, china, furniture and Egyptian mummies. One of the objects now part of a terrace at La Cuesta Encantada is a five-ton wellhead Tessie helped him buy at Verona.

It was reported to have been at the Ziegfeld Follies in 1917 that Mr. Hearst first saw Miss Davies, the daughter of a politician, dancing in the chorus. She was twenty-one years old and aphrodisian; he was fifty-five and paunchy. For eight weeks he sat in a front seat of the show to gaze at her and later take her to dinner. She was sentimental, generous and a born comedienne. She stuttered delightfully, sat on his lap while she rumpled his hair, made him laugh heartily and was completely at ease with him, while his editors, who received up to $260,000 a year each, held him in profound awe.

Friends who saw them at La Cuesta Encantada claimed it was one of the great loves of all time and that it sparked the development of the fantastic castle; and that marriage did not take place only because of Mr. Hearst's inability to divorce his wife or to induce her to divorce him.

The year 1919 was a big one for Hearst and La Cuesta Encantada. His mother died and left him $11,000,000 and full ownership of the property. By this time, he realized that he could not fulfill his ambitions to become Governor of New York State or President of the United States. Still smarting from charges of his responsibility in setting off the Spanish-American War, he became really irked by allusions to "Hearst and Hohenzollern" and a discovery that a butler in his home was a federal agent spying on him. His companionship with Miss Davies had become the choicest bit of gossip in the land.

Frustrated and hurt, but with money pouring into his bank accounts faster than he could spend it, Hearst turned to the development of La Cuesta Encantada and to the attempted promotion of Miss Davies as the greatest movie actress of the century. The goals interlocked, with the castle used as a staging area for the advancement of Miss Davies.

The assembling of the property at San Simeon had been started by Mr. Hearst's father in 1870 when he bought a 40,000-acre ranch for $30,000. The Piedra Blanca (white rocks) Ranch, had been part of the Mission of San Luis Obispo. Added to it later were the San Simeon and Santa Rosa Ranches, which also had been church properties. Twenty thousand head of cattle and thorough-bred horses roamed the range. A simple farmhouse became a home of the Hearst family; it is still there, at the foot of the hill.

In the early years of his marriage, Mr. Hearst took his wife and five sons to the top of the hill on camping trips. He had large tents of gaudy canvas erected by servants, who went ahead with pack mules carrying the tents and provisions. One of the tents was a living room, another a dining room, others had bedrooms and one was a motion picture theatre. On the hill the Hearsts and their guests would "rough it."

Hearst told why he chose the campsite, with its 360-degree panoramic view, for his castle in a letter:

"I love this place. It is wonderful. I love the sea and I love the mountains and the hollows in the hills and the shady places in the creeks and the fine old oaks, and even the hot bushy hillsides — full of quail — and the canyons full of deer. It is a wonderful place. I would rather spend a month here than any other place in the world."

In planning the castle, Mr. Hearst hired Miss Julia Morgan, a young San Francisco architect who could absorb and interpret the architectural inspirations of her client. The result was a plan for a castle that would salve his political wounds, provide a cathedral-like reception center for publishing and movie magnates and absorb some of the art treasures that had been accumulating in Hearst warehouses. One of these had a Spanish cloister of 36,000 stones in 10,700 crates. Another cloister was on its way from Europe. Forty clerks were busy in another warehouse keeping an inventory of the objects there.

The dining room of Hearst's castle has a ceiling carved 400 years ago for a European castle. Hearst and Miss Davies sat at the center of the table.

"Don't spare the costs," Mr. Hearst admonished his buying agents. When some of the objects were sold at bargain prices in Gimbel Brothers Department Store in New York, a Van Dyke painting that had cost Mr. Hearst $375,000 went for $89,000.

Three palatial guest houses were built first at La Cuesta Encantada, later to be merged with the main part of the castle in the center. The guest houses are La Casa del Mar, facing the sea; La Casa del Monte, facing the mountains; and La Casa del Sol, facing the sunrise. La Casa Grande, now the main building, was begun in 1922. It was first occupied in 1925 but work on it continued and never was fully completed. Mr. Hearst had a plaster model showing the castle as he hoped it would ultimately appear.

When Mr. Hearst and Miss Davies traveled in Europe to buy more huge tapestries, carved ceilings, carillon bells and other such items, Miss Morgan redesigned parts of the castle to accommodate them. One day Hearst decided he did not care for twin towers well under construction and had them torn down and built differently. Standing on the roof of the castle one day with Miss Morgan, he exclaimed:

"This view is tremendous. This is where I want my personal suite. Raise the roof and put the suite here."

It was done, and the added rooms were called the Celestial Suite. At one end of a large sitting room, with a balcony facing the Pacific, was Mr. Hearst's bedroom, and at the other end, Miss Davies' bedroom. The bathrooms have spectacular black marble walls and ornate gold-plated fixtures — not solid gold, as some persons believe.

Plenty of space was needed for entertaining and most of the downstairs rooms are enormous. The doorway to the castle is so large that its decorations include carved stone figures of the Duke of Burgundy and friends on a hunting trip, an iron grill from a sixteenth-century Spanish convent, a Gothic sculpture of the Virgin and Child, and a gable of elaborately carved teakwood from India.

The mosaic floor of the vestibule, portraying "Mermen and Fishes," is from a first-century house in Pompeii. Mr. Hearst bought the tile in Rome and sent a crew of Italian artisans to La Cuesta Encantada to lay it. They also worked on the $1,000,000 white-marble and green-tile Neptune Pool and its Greco-Roman temple and the $1,000,000 indoor pool of lapis lazuli mosaics. This took place, incidentally, while the Hearst newspapers were emblazoned with "Buy American" slogans and were editorializing against imports from overseas.

Hearst often swam in the Neptune pool, taking pet dachshunds with him. Telephones were handed to him in the water.

Wherever a visitor turns in the castle he is confronted with objects of art, some 2,000 years old. On the way to the Assembly Hall, the largest of the rooms, are Gobelin tapestries, statues by Jean Leon Gerome and Frederick William Mac-Monnies and a doorway designed by Jacopo Sansovino, architect of the famous library of St. Mark's in Venice.

The Assembly Hall, 100 feet long and rising two stories to an antique ceiling that had been brought piece by piece from a European castle, has French and Italian Renaissance furniture, choir stalls from an Italian monastery, Flemish tapestries once owned by a Spanish royal family, a carved stone fireplace and four 2,000-pound marble medallions from Denmark.

The Refectory, where meals were served in elegant style at night but informally in the morning and at noon, has a dining table fifty-six feet long. An antique from Europe, it cost a fortune; the chairs flanking it cost only $600 each to have made specially. The baronial room has a sixteenth-century fireplace from France, and bright silken banners of old Sienese families.

Guests who stepped into this splendor included Sir Winston Churchill, George Bernard Shaw, Calvin Coolidge and John Nance Garner. All of the chief newspaper lieutenants of Mr. Hearst also came but Miss Davies did not always find their conversation interesting.

"All you talk about is your g-g-g-goddam circulation," she told one group of editors as she peevishly left the room.

More to her liking were Dick Powell, Gene Fowler, Bebe Daniels, Louella Parsons, Beatrice Lillie, Hal Roach, Buster Keaton, and other eminent show people.

Mr. Hearst, who loved youth and could not bear the mention of sickness and death in his presence, also enjoyed the movie folk. Some of them he hired to perform in pictures with Miss Davies and he would slip new contracts for them under their dinner plates as surprises. He also enjoyed spending afternoons with the young people on the bridle paths and the tennis courts. He was a good swimmer and often went in the pools, sometimes taking along one of his pet dachshunds, of which he generally had six or eight in the kennel. Near the castle is the tombstone of a favorite one that says: "Here lies dearest Helena — my devoted friend."

While on his travels inside and outside the castle, Mr. Hearst always had a telephone close at hand. They were in every room, beside the pools, on garden benches and along the walks. The switchboard had three operators and was open twenty-four hours a day.

At La Cuesta Encantada the guests were free to do as they pleased throughout the day but at 7:30 P.M. they were expected to be in the Assembly Room to meet Mr. Hearst when he came down from the Celestial Suite on a small elevator and stepped from behind a panel. The guests were permitted one cocktail each before dinner. Mr. Hearst disapproved of liquor after his college days and he thought cigarettes were a little silly. Liquor was not permitted in the guests' bedrooms and violators of the rule would find their bags packed and taken to the door.

Swimmers in Hearst's $1,000,000 Neptune pool have this view of the castle and guest houses beyond the shrubbery.

Errol Flynn once staggered into the Assembly Hall, to be protected from detection by Miss Davies. Carole Lombard found that the safest place for an extra drink was in "the little girls' room." Servants were fired on the spot if Mr. Hearst caught them serving extra drinks. One day Mr. Hearst found some of the nude statues of La Cuesta Encantada dressed with silk lingerie. He discovered who the culprit was and at dinner that night ordered a pile of empty gin bottles put where the person was to sit.

Dinner generally was served at 9 P.M., with Hearst on one side of the long table and Miss Davies opposite him. Printed menus permitted a choice of food and listed the movies to be shown that night. The table silver and the china were elegant but the waiters provided only paper napkins and the table bore plain bottles of mustard, ketchup and pickles. Napkins and bottles reminded Hearst of his camping days on the hill.

After dinner, everyone had to go to the movie theater where a film not yet generally released was shown. Hearst sat in the front row, with a telephone beside him, and told his guests that if they did not like the picture they could go to sleep in the large, upholstered seats.

New motion pictures were shown by Hearst every night in this theater of his castle. He sat in the front row, beside a telephone.

The game room, with billiard tables, attracted some of the guests after the movie, but Hearst went to the Gothic Study upstairs to work until 3 or 4 A.M. Miss Davies often joined him there, since he appreciated her opinions and outlook on world problems. He would make telephone calls to his editors throughout the country, often getting them out of bed, and write some of the editorials that were to be printed the next day.

The gardens of the castle have flowers and trees from many parts of the world. Drives are lined with citrus and there are plantings of pomegranate, oleander, acacia and eucalyptus. Forty Italian cypress, each weighing five tons, were brought across the mountain from Paso Robles and planted because Mr. Hearst hated to see them cut down to make room for a housing development.

There is a mile-long pergola espaliered with grapevines and fruit trees. One of the jobs of Charles G. Adams, a noted landscape architect, was to plant a mountainside with wildflowers because Mr. Hearst wanted to see them from his bedroom window when he awoke each day.

Another of his pleasures was to surprise his guests by having all the flowers in vast gardens completely changed overnight. Gardeners working under flood-lights would strip out the old plants and replace them with others. On Easter Sundays, fields of lilies were growing where geraniums had been the day before.

The zoo of La Cuesta Encantada had one of the largest private collections of wild animals in the world. In it were zebras, gnus, seven varieties of deer, aoudads, elephants, tigers, water buffaloes, ostriches, yaks, chimpanzees, kangaroos and antelopes. Most of the animals have been sold but some still roam the property and tourists occasionally are delayed in approaching the castle because some strange beast is on the road.

In the assembly hall of the castle, Hearst greeted guests. The room has antique choir stalls, Flemish tapestries and a ceiling from Europe.

At its peak as a private estate, the property had Palomino, Arabian and Morgan horses. It still has an airfield, where Héarst's private planes landed guests from the large cities. He kept a fleet of forty automobiles and occasionally chartered trains to bring guests to San Simeon. When Eleanor Medill (Cissy) Patterson, one of his favorite newspaperwomen, arrived on her own special train he had a brass band at the siding to welcome her.

The daily operating costs of La Cuesta Encantada were $6,000 although the state now is operating the entire establishment on an annual budget of $200,000. At that, it was only one of several homes owned by Mr. Hearst. He spent more on living accommodations than perhaps any other man in history. It cost him $1,370,-000 to buy and improve St. Donats Castle in Wales, where he lived only four months; $400,000 for the castle on Long Island where his wife lived; $7,000,000 for a 110-room Santa Monica beach house in which Miss Davies occasionally lived; $1,000,000 for Wyntoon, a summer home 250 miles north of San Francisco that she found so disagreeable she called it Spittoon; $2,500,000 for a ranch in Mexico, and more for a home site on the rim of the Grand Canyon and large apartments in New York City.

In 1947, Mr. Hearst's doctor advised him to leave the altitude and problems of La Cuesta Encantada for a simpler place near sea level. Miss Davies bought for $200,000 a Spanish stucco house on eight acres in Beverly Hills and she and Mr. Hearst moved into it. He remained there until his death in 1951 at the age of eighty-eight. Beside him when he died was her photograph, on which she had written:

"My bounty is as boundless as the sea, my love as deep. The more I give to thee, the more I have, for both are infinite."

The bulk of Mr. Hearst's personal estate of $59,500,000 and his interest in the $160,000,000 Hearst publishing empire were left to his wife, sons and public enterprises. La Cuesta Encantada was soon found by the heirs to be something of a drain on the pocketbook. In his will Hearst had suggested that it be given to the University of California as a memorial to his mother but the regents of the University looked askance at the idea because of the operating costs.

In 1954 the Hearst sons invited Goodwin Knight, at that time the governor of California, to spend a week-end at the castle and talk about methods of transferring the property to the state. Knight finally referred the problem to Newton B. Drury, the state director of beaches and parks. Drury advocated the property's acquisition by the state; the California park commissioners and legislators took a look at it and in 1957 it was voted into the state park system with only two legislators objecting. The public immediately clamored for a chance to visit the castle.

Mr. Drury set up the parking area at the foot of the hill, and provided buses to transport the sight-seers to the castle. To prevent the visitors from carrying away the art treasures, he arranged for groups to go through the castle under the close watch of guides. And he solved a problem that has pestered many directors who want visitors to see everything at close range but not mar floors and rugs: he put brown rubber matting on the routes the visitors walk.

The results have been phenomenal. Set up to handle 500 visitors a day, the castle soon had 1,000, which later grew to 2,500. People came from all the fifty states to see where Mr. Hearst and "that movie actress" had lived. Reservations may be made by letter a week or more in advance. Motels in near-by Cambria and along the highway have sprung up so visitors may have full days in the area, although the guided tours require only an hour or two. La Cuesta Encantada is far from being a white elephant to California.

✿ ✿ ✿ ✿ ✿ ✿ ✿ ✿

The Hearst San Simeon State Historical Monument, as La Cuesta Encantada is officially known, is near State Route 1 and is open from 9 A.M. to 5 P.M. every day. Reservations for tours are accepted up to sixty days in advance and not less than seven days in advance. They may be made at the Public Tours Reservation Office of the California Division of Beaches and Parks, Sacramento, also at other offices of the division, chambers of commerce and automobile clubs. A service fee of $1 is charged in addition to the $2 tour fee for adults and $1 for children. Admission also may generally be obtained at the gate without reservations.

The Roughneck's Lavish Hacienda

Death Valley Scotty's Castle

GRAPEVINE CANYON · CALIFORNIA

WALTER PERRY SCOTT was a big man, weighing 220 pounds and standing six-feet-three-inches tall. His hobnailed boots, generously cut trousers, five-gallon hat, raucous voice and swaggering gait made him appear even bigger. He was an exuberant, garrulous extrovert, loaded with gold nuggets, and his shenanigans kept him in the limelight for fifty years. The stunts he dreamed up to gain public attention would make a Madison Avenue advertising writer green with envy.

Although illiterate, Scotty was alert and intelligent. He was a storyteller par excellence — generally with either a lively twinkle or a savage gleam in his eyes as a forewarning of what he was going to say or do next. He would roar down Main Street handing out gold coins to strangers and $100 tips to newsboys. As a frontiersman, bronco buster, prospector, disrupter of railroad schedules, hoodwinker of income-tax collectors, confidante of European royalty and builder of a castle, Scotty flamboyantly excelled the exploits of most rivals.

He customarily wore an eighty-dollar sombrero at a rakish angle on the back of his head, red neckties that harmonized with his temperament and pale-blue shirts that matched his eyes. The roughhewn Scotty had what he called "a Ph. D. from the college of hard knocks," drank with two fists and fought the same way, and in leisure moments smoked two-bit corncob pipes that he had carefully soaked in honey.

Oddly, he teamed up with a man who was his direct opposite in virtually all characteristics. In doing so he made it possible to fulfill a long-standing ambition, to build a castle at the desert oasis of Grapevine Canyon, in the upper reaches of California's picturesque Death Valley — a castle that now is one of the most unusual show places and tourist attractions in the Far West. The castle, on a tract of 1,529 acres, is 3,000 feet above sea level. Begun in 1916, the construction was proceeding at full speed in 1924 and continued until the stock-market crash of 1929. It cost $2,200,000 and a replacement at today's prices would exceed $5,000,000.

Scotty's partner was Albert M. Johnson, a chicken-every-Sunday gentleman and scholar from Chicago, who had become a millionaire capitalist and president of the National Life Insurance Company of America. At the height of his business career Mr. Johnson suffered a broken back in a train wreck. Scotty and Johnson had met in Chicago and when Johnson retired he accepted Scotty's invitation to go to Death Valley for his health. Although Johnson was badly crippled, and sometimes given by doctors only a few days to live, Scotty taught him how to ride a horse.

In 1906 the friendship grew into the full partnership that was to continue for forty-two years. With a pack train of mules to carry tents, bedding and supplies, Scotty took Johnson to Grapevine Canyon, and they camped where the castle was later to rise. It was an isolated area then, with only a few straggly cottonwood trees for protection from the sun, although cooling breezes from the northeast eased the 135-degree summer heat.

Both men liked the contrast of snow-capped Mount Whitney, rising 14,496 feet on the horizon, with Bad Water, 279 feet below sea level, not far away. They appreciated the valley's 600 species of plant life and wide variety of wild animals. They enjoyed riding to Suicide Pass, Poison Spring, Deadman's Gulch, Tombstone Flat and the Funeral Mountains — landmarks named for the hardships encountered in 1849 when pioneers sought short cuts across Death Valley to the new gold fields of the West.

A dream of building a castle some day at Grapevine Canyon had come to Scotty in his youth. Born in Kentucky, the son of a racehorse breeder and distiller, he borrowed fifty dollars and ran away from home when he was twelve years old. In Nevada he became a horse wrangler and soon afterward a swamper for Death Valley's twenty-mule-team outfits, hauling borax to Mojave. His job was to apply the wagon brakes on down grades and to run beside the mules on up grades and throw stones at them.

His affection for Grapevine Canyon did not leave Scotty when he joined Buffalo Bill's Wild West Show and became a featured rider along with Annie Oakley. For eleven years he remained with Cody's show, traveling in Europe, hobnobbing with the then Prince of Wales and other royalty and developing an ambition to own European art treasures. On trips along the Rhine he saw castles that merged in his mind with the memories of Death Valley. Scotty saved the money he made in show business and when able he returned to Grapevine Canyon to build a redwood shack that was his first real home.

On a blind date in New York in 1900, Scotty met Josephine Millius, a pretty little salesgirl who worked in a candy store. They were married. Scotty took his bride to the desert in a mule-drawn wagon, sleeping by day and traveling by night because of the intense heat and the hazard of Indian attacks. She later made more trips to the desert with him. They lived in the shack at Grapevine Canyon.

She knew he was blasting open the earth in a search for gold not far from the shack but he never permitted her to see the mines or identify the exact locations. When she had a son she tired of the desert life and took the child to live in Long Beach, California. She said she loved Scotty but not Grapevine Canyon, and hoped he would buy a cattle ranch in some lush countryside and settle down.

(Left) The castle, on which European craftsmen worked, has a Mediterranean beauty. Beyond the inner courtyard is a tower with a clock and chimes. (Right) Scotty was boisterous and generous. He carried gold nuggets and wads of $1,000 bills in the pockets of his baggy trousers.

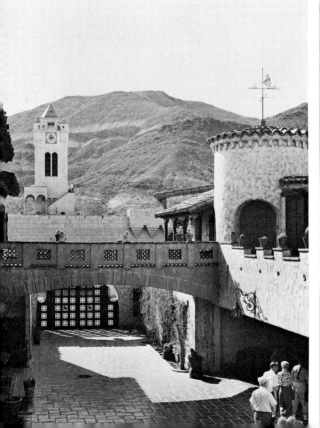

Instead, Scotty intensified his prospecting. At one time he made a deal with Julian Gerard, then a vice president of the old Knickerbocker Trust Company in New York. It enabled Scotty to spend $8,000 of Mr. Gerard's money for grub-staking on a fifty-fifty partnership basis in Death Valley.

Mr. Gerard later felt he had never collected his full share of the gold discovered and there was a long and bitter court battle, which Scotty won. Investigators tried to follow him to his mines but he led them on many a merry chase. He would feed his mules for days to harden them up, then depart in the middle of the night, traverse the summits of jagged peaks and use nitroglycerin to blow up the trails behind him so that neither bloodhounds nor Apache guides could follow.

On one occasion, following a gun battle he waged with pursuers, he was arrested. When he got out of jail on bail in San Bernardino County, where the shooting took place, he rode onto the desert and moved the county-line marker six miles so that the battle appeared to have taken place in Inyo County. He had friends in Inyo and the charges were dropped.

When he ceased to get much attention by tossing gold coins from hotel windows and publicly clipping $1,000 bills from treasury sheets — the form in which bills then were available to banks and favored customers — he hired a Santa Fe train for $5,500 to set a record for the 2,267-mile run from Los Angeles to Chicago. He gave $100 tips to crew members on the twenty-eight locomotives used on the trip. The train, shaving thirteen hours from previous records, rolled into the Dearborn Street Station in Chicago so fast under Scotty's urgings that it crumpled the end-of-the-line bumper and sent railroad shares soaring in the stock market.

Not long after that, Scotty teamed up with Mr. Johnson. Just how much money Scotty actually had and whether the productivity of his gold mines was largely will-o'-the-wisp have never been established. When cornered by the authorities he admitted only that he had a "little hole in the ground" and "minted a little money" when needed. But in Mr. Johnson he had a quick and ample source of funds. Building a castle consequently was no problem financially, when the idea of it became as appealing to Mr. Johnson as it had been for years in Scotty's dreams.

They considered hiring Frank Lloyd Wright and other architects noted for merging houses into desert surroundings. Finally they chose C. A. MacNeilledge as a consultant and Matt Roy Thompson as an engineer. They decided they wanted a white concrete castle with red tile roofs — a structure that would be mixed Moorish, Spanish, Italian and Mexican, with a strong resemblance to some of the early California missions.

So there rose in Grapevine Canyon a building that now has twenty-one oversize main rooms, eight master baths and six large fireplaces. Besides the main part of the castle, there is a music wing, although Scotty could not play a note on any instrument and Mr. Johnson was physically unable to do it. There also are a Spanish clock-and-chimes tower, stables and guest houses. A 185-foot outdoor swimming pool beside a patio was built but some of the tiles never were laid.

"We had no plans — no blueprints," Scotty said after he had moved into the castle. "We'd just throw up a piece and if it looked good we'd leave it and throw up some more. If it didn't look good, we'd tear it down and try something else."

One of the first things completed was a hydroelectric plant and water system large enough for a small town. One of the springs that had originally made the site desirable to Scotty produced 600 gallons a minute of clear, sparkling water.

Four thousand men worked on the construction of the castle at various times. The jobs on the desert were not too appealing to many artisans and often there were three crews — one that was at work at the castle, one that had just quit and was on its way back to Los Angeles and one that had just been hired and was on its way to Grapevine Canyon.

Scotty had no unions to annoy him but his labor difficulties included carpenters who would not eat with plumbers, bricklayers who would not fraternize with Austrian woodcarvers imported for the project, and chefs who would not get along with anybody. On one occasion there were complaints about an Indian chef because he would not serve griddlecakes for breakfast. Scotty, who liked to cook, got up early one morning, stirred up a bucket of griddlecake batter and slipped into it a package of Epsom salts. There were no more criticisms of the Indian chef, nor were there any more demands for griddlecakes.

The cost of trucking building materials over the mountains and across the valley was staggering. The nearest railroad station was at Bonnie Clair, twenty miles away, on the Tonopah & Tidewater Railroad. Some idea of the trucking costs is indicated by the $25,000 that Scotty paid to have delivered to the castle a quantity of old railroad ties that he had bought from the Tonopah & Tidewater for $1,500. He wanted the ties for firewood and hundreds of them are still stacked outside the castle and doubtless will be for decades. The freight charges did not discourage Scotty; he even had huge palm trees trucked from San Bernardino and planted near the castle.

When the place was partly built, Scotty came along a trail one day and seeing the walls from a distance declared: "Hell, that don't look like any castle I saw on the Rhine." So the walls were torn down, somebody thought of a different way to pile the rocks and the construction was started over again.

While the castle was still rising and Scotty was neglecting his outside publicity he got a taste of notoriety he had not expected. Eva Mudge Jorgensen, who had been the Little Eva in Buffalo Bill's Wild West Show when Scotty was one of its star performers, became entangled in marital litigation with her husband. Scotty had demonstrated his marksmanship in the Wild West show by shooting apples from Little Eva's head; now her husband claimed she had spent two years at Scotty's ranch on the pretense of writing his biography although the book had never appeared.

Despite all his troubles, Scotty remained steadfast in his determination to build a show place. He spared no cost in the decorative tile work, especially.

Visitors who now enter the castle are often surprised to find large containers of cotton boots at the door. Guides give instructions for slipping the boots over walking shoes so that the colorful tile floors will not be scratched.

The rooms are of generous dimensions; some are forty feet high. Their beauty on first glance seems to stem from a Mediterranean variety of simplicity and soft light. Windows admit adequate sunshine without flooding the rooms with glare. The temperament of the desert has been captured by the ample use, in tiles, furnishings and wall decorations, of pastel greens, soft blues, Spanish yellows, grays and Indian reds.

The doors and the exposed redwood timbers are massive, heavily adzed, hand-embellished, brushed and burnished to old age by the imported Austrian craftsmen. Hand-wrought door latches, grills and wall adornments include some made at the castle and others that are centuries old and were bought by Scotty in Europe.

The living room has a balcony and a high rock fountain and grotto of Oriental design, with water cascading down the front of brilliant jasper that colored lights play upon. Scotty had the idea for the waterfall, believing that it would add moisture to the air in the room and help reduce the heat. He was right. It was like an early grass-root air conditioning system. Still in use, it keeps the indoor temperature several degrees cooler than that outside, even in the shade of the palm trees.

Draperies in the downstairs rooms were made of hundreds of carefully matched goats' skins, hand embossed and colored. The rooms have Don Quixote plaques, sterling silver lamps and pictures of Bill Cody and Annie Oakley — among Scotty's best friends in the old days.

A majolica bowl on a table is twenty-four inches in diameter. Its opaque glaze and richly embossed aqua enamel on a fluted contour, with figures of deer and a castle superimposed, were so appealing to a visitor that one day, when Scotty was not looking, he walked off with it. "The damn rascal swiped it and sold it for one hundred dollars," Scotty said later. "But we caught up with him and made him get the bowl back to us."

Much of the ironwork in the castle is from Italy and some of the rugs were specially woven on Majorca to meet the specifications sent by Scotty. Besides working on the handhewn timbers of the castle, the craftsmen from Austria also made some of the beds, chairs and tables. They are used in close relationship to beds, chests and other items from European palaces.

A bedroom that cost $40,000 was specially built for Scotty but he generally shunned it. Ports were built in the walls of this room ostensibly so he could poke rifles through and fire on unwelcome visitors. He never indulged in such inhospitable conduct although visitors sometimes annoyed him. He liked to reply to letter writers that "the castle won't be finished for forty years but when it is, you will be welcome to come and see me and be waited on hand and foot."

He enjoyed eating in the castle, meeting close friends there and telling his fanciful stories to wide-eyed listeners. When it came time to go to retire he generally rejected the 150-year-old bed in his room and went down the road to a small, primitive shack among the cottonwoods. It was away from prying eyes and it was where his collies could run without restraint. Windy, his favorite, slept at the shack's entrance as a guard.

Mr. Johnson had a bathtub taken from the castle and installed in the shack as a surprise for Scotty. He had the tub ripped out immediately. He preferred to bathe under a shower outdoors, sitting naked in an antique Spanish mission chair while the water splashed upon him.

The castle's upstairs music room, splendid enough for royalty, has carved beams and ninety-six carved panels, none identical. The chandeliers are of hand-wrought iron and antique brass. Around a table are chairs from a palace in Spain. A control panel in this room governs the playing of the organ, the tower chimes and a piano, either manually or electrically by music roll. The organ's iron grill, six centuries old, is from Toledo, Spain.

The Spanish guest suite of the castle has a wooden chest that was made in the era of Columbus. The Italian room has a rug that a family in Italy spent seven years weaving. There are European art treasures everywhere in the castle except in the Will Rogers Room. That room is strictly Early American in its design, furnishings and stark simplicity — as Scotty said Will wanted it. Rogers, a close friend of Scotty, often visited the castle and the simple room was reserved for him.

Mrs. Albert M. Johnson, Scotty and Mr. Johnson relaxed in the castle.

The dining room has redwood beams, carved by the Austrian craftsmen. The table and chairs are Spanish. A crest in the dining room is inscribed: "By our perseverance we will succeed." The use of slogans is continued in the kitchen, where an inscription reads: "Serve yourself with all you desire. Be seated, you are welcome."

The colorful bathrooms are rich in imported tile and decorations. The clear water and the pressure, sufficient to fill the tub rapidly, shows that a great job was done of developing a water system that gives no evidence of failing in the future.

Scotty's spending for luxuries at the castle, coupled with his wild distribution of money on his visits to the big cities, caused federal income-tax collectors to visit him one day at Grapevine Canyon. They called his attention to newspaper reports that he had spent several millions of dollars in the previous twenty years and they noted that they had no records of his having paid income taxes.

"Well, gentlemen," Scotty said, slapping his knee and laughing loudly, "it's true that I didn't pay any taxes. But it's this way. All that I have earned or stolen I got before 1913, when the income tax went into effect."

The revenue men could not think of any way of proving otherwise, so they marked the case closed.

Scotty was equally successful in convincing others that his money was untouchable. When asked by lawyers in a courtroom for a disclosure of where his gold mines were, he said he had no mines but just "holes in the ground" where he picked up gold occasionally. Nobody ever located any sizable tangible asset of his that could be attached. Even the castle that bore his name was recorded in government offices as being owned by Mr. Johnson. When Johnson was asked about Scotty's wealth he said:

"Scotty doesn't have a nickel to his name."

In recording a title to the vast acreage that Scotty and Mr. Johnson contended was "the yard of the castle," however, there had been a serious mistake. Scotty generally looked upon most of the 3,000 square miles of Death Valley as something of an unofficial private preserve of his own. When the National Park Service was studying the valley's markers in 1933 to set up the Death Valley National Park, Scotty was asked for the deed to the castle's land.

"What deed?" Scotty replied.

It developed that there had been errors even in the homestead claims and the castle probably occupied a claim somebody else had staked out. Congress finally passed a special act allowing Johnson to buy 1,529 acres at $1.25 an acre, which he did in 1938. The government retained mineral rights on the property and it also obtained limited privileges to repurchase all the castle's acreage.

Scotty did not take kindly to the "invasion" by the government. "I've got my hair in braids," he said. "It's the government. Why, doggone 'em, they're making Death Valley — MY Death Valley — into a goddam national park for dudes."

Scotty's Castle has Moorish, Spanish, Italian and Mexican influences. The courtyard resembles those of California missions.

Mr. Johnson's wife, who lived at the castle with him, was killed in a highway mishap in Grapevine Canyon in 1943. Johnson continued his close association with Scotty although, as Scotty once explained it, "We got in each other's hair quite often and we got awful mad at each other."

In 1946 the castle and its acreage were conveyed by Mr. Johnson and Scotty to the Gospel Foundation of California, a nonprofit organization devoted to charitable activities. Johnson died in 1948 and Scotty was so shaken that he could not get himself to go to the funeral. Instead, he wrote a note addressed to his friend that said:

"We rode the mountain trails together and they were terribly rough. This one will be easier. I hope you will find the mules and the pasture good. This trail you will have to travel alone, but I'll meet you at the end. Your partner, Death Valley Scotty."

When Scotty died in 1954 he was buried on a hill overlooking the castle. A plaque on the grave is inscribed with words that he had once spoken:

"I got four things to live by. Don't say nothing that will hurt anybody. Don't give advice — nobody will take it anyway. Don't complain. And don't explain."

The consensus in Death Valley today is that Scotty never had the big gold mines that he tried to make people think he had except when he was in court pleading poverty, but that he did have limited resources of gold underground in the valley and a very big resource in Albert Johnson. Just before his death, Johnson said: "I've been paying Scotty's bills for years and I like it. He repays me in laughs."

In one of his probable moments of truth-telling, Scotty said:

"I haven't got any mines. I just know where I can get gold. I got it cached away in the mountains. It is in the rocks, so I can't be taxed or accused of hoarding. I have a money mill of my own. I can grind out money when I need it."

Death Valley Scotty's Castle now is "grinding out money" more effectively than Scotty or Mr. Johnson probably ever expected. About 100,000 visitors a year pay fees to tour the castle. One of the adjacent buildings has been converted into a motel for sixty guests. The entire property is in harmony with the Death Valley National Park, which is adjoining. The isolation is so great that anyone at the castle today who wants to use a telephone to say "hello" to some distant friend must make a fifty-two-mile roundtrip on the highways just to use an old-fashioned turn-the-crank wall telephone. For emergencies, a ranger five miles down the road has a two-way radio linking Grapevine Canyon to the outside world.

❀   ❀   ❀   ❀   ❀   ❀   ❀   ❀

The castle, 304 miles from Los Angeles and 541 from San Francisco, can be approached by way of U. S. Route 6 to Olancha, then by following directional signs. The castle is open every day in the year and the entrance fee for adults is $1.10. A business office of the castle is at 1462 North Stanley Avenue, Hollywood 46, California.

The Orange-Grove Haven of the "Blue Boy"

Henry E. Huntington's Treasure-Trove

SAN MARINO · CALIFORNIA

IN 1870, when Henry E. Huntington was twenty years old, he took a job as a porter in a New York City hardware store rather than go to college. Big fortunes were being made in business after the Civil War and he wanted to get started on one of his own while he was still young. He was imaginative, clear-eyed, tall, slim and neat, and he walked with a military bearing. Tireless and meticulous, he soon was promoted to a clerkship; and in time moved on to the ownership of saw-mills, railroads, street transportation systems, utility companies and tens of thousands of acres of orange groves and ranches in Southern California.

As though he had undertaken to prove the wisdom of Horace Greeley's well known advice to young men, he became a director of sixty corporations on the West Coast and a dominant power in politics. Although kind and gentle with his friends, he was shrewd and ruthless in business.

Huntington 143

Mr. Huntington gained his first fortune by earning it. He gained another by inheritance from his uncle, Collis P. Huntington. He gained a third by marrying his uncle's widow after he was divorced from his first wife, who was the mother of his four children.

With all this wealth he decided at the age of fifty-eight to retire and try to do something for the public that might justify a place for himself in a hall of eternal fame. Until his death nineteen years later he worked just as hard at spending his money for the public good as he previously had in amassing a multimillion-dollar bank account.

His biggest stride toward immortality was the development of a marble and concrete Georgian home at San Marino, in the foothills of California's Sierra Madres eleven miles from Los Angeles, and the subsequent conversion of the palatial structure, the gardens and additional buildings into a public art museum, library and horticultural wonder. To perpetuate his achievement, he endowed it with $20,000,000.

One of the art treasures that he acquired for the mansion is Thomas Gainsborough's famous painting, the "Blue Boy," which now hangs in an earthquake-proof, burglarproof, fireproof wing of the building. Whether the "Blue Boy" rates among the finest paintings in the world is a moot question; certainly it is one of the most popular, being the magnet that attracts the most attention from the 250,000 persons who visit the Huntington mansion every year. Picture-viewers flock to it just as they do to the "Mona Lisa" in the Louvre.

There was some similarity in the rise to fame of the model who sat for the "Blue Boy," a London ironmonger's son, to that of the megalomaniacal climb of Mr. Huntington. The model, Jonathan Buttall, and Mr. Huntington had parents in the hardware business; in their youth both lacked rank, title and social position, and both rose rapidly to fame in the arts without being practitioners of the arts.

As a collector, Mr. Huntington distinguished himself at San Marino by acquiring incunabula — venerable volumes printed before 1500. The greatest of these is the Gutenberg Bible, generally conceded to be the first important book ever printed with movable metal type. The two volumes of it are printed on vellum, probably sheepskin, and are bound between heavy wooden boards. Over the boards is stretched the original fifteenth-century stamped leather, held fast by metal bosses. It is just one of the 200,000 rare books, 500 art objects, 1,000,000 manuscripts and 150,000 reference works that Mr. Huntington acquired to make his mansion and adjacent library renowned in a way that no other man has equalled.

The emergence of Mr. Huntington as a shrine builder had a dynamic background. After his jobs in the hardware business he went to work for his uncle, Collis P. Huntington, in the development of the Chesapeake, Ohio & South Western Railroad, the Kentucky Central Railroad and other lines. When he was forty-one years old he joined Collis in San Francisco to manage the Southern Pacific Railroad and to develop street transportation systems in San Francisco and Los Angeles.

The present art gallery was the Huntington residence. (Right) Huntington, shown on the steps of his home, strolled through his vast gardens every day.

The Huntingtons feuded with another mogul who was to become a mansion builder — newspaper tycoon William Randolph Hearst. Hearst editorials were critical of the "Huntington Plantation," as some persons called California, and of the big assortment of senators, representatives and other officials that the Huntingtons assertedly "owned." Collis spent much of his time in New York, so his nephew — who was known to associates as "Ed" or "H. E." — bore the brunt of the battle to retain control of banks, railroads, stores, universities and politics.

Mr. Hearst's father, George, had become a senator and wanted to become governor of California. A deal was made with the political machine in power, operated by Chris (Blind Boss) Buckley. But Mr. Buckley took orders from an elusive gentleman named Bill Stow, who was an agent of the Huntingtons, and George Hearst was thrown to the political wolves. The Hearst crusade against the Huntingtons continued until $30,000 worth of Huntington advertising suddenly appeared in Mr. Hearst's *San Francisco Examiner*. Hearst executives now contend it was only a coincidence, since the amount of money was insignificant in the great newspaper empire. Moreover, Hearst soon obtained the legislation he demanded to curb some of the "arrogant independence" of the Southern Pacific.

In 1900, Collis died and left most of his fortune to his wife, Arabella Duval Huntington, and to his nephew, Ed. Becoming head of the Southern Pacific, Ed operated it until 1902, when he sold it to E. H. Harriman, got a divorce and began thinking seriously about mansions. He had been married in 1873 to Mary Alice Prentice Huntington, a sister of Collis's adopted daughter.

In 1913, Huntington married Collis's widow, Arabella, who had a son by her first marriage. This meant a merger of the fortunes he had variously earned, inherited and married. He and his new wife both desired to develop a mansion and great center of the arts at San Marino. The shrine that resulted has been spoken of as a $100,000,000 repository of beauty. The figure is more than Mr. Huntington spent on the shrine and its contents before his death in 1927 but a replacement at today's prices could exceed that amount. The incunabula, the paintings, the porcelains, the tapestries and the furniture rival the collections of great museums that required generations to assemble.

While traveling through the Los Angeles area in 1892, Mr. Huntington had visited the San Marino Ranch, owned by J. de Barth Shorb. The view of the sunset from the south veranda, overlooking the San Gabriel Valley, made a lasting impression on him. To the north of the ranch could be seen the majestic Sierra Madre range of mountains, with Mount Wilson, Mount Lowe and Old Baldy. To the south was the rolling countryside of citrus trees and fields of hay and grain; to the southeast, a panoramic view of the Whittier hills.

As the years passed, Mr. Huntington became convinced that some day Southern California would be a cultural center of the world. Certain that it was his favorite place to live, he bought vast properties there. In 1902 he purchased the 550 acres of the San Marino Ranch, part of which was in Pasadena.

He still spent considerable time in the East on business. The Newport News Shipbuilding and Dry Dock Company was one of his concerns. While in New York City one day he was caught in a rain squall. He happened to be near the Fifth Avenue and Fifty-Seventh Street colony of art galleries and he ducked into a doorway to keep his white mustachios dry. Before he returned to the street again he had bought a painting by Sir Henry Raeburn. His love of the arts increased with his affection for Southern California and he began stockpiling his rooms at the Metropolitan Club in New York and the Jonathan Club in Los Angeles with items that struck his fancy.

Rough sketches for the San Marino mansion Mr. Huntington hoped to build were made in 1905 by E. S. Code, a railroad engineer. In 1906 Mr. Huntington hired Myron Hunt and Elmer Grey of Los Angeles as architects for the mansion. The Shorb house, a Victorian structure built in 1878, was razed and its lumber used for six houses of workmen. The Huntington mansion began to rise on the site of the old residence. It was completed in 1910 but Mr. Huntington did not continuously occupy it until he was married to Arabella in 1913 and had made his first trip to Europe. By that time he had decided to strengthen and remodel the second floor for some of the heavy works of art he was collecting.

The Huntington dining room has a chandelier, made in 1780, that gives an effect of a handful of diamonds tossed into the air.

The design of the building, called "modified" Georgian by the planners, is similar to that used for small palaces in England and France in the eighteenth century. The house has three floors and the exterior is of white cement, with black iron railings, Georgian pillars, red-tile roofs and terrace floors, marble steps and three-foot cement urns containing evergreens. The width of the house, with its covered portico, is 344 feet.

On entering the great hallway, visitors see a broad double stairway of marble, which swoops upward in two directions. There also is an elevator. The first floor has a living room, drawing room, library, den, terrace, dining room, kitchens and service rooms. The second floor has a paneled Georgian drawing room, seven bedrooms with marble fireplaces, six master baths, sitting rooms and dressing rooms; also seven servants' rooms and baths. The third floor has ten rooms.

The original plans called for a wing with bowling alleys and billiard tables but it was decided to construct a separate building as a center for games. This structure now is a cafeteria.

The northeast section of the huge basement is a wine cellar. Mr. Huntington owned the San Gabriel Winery, which he obtained in a land deal, and he kept large supplies of its product in hogsheads, as well as rare vintage wines from France. He drank little of the wine himself but served it liberally to guests.

Mr. Huntington was a naturally frugal man but he permitted no scrimping in the construction of the mansion. All interior woodwork received six to ten coats of paint, each rubbed smooth before the next one was applied and the final coat of enamel rubbed with pumice and rottenstone to produce a satin finish.

There was one big mistake, which the servants quickly discovered. When the doorbell rang, a butler or maid had to walk the entire length of the main hallway from the servants' quarters to greet a visitor. That meant that the servants generally had to run along the long hallway so that visitors would not be left waiting. This fault was never remedied.

The servants were not the only persons inconvenienced. Mr. Huntington roamed the new mansion turning out electric lights in unoccupied rooms and corridors. His wife told friends that while deciding to spend $10,000 for a book he would tour the house to save a few pennies' worth of electricity.

"My dear Arabella," Mr. Huntington said, "if I did not save pennies I would not be able to buy ten-thousand-dollar books."

One of his extravagances at San Marino was a railroad spur to the door of the mansion that enabled him to ride from there to Grand Central Terminal in New York without leaving a private car. He had three private cars at the estate and a big concrete garage to keep them in. The cars were the "Alabama," "San Marino No. 1" and "San Marino No. 2." Often he would ride in one of them and have another one attached to the same train for servants, baggage and some of the statues and paintings he was transporting across the country.

Mrs. Huntington, who liked birds, had an aviary at the mansion with twenty-six varieties of parrots and sixty-five other species of birds, including blue-crowned Victorian pigeons, pheasants and talking mynahs. One of her favorite mynahs made trips to New York with her and Mr. Huntington, talking all the way and apparently enjoying the travel.

Mr. Huntington built a lily pond for waterfowl, houses for 1,000 chickens, garages and stables. Until the automobile became common he always had a surrey and a handsome pair of chestnut-brown horses for travel around San Marino. One of his problems was that of getting a flagpole of suitable size for the estate. He bought a 148-foot Oregon fir and had it trucked through the hilly country of San Marino.

Early in the development of his estate, Mr. Huntington began building an arboretum, cactus garden and vast flower beds with plantings from all the hemispheres of the world. As a director of this work he hired William Hertrich, a young horticulturist from Germany, who laid out the gardens, pagodas, ponds and groves of citrus and redwood trees.

In 1912, when Mr. Huntington wanted a Japanese garden, Mr. Hertrich found one in Pasadena whose owner agreed to sell the entire property intact including buildings and bridges. It was bought and the structures were moved to San Marino to become part of the gardens there.

A cactus garden, with 1,500 varieties of the plant on several acres, was developed. Cacti imported from deserts throughout the world constitute probably the greatest collection ever assembled in one area. Three carloads of cacti were brought from the Arizona desert, along with five carloads of volcanic rock to provide a suitable background. Visitors who find little interest in Huntington's other collections often are fascinated by the cactus garden; the strange contours and colorings make it a paradise for photographers.

In a camelia garden, 1,000 varieties of the plant provide a dramatic blanket of flowers in the spring, and there are rose gardens with bowers of flowers. One of the first avocado orchards in Southern California also is on the estate, along with groves of grapefruit, navel and Valencia oranges, tangerines, mandarins, blood oranges and oriental kumquats. Other parts of the gardens have Kadota figs, apricots, nectarines, peaches, plums, cherries, walnuts, sapotas, cherimoyas and guaves.

Mr. Huntington, wanting a mature forest at once, had fifty-foot trees weighing twenty tons each transplanted, as an ordinary home-builder would put shrubs around a foundation. No heavy tractors or power-shovels were available at that time, so all the digging and boxing of the trees had to be done by hand. When one of the trees fell from a truck and interrupted highway traffic for days, Mr. Huntington decided to build the railroad spur to his home for further transplantings.

In his search for unusual foliage, Mr. Huntington obtained palms from all parts of the Los Angeles area, also from San Diego, Ventura, Santa Barbara, Eng-

In the Huntington living room are Boucher tapestries and eighteenth-century French furniture.

land, Belgium, Germany and Japan; ferns from New Zealand, Australia, Mexico, Central America; and cyclamens, primulas, azaleas and rhododendrons from many nations.

Inside the mansion there were many conferences to plan new acquisitions of art objects and books. Participants often included Sir Joseph Duveen, later Lord Duveen of Milbank, who advised Mr. Huntington on art, and Dr. A. S. W. Rosenbach, the bibliophile, who considered Mr. Huntington the biggest private collector of books the world has ever known.

Among the house guests were John D. Rockefeller, Jr. and his entire family; Prince Paul Troubetskoy, who modeled a bust of Mr. Huntington; Homer Ferguson, the ship builder; Otto H. Kahn, the New York banker; Mortimer Schiff, the New York financier; John Drinkwater, the English novelist and playwright; Sir Esme Howard, a British ambassador to the United States; and Crown Prince Adolf and Crown Princess Louise of Sweden.

The grand staircase of the mansion was a noble setting for the royal visitors as they descended in evening gown and white tie and tails for the Huntington parties. So were the spacious rooms, with the "Blue Boy" now flanked by paintings such as Sir Thomas Lawrence's "Pinkie," a portrait of Sarah Moulton-Barrett, aunt of Elizabeth Barrett Browning.

Other Gainsboroughs also were added, along with noted paintings by John Constable, William Hogarth, John Hoppner, Sir Henry Raeburn, Sir Joshua Reynolds, George Romney, Gilbert Stuart, Benjamin West and J. M. W. Turner. French porcelains, European furniture, historic bronzes, statues and primitives also were added, but perhaps the most distinguished items now on display are ten Boucher wall tapestries woven in the royal factory at Beauvais in the reign of Louis XV. The success of the factory was due partly to its wealthy, luxury-loving patrons, but mainly to the superb designs of François Boucher — and Mr. Huntington bought some of the best. Among these are the "Italian Hunting Scenes," first put on the looms in 1736 and so popular that they remained in production for twenty-six years.

The Sèvres porcelains of the Marquise de Pompadour in the collection have blues and greens that stir the enthusiasm of experts. To protect these and other delicate items from earthquakes, Mr. Huntington had them fastened down securely. The home of his uncle, Collis, had been wrecked in the San Francisco earthquake, with a loss of more than $1,000,000 worth of Rembrandts, Van Dycks and other art objects.

The persons responsible for the collection after Mr. Huntington's death, even more sensitive to the earthquake hazard, added to the mansion a wing with special protections, where many of the more precious objects now are displayed. The new gallery has excellent skylighting but for some reason the pictures in it are hung so high that they strain the necks of viewers.

The library, which includes a wing Mr. Huntington built as a memorial to his wife, is 200 feet east of the old residence. Of classical design, it is in the form of an *E* so that natural light penetrates most of the interior. The library was completed in 1920 and the wing in 1927.

Besides the Gutenberg Bible, which cost $50,000, the library has manuscripts of Chaucer, Stevenson and Shakespeare. One of the first printings of *Hamlet* is in the collection. There are specimens of Christopher Columbus's handwriting, John Hancock's letter naming George Washington Commander-in-Chief of the armed forces and the neatly penned autobiography of Benjamin Franklin.

One of Mr. Huntington's first big book purchases was that of the Henry W. Poor library in 1909, which included 1,600 lots of beautifully printed and bound volumes, illuminated manuscripts and incunabula. Subsequently, he bought more entire libraries, competing with the biggest dealers in the world. He would spend a million dollars as quickly as a thousand at an auction if the books coincided with his interest in English literature and Americana. A check of the library recently showed that 500 volumes of Shakespeare had come from eighty sources.

Four hundred bidders sought the Gutenberg Bible when it was auctioned in New York City in 1911. The bidding started at $10,000 and when Mr. Huntington got it for $50,000 everybody stood up and cheered. Later vitriolic criticism replaced the cheering in the East when Mr. Huntington announced that all his books would be taken to the mansion at San Marino. He had joined the Grolier Club in New York and, with other bibliophiles, founded the Hobby Club there, which led to a general belief that he would keep his books in the East. The first indication to the contrary came in 1913 when he issued orders for a strengthening of the floors of his home at San Marino.

In the same year Mr. Huntington, with his new bride, made his first trip to Europe. He rented a château near Paris, but on his return to Southern California he said: "This is Heaven to me. I intend to remain here."

Air-conditioning systems were installed by Mr. Huntington to protect his manuscripts and the glue and pages of his books. Bookworms do not work at temperatures below 70 degrees F., he learned, so the books are kept at 63 degrees F. Every new acquisition still is fumigated, and a bookbindery is maintained to keep all the volumes in repair.

One of the books receiving this care is William Blades's *The Enemies of Books*, published in London in 1880, which has this to say about bookbinders:

Adjacent to the Huntington residence on the north is a croquet court flanked by European statues and rare trees and shrubs.

The pillared structure beyond the terrace is a mausoleum, designed by John Russell Pope. In it Mr. and Mrs. Huntington are buried.

"Dante in his *Inferno* deals out to the lost souls various tortures suited with dramatic fitness to the past crimes of the victims, and had I to execute judgment on the criminal binders of certain precious volumes I have seen, I would collect the paper-shavings so ruthlessly shorn off and roast the perpetrators of the outrage over their slow combustion."

To protect his volumes from hazards other than bookbinders, Mr. Huntington built an underground steel vault, with an elevator leading to it. According to Robert O. Schad, curator of rare books in the collection, the vault rivals anything at Alcatraz Prison, so far as protections are concerned. A person entering the vault is protected by thirty tons of four-inch steel armor plate recessed in a casing of reinforced concrete nine feet thick. Even if a Hiroshima-type atomic bomb hit the state, the contents of this vault probably would survive.

Besides containing some of the more precious books and manuscripts, the vault contains a microfilm record of everything in the Huntington collection. In wartime, the items that probably would be locked constantly in the vault include the Gutenberg Bible, the "Blue Boy," "Pinkie," Shakespeare's "Venus and Adonis" and many of the personal letters of the great figures of history.

A perpetual deed of trust for the maintenance of his estate, now reduced to 200 acres, was signed by Mr. Huntington in 1919. The instrument centers the responsibilities in a small board of directors, the first five members of which were Howard E. Huntington, his son by his first marriage; Archer M. Huntington, his wife's son by her first marriage; Dr. George E. Hale, then the director of the Mount Wilson Observatory; and George S. Patton and William E. Dunn, friends and business associates of Mr. Huntington.

After completing his home, Mr. Huntington joined with friends and neighbors in founding the City of San Marino. He donated much of the property for it, built broad highways and planted its trees and flowers. He also contributed a site for the city hall when incorporation papers were drawn. Under his planning the city became a community of fine homes, ornamental highways and little commerce. He even bought the old and dilapidated Hotel Wentworth and redeveloped it into the spacious and splendid Hotel Huntington, which continues to operate. The architects for the hotel were Myron Hunt and Elmer Grey, who had designed the Huntington residence.

The name "San Marino" was first used on the West Coast by Mr. Shorb, who called his estate the San Marino Ranch because his grandfather had had a plantation by that name in Frederick County, Maryland. The grandfather had used the name because he was fond of the tiny independent San Marino nation in the mountains of Italy.

In 1926 Mr. Huntington commissioned John Russell Pope, the distinguished New York City architect, to plan a mausoleum for a high knoll of his estate at San Marino. It was under construction when Mr. Huntington died, and he and his wife now are buried there. He had tried to avoid the limelight except at the estate and when asked to write an autobiography he had declared:

"No, never. This home and library will tell the story. They represent the reward of all the work I have ever done. The ownership of a fine home, a fine art collection and a fine library is the swiftest and surest way to immortality."

✿   ✿   ✿   ✿   ✿   ✿   ✿   ✿

The galleries and gardens, which are entered from Oxford Road, are open to the public from 1 P.M. to 4:30 P.M. every day except Monday and a few holidays. They are closed during the entire month of October. Admission is free. Children under six are not admitted to the buildings.

The Only Royal Palace in the United States

Iolani, Built by the Merry Monarch

HONOLULU · HAWAII

THE POLYNESIAN guide put a lei of colorful orchids around the neck of each woman on the tour as she entered the grounds of the ornate home that fun-loving King Kalakaua, the Merry Monarch, had built under the spreading banyan trees in Honolulu. As the guide dropped a lei in place he kissed each woman and said, "Aloha!" Then he handed leis to the women to perform the same ritual on their husbands.

"Just what do you Hawaiians mean by all this 'Aloha'?" one of the curious visitors asked. "We've been hearing it morning, noon and night, and now you say it to us with special emphasis when we come to the royal palace."

Leading the visitors under bowers of bougainvillaea, oleander and plumiera, the guide smiled as he replied; "Yes, 'Aloha' means we welcome you. It means more than words can say. It means good luck to you, and good night at the close of day. It means we love you, and it means please come back again.

Iolani Palace 155

"And," he continued, "when we welcome you to one of the wonders of Hawaii especially dear to us, we pronounce the word 'a-lo-HA!'"

In the throne room of the palace he turned to the visitors and exclaimed "A-lo-HA!" He noted that this was the Iolani Palace that the Merry Monarch built in 1879-82 and today is the only royal palace in any of the fifty states. In the Hawaiian tongue, Iolani means "Bird of Heaven."

Although sugar remains the chief revenue producer for the Hawaiian islands, tourism has reached second place and a chief point of interest at Honolulu, on the island of Oahu, is the palace. It rivals in interest Pearl Harbor, tropical forests, dazzling flowers, pineapple fields, active volcanoes, waterfalls and beautiful Polynesian women.

After a trip through the palace, visitors know that they have taken a step into the fabled islands of the South Seas. They realize that they have reached the only tropical state and finally are getting a first-hand look at "hoomanawanui" — the Hawaiians' easy way of life.

It was not easy in 1874, however, for the Merry Monarch to get his job as king. He did not inherit it, as all his predecessors had done; he ran for election at a legislative assembly of the second-string leaders of the islands. The previous king had died without naming a successor. His widow, the Dowager Queen Emma, wanted to become the ruler and most of the common people thought she should be elected but the legislative assembly voted 36 to 6 in favor of the Merry Monarch.

When the crowd outside the palace heard about the decision later, the legislators were knocked into the gutters and beaten, the clothes were torn from their backs and their carriages were smashed. The courthouse was wrecked. Sailors from British and United States warships helped to restore order, and the Merry Monarch began a seventeen-year reign that occasionally resembled a Viennese comic opera.

The palace that he built is confusingly Continental and Victorian in architecture. It resembles some of the old mansions of Vienna, as well as several of the gambling casinos along the Mediterranean coast of the French Riviera. The Hawaiians prefer comparisons with the palaces of European royalty.

During his first year on the throne, the Merry Monarch visited the United States to promote the signing of a reciprocal treaty that would make sugar the real king of the Hawaiian islands. He was the first king to visit the mainland. He enjoyed it all so much that he decided to make a trip around the world: the first such journey of any king in history.

After laying the cornerstone of Iolani Palace in 1879, the Merry Monarch started on his great globe-circling adventure. Accompanying him was his valet Robert, a decrepit German baron, who was his interpreter. In Japan, China, Siam, India, Italy, France, Germany and England they received royal welcomes. The Merry Monarch was greatly impressed by the palaces he visited, and he began re-planning Iolani Palace.

Queen Liliuokalani, the last ruler before Hawaii became a republic in 1893, was a prisoner in the palace for nine months. (Right) King Kalakaua, the Merry Monarch, died after building the palace and was succeeded as the ruler by his sister, Queen Liliuokalani.

Returning to Honolulu, he discharged the architects and builders who had been working on Iolani. He hired new ones and ordered vast changes in the structure to conform with the grandiose ideas he had formed in his world tour.

In 1883, nine years after the Merry Monarch's election as king, Iolani Palace was completed at a cost of $350,000, which was a huge amount to the islanders. One of the first events in the palace was a coronation ceremony, with the Merry Monarch becoming the first Hawaiian ruler to be crowned. For the event he wore a costly jeweled crown he had bought in England. There was a similar crown for his royal consort.

The Merry Monarch wore a robe of 5,000 feathers of the o-o bird. Attending the ceremony were 8,000 persons, including diplomatic representatives of American, European and Asiatic nations. Soon afterward the King had a Masonic dinner for 120 guests at the palace. Kalakaua was a thirty-third degree Mason.

All-night poker games for the Merry Monarch and his cronies became common at the palace. There were heavy drinking, cigar smoking and storytelling. Occasionally irked by the luck of some of the other players, the Merry Monarch would set new rules to suit his fancy.

Iolani Palace 157

While playing with Claus Spreckels, the California sugar tycoon, the King found himself losing to four aces held by Mr. Spreckels. Tossing four kings onto the table, he scooped up the money, declaring: "Five kings beat four aces any time. I have four kings on the table and I am the fifth!"

The Merry Monarch introduced yachting as a sport in Honolulu and installed the first telephone in the palace so he could talk to the crewmen of his boats at the near-by wharf.

Across the street from the palace lived Walter Murray Gibson, a wealthy Mormon from the United States. He was reported to have become such a close friend of the Merry Monarch that he really was the power behind the throne. Legislators of the monarchy became resentful and in 1887 ordered the Merry Monarch to stop dealing with Mr. Gibson and replace the entire royal cabinet.

The Merry Monarch complied. In 1890 he left for California so that doctors there could study the cause of his declining health. He was feted in Los Angeles, San Diego and Santa Barbara but on arriving in San Francisco he was found to be suffering from Bright's Disease and he died there, in the Palace Hotel.

Back in Honolulu, his sister Liliuokalani was made queen and she moved into Iolani Palace for some of the unhappiest years that any queen ever endured. There was frequent bickering with the legislators. In 1893 the monarchy was overthrown, a provisional government was set up and the Queen was placed under house arrest in Iolani Palace. She spent nine months there as a prisoner.

Soldiers rolled dice in the palace for jewels pried from the crowns. An Irish sergeant won the largest diamond among the stones and mailed it to his fiancée in Indiana along with a note that it was "just one of those Hawaiian stones." Not until many years later did the woman discover that the stone, kept by her in a drawer full of junk jewelry, was worth several thousand dollars.

When Hawaii became a republic in 1894, Iolani became a home for the president, and after annexation of the islands as a territory of the United States the palace became a home of the governors. Since becoming the fiftieth state in 1959, Hawaii has used the palace for government offices and meetings of the legislature pending the construction of a state capitol. It is destined to become a permanent public shrine and museum when the capitol is completed.

Although nobody is quite certain who planned the palace, it is known that the walls are brick faced with concrete and trimmed with stone. Hawaiian koa, ohia, kamani and kou woods are used lavishly in the interior, along with white cedar and walnut from the mainland. The grand stairway is of koa, ornamented with carved cedar, ohia and kamani.

To the right of the stairway on the first floor is the throne room, where most of the royal entertaining took place. The room has crystal chandeliers brought from Europe by the Merry Monarch, two canopied gold thrones and velvet-draped French windows.

Iolani's throne room still has feather kahilis flanking twin thrones under a red velvet canopy.

The throne room also has rows of feathered kahilis, which are plumes signifying royalty. They are on standards several feet taller than the royal guards who once carried them in processions as soldiers might carry national flags. The rarest of all the kahilis is made of 10,000 flaming-red feathers from the Ko'ae bird, which is generally found at Kilauea, the volcanic home in Hawaii of Pele, the legendary fire goddess. Since each bird has only one red feather, 10,000 of the birds had to be plucked.

As impressive as the plumage of the kahilis are the standards, which have alternate rings of tortoise shell and human bones. Other decorations in the throne room include the Merry Monarch's coat of arms and portraits of the old Hawaiian royalty.

Across the hall is the old State Dining Room and its adjacent Blue Room, which was decorated in blue mohair and served as a lounge and music room. Lavish luaus, or Hawaiian feasts, once were held throughout this side of the house.

On the second floor, four royal bedrooms have been converted into a library and offices for the governor and his staff. Portraits there include one of Louis Philippe, given by the French monarch to the Hawaiian royalty in 1848. It has a bullet hole through it, caused by a revolutionist's wild shot in 1893.

Uses of the rooms change occasionally. Recently the Merry Monarch's bedroom was the office of the governor, the throne room was occupied by the House of Representatives and the dining room was occupied by the Senate. In the basement a former billiard room and a workshop of the Merry Monarch have been converted into offices for the fiftieth state.

✿　✿　✿　✿　✿　✿　✿　✿

Iolani Palace is at King and Richards Streets in downtown Honolulu. It is open to visitors from 8 A.M. to 4 P.M. Monday through Friday and from 8 A.M. to noon on Saturday, although sessions of the legislature may occasionally exclude visitors from some rooms. Guides are provided. Admission is free.

Way Down South

Walter D. Bellingrath's Abode

THEODORE · ALABAMA

TWENTY MILES south of Mobile, Alabama, are the Bellingrath mansion and gardens which, among tourist meccas are on a pinnacle by themselves. Compared with other places they are virtually new: the gardens were started in 1927 and the mansion in 1935. Yet they are patterned after those of past centuries. They are extraordinary works of new art in old designs. The mansion, its furnishings and the gardens are integral parts of an indivisible symbol of the culture of the Deep South.

Bricks, flagstones, lacy ironwork, fountains and artistic curiosities hundreds of years old have been used to capture the atmosphere and grandeur of the past. Withal, the monstrosities of design, the structural pitfalls, the common inconveniences and the economic impracticalities of bygone days have been avoided. Neither the dwelling with its picture windows and air conditioning nor the 60 acres of manicured gardens nor the 750 acres of plantation would be shunned by a modern owner — provided he could meet the payroll of fifty-five servants.

Bellingrath was developed by the late Mr. and Mrs. Walter D. Bellingrath. In 1955 the property and the family fortune were inherited by a philanthropic foundation that benefits three colleges and two churches. The mansion and gardens are open to the public every day in the year.

The bricks of the building, made by slaves long before the Civil War, were salvaged from old Mobile buildings being demolished. The intricate lacy ironwork which distinguishes the exterior of the mansion was obtained from an old waterfront hotel that was razed. The flagstones of the terraces were brought from distant lands as ship ballast and used for public sidewalks in Mobile; Mr. Bellingrath acquired them by paying for new concrete sidewalks in the city.

Noting the mansion's Colonial profile, Roman arches, Italian fountains, New Orleans ironwork, English dolphins and Chicago roof tile, George B. Rogers, architect of the structure, said the design was a mingling of English, Mediterranean and American influences. To most visitors it is a successful mingling, although some architectural purists are critical.

Having been under five flags — French, English, Spanish, United States and Confederate — Mobile takes the mongrel design for granted. Historians, however, speak of Bellingrath as a "new shrine" that is not in the same league with the stark, white comfort-defying ante-bellum mansions.

Especially appealing to modernists is the sweeping view from the front hall through seventy feet of pleasant rooms. Of interest also is a huge sunburst medallion on the living room ceiling and the cornices, made by European craftsmen, in five designs — Tudor rose, Greek key, acanthus leaf, egg-and-dart and trypanocidal.

A son of German immigrants, Mr. Bellingrath was born in Atlanta, Georgia. At the age of seventeen he went to work for the Louisville and Nashville Railroad as a station agent and telegrapher. In 1903 he moved to Mobile to become a Coca Cola distributor. He bottled three cases of it each night in his basement and then tried to sell it from door to door the next day, but his customers were accustomed to orange pop. To get them acquainted with Cola Cola he "accidentally" put a few bottles of it in cases of other drinks.

The business grew until Mr. Bellingrath became one of the biggest bottlers of Coca Cola in the South. He received sixteen loving cups as trophies on his eightieth birthday and was honored as a 500,000-gallon-a-year tycoon of the industry; he bought that much of the syrup, only one ounce of which was required to a bottle. He died at eighty-six, in 1955, twelve years after the death of his wife, Bessie Morse Bellingrath. They had no children.

Aside from the bottling business, the Bellingraths had other good fortune. In the depths of the depression in the nineteen thirties, while Mississippi River floods were washing out wealthy cotton growers, the Bellingraths had millions of dollars to spend for the construction and furnishing of their unusual mansion. For 200 years prosperous French, Spanish, Italian, German and English families had settled in this part of the nation, bringing furniture, porcelains, china, silverware, rugs and statues from Europe. When financial troubles developed these art treasures were sold.

Mrs. Bellingrath haunted the auctions and had abundant cash in hand, while other potential bidders were pauperized. She often bought the entire contents of a mansion, transferring to her home only those items that were choice and storing the others until they could be sold.

As a result, Bellingrath has Charles Lamb's dressing table in a bathroom; the contrast with the modern pink-and-green tile walls and square bathtub is startling. Sir Thomas Lipton's dining-room table and chairs are in one of Bellingrath's three dining rooms. Tall cabinets are filled with Meissen, Sèvres and English porcelains, and throughout the house there is more fine silver than one might expect in Tiffany's.

Other furnishings include a mirror that Louis XVI once used, a rosewood table that had belonged to the mother of Kaiser Wilhelm II, Bennington chairs, a Vermont melodeon and a Meissen "table plateau" of sterling silver and big mirrors that Robert Livingston owned in the Revolutionary War era.

"I don't know how much it all cost and I don't want to know," Mr. Bellingrath said just before he died. "If I did know, I wouldn't enjoy it."

The main dining room is international. Besides the Lipton furniture it has Russian candelabra and teapots, Chinese urns, Early American beehive candlesticks, hand-painted English china and Italian milk glass.

The Bellingrath mansion has ironwork salvaged from pre-Civil War hotels in Mobile. Bricks, made by slaves, also were salvaged for the home.

The Bellingrath dining room has a table and chairs once owned by Sir Thomas Lipton. The centerpiece is Meissen porcelain with ormolu.

The Bottle Room has shelves filled with Venetian, Waterford and other fine glass. It also has some sturdy soft-drink bottles, the first that Mr. Bellingrath used in his business, standing beside delicate liquor glasses.

Luther Harris, a houseman who worked for the Bellingraths and is still on the job, recalls that Mr. Bellingrath always drank from bottles — Coca Cola in public and whisky in private. Mrs. Bellingrath, he also recalls, "hated liquor worse than God hates sin" and even at the frequent big receptions in the mansion served nothing stronger than pop in the fine old liquor glasses.

In the collection are four sets of twenty-two-carat gold service plates, nine complete dinner services of Royal Doulton, Worcester, Haviland and Black Knight; embossed sterling silver punch bowls; sterling silver trays as large as card tables; and a dazzling array of sterling bun warmers, pitchers, baskets, centerpieces and candelabra. Oriental rugs and 300-year-old Aubussons from France are on the floors.

There are reminders of Mr. Bellingrath everywhere. The colorful tiles of some floors were made in his tile factories, one of his subsidiary enterprises. There is an occasional harmonica on an inlaid table; playing hillbilly tunes on a mouth organ was his chief musical entertainment up to the last day of his life.

The dwelling is on the Isle-aux-Oies River, better known to residents as the Fowl. Mr. Bellingrath started the estate as a fishing camp in 1917. On a trip to Europe in 1927 he and his wife were so impressed by the gardens of various castles that they hurried home to start their own.

Visitors entering the wrought-iron gates, originally owned by the first governor of Louisiana, gain an initial impression that Bellingrath is a semitropical wonderland. The lofty limbs of aged oaks are laden with wispy Spanish moss. Along the sun-dappled paths and beside a lake are azaleas, hydrangeas, roses, camellias, oleander, hibiscus, African violets, Confederate jasmine, sweet olive, laurel, magnolia, beech and pine. The property has seventy varieties of trees.

"We have no season here," Mr. Bellingrath once commented. "Something is in bloom every day. The beauty changes by the week. Our gardens are like a lady with fifty-two gowns."

The latest count of azalea bushes showed 250,000 including 200 varieties. Some are estimated to be 150 years old, the biggest being eighteen feet tall and thirty feet wide. The gardens have 2,500 specimens of camellias, with some of the bushes an estimated one hundred years old; the biggest are twenty feet tall and sixteen feet wide.

In setting up the trust for perpetual operation of the property as a public shrine, Mr. Bellingrath said: "In the evening of our lives my beloved wife and I found untold happiness in the development of the gardens. Thousands of our fellow citizens have enjoyed the rare and lovely spectacle which nature, with our help, has provided in this 'Charm Spot of the Deep South.' The inspiration which we received as we carried on our work and the appreciative reaction of many visitors resulted in plans for the perpetuation of this beauty."

The continuing profits from Mr. Bellingrath's bottling business are part of the trust. The beneficiaries of the trust's net income each year are Southwestern College at Memphis, Huntingdon College at Montgomery, Stillman College (for Negroes) at Tuscaloosa, Central Presbyterian Church of Mobile (as a memorial to Mr. Bellingrath's parents) and St. Francis Street Methodist Church of Mobile (as a memorial to his wife's parents).

Fred W. Holder, general manager of Bellingrath, reports that 16,000 people a day have visited the property for big events and the average for a year is 150,000. He adds that "We're open from cain to cain't," which in Gulf Coast parlance means from the time you can see at sunrise until you can't see at sundown.

❖   ❖   ❖   ❖   ❖   ❖   ❖   ❖

The gates are near Theodore, just south of U. S. Route 90. The admission to the gardens is $2, and to the mansion, $2.50 additional. The official hours for visitors at the gardens are from 7 A. M. to dusk and at the mansion from 8 A. M. to 5 P. M., every day.

Longwood is an octagonal Moorish castle begun in 1861 and still not finished. (Opposite page) Because of its pillars and balconies, Dunleith is one of the most-photographed mansions in Natchez.

Cotton and Southern Comfort   *Dunleith*

The River-Front Pageant

NATCHEZ · MISSISSIPPI

ON THE MISSISSIPPI RIVER bluffs 150 miles northwest of New Orleans, the early Indians had tepees. De Soto explored the bluffs and La Salle colonized them. The Spanish massacred rivals there, and the French and the British set up trading posts. Natchez, as the community was named, became a rowdy river-front way station of saloons, gambling dens, tinny pianos, squawking parrots, boisterous sailors and women touting their charms.

Then cotton became the King of the South. The new culture that accompanied the new wealth caused a constellation of elegant mansions to rise on the bluffs. Today's tourists have discovered the Natchez pageant of homes and the money they spend there is providing a prosperity that neither the southern planters nor their predecessors could have anticipated.

The mansions of Natchez, like those of Charleston, are not enormous in size but collectively they are a giant in architecture and in drama. The walls of the

Georgian and Greek Revival houses have witnessed slavery, warfare, political shenanigans, skyrocketing incomes, abject poverty, family feuds, murder. . . .

Some of the continuing melodrama is seen at Longwood, also known as Nutt's Folly. It is an eight-sided Moorish castle, begun in 1861 and still not finished. In fact, carpenters' tools are on the floors and paint brushes in the buckets just as they were left when Confederate Army bugles echoed through the countryside to herald the outbreak of patricidal conflict. Most of the workmen at Nutt's Folly were Pennsylvanians and they fled north to join the Union Army.

Haller Nutt, who built the octagonal house, came from a family of adventurers. His father, Dr. Rush Nutt, who left a medical practice to see America on horseback, perfect a cotton gin and visit Europe, set up Haller in business as a cotton planter at Natchez. He fell in love with Julia Williams, a young and pretty girl who had been disappointed in a love affair, and they were married. In his eagerness to make his bride happy, Haller decided to build a mansion that he believed would be so different and elegant that it would be the pride of Natchez.

His father had gotten him interested in arabesques, Oriental buildings and Moorish palaces. Other persons had fired him with enthusiasm for octagonal buildings. Taking his numerous ideas to Philadelphia, he submitted them to Samuel Sloan, an architect there, and the blueprints for Longwood were drawn.

The plans for the six-story residence stemmed largely from a style fostered by Orson Squire Fowler. Mr. Fowler specialized in reading skull bumps and writing marriage manuals before he turned to architecture. He lectured on "how to promote sexual vigor" and had three children when he was over seventy years old. He also undertook to convince the nation that octagonal buildings were logical because eight walls would enclose more space than four walls of the same length.

Octagonal homes were built from Maine to California but Nutt's Folly is the most famous one still standing. It is on Lower Woodville Road, among trees laden with Spanish moss. It has thirty-two rooms, nine of them completed. On the top is an onion-shaped dome. On each of the outside brick walls Mr. Nutt built galleries, with narrow fluted pillars topped by gingerbread ornamentations. In the walls are scores of narrow, arched windows.

Every main floor of the house has a central eight-sided room, with eight doors leading to eight outer rooms that were to have eight decorative panels and eight-sided furniture. One of the architect's aims was to enable a person to walk throughout the house without passing twice through the same door.

The inventive Mr. Nutt also arranged for indirect lighting by using large mirrors in the dome and smaller ones downstairs to direct the sunbeams wherever they were needed.

Wooden decorations were carved in Philadelphia by Yankee artisans, who also built marble mantels and ornate plaster ceilings. Mr. Nutt ordered fabrics from Ireland, a marble stairway from Italy, furniture from France and silverware

Stanton Hall, built by an Irishman from Belfast, now has rooms for tourists.

from England. Many of the items were in warehouses when work on the mansion was abruptly halted; some of them now have been bought by museums.

Mr. Nutt, believing the war would not last long, moved his wife and children into completed basement rooms of the house until work on the upper floors could be completed. The basement had been intended for a billiard room, wine cellar and playroom. Mr. Nutt died before the war ended but his family continued to live there and another family is still living in the basement rooms. The building is owned by Mr. Nutt's grandchildren, who live in New York City and Wisconsin.

A vastly different type of house is one with Grecian pillars that Frederick Stanton, an Irishman from Belfast, built in 1851 at High and Pearl Streets. Stanton had made a quick fortune in cotton and wanted to impress his neighbors. He also wanted a home somewhat like the "white house" he had left on the other side of the Atlantic.

To furnish the new home he returned to Europe on a buying spree, leaving his wife in Natchez for fear she might curb his extravagances. He bought so many tapestries, tables, chairs, rugs, draperies, chandeliers and slabs of marble that he had to charter a ship to bring them home — with an overflow stowed aboard other ships.

Stanton Hall, as the house is known, has two outside galleries that are noted for their wrought-iron balustrades. The house, of brick, stucco and wood, with marble floors, has carved decorations with grapes and roses as motifs.

On the main floor is a hall seventy-four feet in length and a drawing room nearly as long. An entrance to a reception room did not seem sufficiently large to Mr. Stanton, and he had the workmen install a broad Italian arch that has no direct support from the floor. The mantels are of white Carrara marble, carved with fruit, flowers and cherubs.

A forty-foot banquet room has two marble fireplaces. The chandeliers, made overseas from designs Mr. Stanton provided, bear images of Indians, soldiers and wild buffaloes to depict the history of Natchez. The Stantons had no trouble getting seventeen servants to operate the mansion but they had to send to New Orleans for more furniture.

Mr. Stanton died suddenly, less than a year after moving into the new home, and his wife soon was groaning under the cost of maintaining the property. During the Civil War, soldiers moved into Stanton Hall. Two of the Stanton daughters hid the silverware upstairs but one night they were chloroformed and by the time they revived, the silverware had vanished. The mansion later was sold for less than the original cost of the iron fence around it.

The Stanton College for Young Ladies occupied Stanton Hall for a time; later, other owners moved into it and the building became dilapidated. Now the Pilgrimage Garden Club owns it, is steadily restoring the original splendor and is using the building as a headquarters and for overnight lodging for tourists.

Quite a different house among the Natchez adaptations is Elmscourt, which has a Mediterranean atmosphere. Its iron grillwork, around two galleries on the front, was brought from Italy and is rated among the finest anywhere.

Elmscourt has lacy ironwork from Italy. Jennie Merrill, who was murdered, lived here in girlhood.

Another distinction of Elmscourt is that it was the girlhood home of Miss Jane (Jennie) Merrill, whose murder in 1932 held the attention of newspaper readers throughout the country and is still something of a mystery.

Elmscourt, on U. S. Route 61, was built in 1810 and in 1830 was a wedding gift to Mr. and Mrs. Ayres P. Merrill from Mrs. Merrill's father. It was a simple, square, planter's house but the Merrills added large wings, the grillwork and considerable interior fretwork. Its chandeliers held hundreds of candles and the house became known as The Mansion of a Thousand Candles.

The mansion was a center of brilliant parties. Jennie, one of seven children, grew up there amid a rustle of silk. She helped to entertain General Ulysses S. Grant, and when her father became Ambassador to Belgium she went overseas to meet the kings and queens of Europe.

Returning to Elmscourt, Jennie often met with three close friends — Duncan Minor, member of one of the oldest Natchez families; Octavia Dockery, the beautiful daughter of a Confederate general; and Dick Dana, son of a clergyman and relative of Charles A. Dana, the New York editor, and Charles Dana Gibson, the artist. Although normal in their youth, the four became eccentric after passing the age of fifty. . . .

Jennie moved to Glenwood, a mansion once occupied by the Stantons; then to Glenburnie, next door. Both of these houses are across the road from Elmscourt. Because of family objections, Jennie did not marry Duncan Minor, but he was a frequent visitor in her home. As she aged, Jennie got a reputation for driving through red traffic lights; when policemen saw who was at the wheel they just shook their heads.

Dick Dana moved into Glenwood and Octavia Dockery later joined him. They kept goats in the mansion and it became known as Goat Castle, with Octavia called the Goat Woman. As the house became a slum, Dick dressed in burlap sacks, grew a beard and climbed trees to stare down at people. Quarrels between the couple in Glenwood and the couple in Glenburnie became notorious, and occasionally Jennie got out her rifle to shoot goats that roamed onto her property.

On the night of August 4, 1932, shots echoed through the woods. The next day a trail of blood in Glenburnie led to the body of Jennie in a thicket near the house. Shoeless and in a tattered cotton dress, Jennie had been shot to death.

Accused of the murder, Dick and Octavia later were exonerated. Duncan was questioned repeatedly and each time was released. A Negro "confessed" the murder but his statements were found to be untrue. A woman went to jail as an accessory to the crime but later was freed. A vagrant, considered a prime suspect, was killed while resisting arrest. The people of Natchez, especially members of the prominent families involved, today are reluctant to talk about the strange affair.

As for Elmscourt, it now is owned and elegantly maintained by Mrs. Douglas H. MacNeil.

Rosalie, built for a fourteen-year-old bride, now is owned by the Daughters of the American Revolution.

Rosalie, a Georgian mansion at the south end of Broadway, was built in 1820 by Peter Little, a wealthy operator of sawmills, for his child bride, Eliza Low, fourteen years old. Eliza was Peter's ward before she became his bride; too young to manage a mansion, she was sent to a finishing school in Baltimore by her husband.

When Eliza finally became the mistress of Rosalie she was so religious that a parade of clergymen came to visit the Littles and many stayed overnight. Wanting some privacy, Mr. Little finally built another mansion, the Parsonage, around the corner for the overnight guests.

Rosalie, designed by James S. Griffin of Baltimore, is a white-pillared, red-brick house with double galleries on the front. During the Civil War its large French mirrors were hidden in caves near by so that soldiers would not destroy them. Its brass fenders and andirons were buried on the grounds and then could not be found for many years, until children digging in play came upon them.

General Grant stayed at the house and General Walter Q. Gresham, also of the Union Army, made it his headquarters. General Gresham allowed the owner,

Mrs. Andrew L. Wilson, to remain in the house until he discovered she was working for the Confederates; he then banished her to Atlanta, but after the war the Gresham and Wilson families resumed the war-born friendship.

The Daughters of the American Revolution now own, maintain and exhibit the mansion. It is on the original site of Fort Rosalie, which, built by the French, had flown the flags of France, England, Spain and the United States.

Dunleith, which the casual visitor to Natchez often considers its most impressive mansion, is a symmetrical Greek Revival structure rimmed by two-story pillars and double galleries. Facing U. S. Routes 61 and 65, it is on the site of an earlier mansion that burned. It was built in 1847 by Charles Dahlgren, a member of the royal family of Sweden who had migrated to Natchez. The present owners are Mr. and Mrs. N. L. Carpenter, members of the fifth generation of Carpenters to occupy it. (See photo on page 167).

A parlor of Rosalie has an Italian marble fireplace, Dresden china cuspidors and an 1850 English harp.

D'Evereux has no measurement not divisible by three. A schoolteacher from the North fell in love with the house and bought it.

D'Evereux, a Greek Revival house built in 1840, has no parts or measurements that are not divisible by three. The structure has six Doric columns that are three feet thick and twenty-four feet tall. Double parlors are eighteen by twenty-four feet. The hall is thirty-three feet by twelve feet, and the ceilings are twelve feet high. The divisible-by-three fixation of the designers is evident in steps, woodwork and the thickness of walls.

St. John Elliott built D'Evereux, which is on U. S. Routes 61 and 84. Mr. Elliott, a cotton broker, wanted to perpetuate the family name and tried to give the house to a nephew if he would change his name to St. John Elliott. The nephew refused. Consequently, the house was left by Mr. Elliott's will to a Roman Catholic orphanage. Mrs. Elliott gave $20,000 to the orphanage, got full title to the house and bequeathed it to relatives.

Tenants then stored yams and kept horses in D'Evereux. In 1923 Miss Myra Virginia Smith, a schoolteacher from Illinois and Minnesota, bought the house and restored it. Despite the years of neglect the walls are firm and straight today. Miss Smith, demonstrating with a plumb the trueness of the walls, said she could not understand the refusal of St. John Elliott's nephew to change his name, adding that "I would have changed my name to mud to get a house like this one."

Miss Smith also commented that D'Evereux faces north, as "all good houses do." This permits the living quarters on the sides and rear to face gardens and get maximum sunshine and breezes, she explained. "Only an ignorant Yankee would buy a house here facing south," she added.

Melrose, a blend of Greek Revival and Georgian designs, is considered one of the most complete and architecturally perfect houses in Natchez. On Melrose Avenue, it was built in 1845 by John T. McMurran, a lawyer from the East, who was a spellbinder in the courtrooms and a successful speculator in cotton plantations. His wife, Mary Louise, had long been a social belle of Natchez and like the others in her set wanted the biggest and most elegant mansion in town.

Mr. McMurran spared no expense in providing it. He built a red-brick house with double galleries and four Doric pillars on the front. On the roof he built a widow's walk like those of New England coastal homes.

The hallways and rooms of the house are king size, with candles in rows over doorways, and fireplaces of Egyptian marble. Near one fireplace are twin horsehair seats with a hard stool between them. This was a courting set, with the stool for the chaperone so that she could watch the love-making and not fall asleep.

One of the tables that Mr. McMurran displayed with great pride is circular, has a pattern of birds in mosaics and originally had small diamonds for the birds' eyes. The diamonds vanished — pried loose by the bayonet tips of Union soldiers and stolen, so the story goes.

Melrose is one of the finest houses, architecturally, in Natchez.

In the financial debacle of 1865 Mr. McMurran sold Melrose to George M. Davis, a law associate, and the house has been owned by the same family ever since. The present occupant is Mrs. George M. D. Kelly, whose late husband was a grandson of Mr. Davis and who inherited the mansion at the age of eight.

Soon after losing Melrose, Mr. McMurran boarded a river boat for New Orleans to improve his fortunes. On board also were 300 other persons and 2,500 bales of cotton. Embers from the smokestacks of the boat ignited the cotton. The passengers and their horses soon were wallowing in the mud of the river, trying desperately to get away from the boat before it exploded. Mr. McMurran, mortally injured, was never to see Melrose again, even as a guest.

✿ ✿ ✿ ✿ ✿ ✿ ✿ ✿

Thirty ante-bellum houses in Natchez are opened for conducted tours each March. The six tours of all thirty houses require three days and cost $20. One tour of five houses costs $4. Longwood, Rosalie, Stanton Hall and several other houses can be visited from 9 A.M. to 5 P.M. on most days of the year for fees averaging $1. Brochures are available from the Association of Commerce, the Natchez Garden Club and the Pilgrimage Garden Club, all in Natchez.

Old Hickory's Haven

The Hermitage of Andrew Jackson

NASHVILLE · TENNESSEE

MILITARY CONFLICTS, political maneuvers, an illegal marriage and a duel-to-the-death by the seventh President of the United States are among the events that a stately Greek Revival mansion near Nashville could talk about intimately if it had a tongue. It was the home of Andrew Jackson during the most exciting years of his tempestuous life.

Jackson's best friends conceded that his crudities in spelling and grammar "would make the angels weep." But he was self-confident, energetic, honest and straightforward; he also was very proud and he loved a good fight. If architecture can reflect such traits of a man, they stand out in bold relief at the Hermitage, the 425-acre plantation Jackson bought in 1804 and developed steadily until his death there in 1845.

Jackson never saw his father and he lost two brothers in the Revolutionary War, in which he himself fought at the age of fourteen. In 1791 he married Rachel Donelson only to discover later, to the amazement of both, that her first husband, Lewis Robards, had not obtained a divorce in a suit that had been started. In 1794, after a divorce decree finally had been issued, Jackson went through the formality of remarrying Rachel. The marriage was one of the happiest in history but the unintentional irregularity was long used against Jackson, especially in the bitter Presidential campaign of 1828, when he defeated John Quincy Adams despite the so-called scandal.

Jackson and his wife generally had simple tastes. However, when they began looking for a home they decided they wanted something that would provide not only comfort but social and political status. At first they occupied a converted blockhouse on the plantation, meanwhile dreaming of building something as splendid as the mansions they had seen in Charleston and Natchez.

During the planning, Jackson had a steady procession of military and political visitors at the plantation and he listened to some of their ideas about architecture. He did this while performing such feats as mobilizing militiamen of Tennessee, Kentucky and Louisiana; Baratarian privateers; free Negroes; Mississippi dragoons and Choctaw Indians into an army of 5,000 to win the Battle of New Orleans. He also was a United States Senator and governor of the new territory of Florida.

Jackson was at the plantation in 1806 when he heard that Charles Dickinson, a local leader, had said "Jackson was entitled to great military honors because he captured another man's wife." Jackson extracted an apology from Dickinson, who said he must have been drunk; but later in a wrangle over race horses Dickinson demanded a duel and at seven o'clock on a May morning the pair, with their seconds, met in the woods.

It was agreed that Jackson and Dickinson were to stand twenty-four feet apart, with pistols upright, either one to be shot dead instantly by the seconds if he fired before a signal was given. When "Fire!" was called, Dickinson shot Jackson in the chest, causing a slight injury. Then Jackson fired calmly and Dickinson fell with a wound from which he soon died.

The gossip made the Jacksons even more determined to build a prestigious home that would be a show place of the South. They decided on a white-pillared brick mansion with a Corinthian portico and upper gallery.

It was constructed in 1818-19, partly with slave labor. Jackson, like most of the Presidents who preceded him, was a slave owner. Some of the master craftsmen for the construction were adventurers who traveled from job to job throughout the country. Bricks used in the structure were made on the property and the timbers were cut from near-by forests.

The Hermitage was the headquarters of Jackson's campaigning in 1828. His wife was distressed when the divorce and the duel again were used against him and she died at the mansion after he won the election and before he went to the White House. He sat at her bier in the Hermitage and said: "What are all the world and its honors to me since she is taken from me?"

The back parlor of the Hermitage has furnishings that the Jacksons used. The clock is set at the hour Jackson died.

The new mistress of the Hermitage, as well as of the White House, was Sarah York Jackson, wife of Andrew Jackson, Jr. The Jacksons had no children of their own but had adopted Andrew, Jr., who was Rachel's brother's child.

Another newcomer at the Hermitage was Henry (Black Horse Harry) Lee. After his philanderings in Virginia while the owner of Stratford Hall, Lee became a speech writer for Jackson. At the Hermitage a reconciliation of Lee and his wife Anne was achieved, although it did not endure long.

In 1831, wings were added to the Hermitage. Jackson also built a new kitchen, a smokehouse and a tomb on the lawn. A fire in 1834 destroyed the roof and much of the interior of the mansion. The sturdy brick walls were not badly damaged, except for discoloration by smoke. Jackson ordered immediate renovation of the house. Gables and pillars considerably more attractive than the original ones were added.

Andrew Jackson, Jr., sold the Hermitage to Tennessee for $48,000 in 1856. He and his wife moved from it, but four years later they returned to become its custodians at the request of the state. Uncertain what to do with the property, the state offered it to the federal government for conversion into a southern branch of the United States Military Academy. The Civil War ended discussion of the proposal.

In 1865 Andrew, Jr., died at the Hermitage. His widow and her sister, Mrs. Marion Adams, remained there while their five sons continued to serve in the Confederate Army. Only one of the sons, Colonel Andrew Jackson III, returned from the war.

In 1889 Mrs. Andrew Jackson III conceived the idea of a Ladies' Hermitage Association to preserve and display the property. The association was incorporated and the state gave acreage to it piecemeal until 1935, when the original tract plus additions reached a total of 500 acres.

An option on the original furnishings and relics was given the association by Andrew Jackson III in 1889 but the association was unable to complete the payments. The Colonel shipped the possessions to Cincinnati for exhibit for pay. This failed, and he brought them all back to Nashville. Gradually the association acquired them for return to the Hermitage, obtaining funds from benefits, lectures, concerts, balls, membership fees and state and federal appropriations.

Despite a façade resembling that of a Greek temple, the Hermitage has a colonial air. There are large verandas, a wide center hallway flanked by double rooms and supplemental wings. The eleven main rooms are spacious, designed for elegant living with a bevy of servants.

The hallway has a superb flying staircase, cantilevered from the walls as it winds upward. The pictorial wallpaper, printed by du Four in Paris in 1825, was ordered by Jackson after the 1834 fire. In distinctive colors, it represents the legend of the travels of Telemachus in search of Ulysses on the island of Calypso. In 1930 the wallpaper was removed by experts from the New York Metropolitan Museum of Art, and the walls were treated to insure preservation of the wallpaper, which then was put back in place.

Unlike many such shrines, the Hermitage is furnished largely with original furniture and curios. In the front parlor are a crystal chandelier, French vases, an Italian marble mantel, Dresden urns, a Japanese bronze clock, mahogany chairs, Bohemian glass, Victorian carpets, colonial whatnots and other objects that belonged to the Jacksons. However, the lace curtains and red brocatel draperies are reproductions of the originals. In the back parlor, the furnishings are original, except for those that had to be duplicated recently because of deterioration.

Jackson's bedroom contains the bed on which he died, also his chairs, bureau, wardrobe, washstand, shaving paraphernalia, sofa, candlesticks and mirrors. Even the same pictures are on the walls as when he was there. Curiosities include a silver cup presented by Martin Van Buren to his godson, Andrew Jackson III, cradles, hatboxes, Rachel Jackson's guitar and sewing boxes and silver luster vases sent by the Czar of Russia.

In the dining room, an oaken floor that replaced the deteriorated original one has been torn up by the ladies' association, and a pine one of the Jackson era installed. There is a table at which nine Presidents have dined, some in recent years. The Hermitage was a favorite mansion especially of Franklin D. Roosevelt.

Andrew Jackson's mother, the former Elizabeth Hutchinson, was a remarkable woman. Her last letter to Jackson as she lay dying of yellow fever was read by him later to generals and politicians he was coaching. Today, it is available at the Hermitage and visitors comment that its advice is better now than ever before. In it the mother wrote:

"Andrew, if I should not see you again, I wish you to remember and treasure up some things I have already said to you. In this world you will have to make your own way. To do that, you must have friends. You can make friends by being honest, and you can keep them by being steadfast. You must keep in mind that friends worth having will in the long run expect as much from you as they give to you.

"To forget an obligation or to be ungrateful for a kindness is a base crime — not merely a fault or a sin, but an actual crime. Men guilty of it sooner or later must suffer the penalty.

"In personal conduct be always polite but never obsequious. None will respect you more than you respect yourself. Avoid quarrels as long as you can without yielding to imposition. But sustain your manhood always.

"Never bring a suit in law for assault and battery or for defamation. The law affords no remedy for such outrages that can satisfy the feelings of a true man. Never wound the feelings of others. Never brook wanton outrage upon your own feelings. If ever you have to vindicate your feelings or defend your honor, do it calmly. If angry at first, wait until your wrath cools before you proceed."

Near the Hermitage are gardens that Rachel Jackson planted and also Hermitage Church, which Jackson built to please his wife. The church is a severely plain structure of weathered brick. Members of the Jackson family still occupy a pew that ancestors used more than a century ago.

✿　✿　✿　✿　✿　✿　✿　✿

The Hermitage is twelve miles east of Nashville, near U. S. Route 70-N. The house is open from 8 A.M. to 5 P.M. from April 1 to September 30, and from 8 A.M. to 4 P.M. the rest of the year. Admission is 50 cents for adults and 10 cents for children.

Gillette Castle (opposite page) is on a lofty hill overlooking the Connecticut River. Gillette, at the cab of the locomotive, personally operated a three-mile shortline to amuse himself and frighten guests.

The Rhapsody in Granite

William Gillette's Castle

HADLYME · CONNECTICUT

FAME IN THE THEATER is fugitive, but the name of William Gillette was emblazoned on marquees of the largest theaters across the country in the early part of the century. He was something of a John Barrymore, Tyrone Power, Henry Fonda and Maurice Evans all rolled into one.

He starred as Conan Doyle's famous detective in so many plays from 1899 to 1932 that he became known as Mr. Sherlock Holmes. He personally wrote thirteen plays and adapted seven others, and he toured the nation to play the leading roles. His earnings ran as high as $310,000 a year, in an era when a dollar was worth a dollar and the government took virtually none of it in taxes.

Mr. Gillette started to build a mansion in 1913 near Greenport, Long Island, but one sunny afternoon while cruising up the Connecticut River in his old and queer houseboat, the *Aunt Polly*, he saw seven wooded hills rising picturesquely from the shore at Hadlyme. He had a natural fondness for Connecticut, having been born there, and that very day he decided he preferred the greenery of the Nutmeg State to the sand dunes of Long Island.

Anchoring the *Aunt Polly* near the Hadlyme ferry slip, Mr. Gillette climbed the loftiest of the hills, known as the Seventh Sister. Soon afterward he bought 122 acres there and began building his new home, which he called the Seventh Sister. His property extended down to the river and had a frontage of three-quarters of a mile on it. The steel, timbers and other materials he had assembled at Greenport were barged to Hadlyme. To get the materials and workmen up the steep hillside, Mr. Gillette built an aerial tramway.

The construction of the castle began in 1914 and continued for five years. Mr. Gillette was reported to have spent $1,200,000 on the property. He kept twenty-two masons and a dozen carpenters busy almost constantly following plans that he personally drew and frequently revised.

The walls of granite are four to five feet thick and they rise four stories. Timbers, doors and woodwork are of hand-hewn white oak. Similar material was used for garden arches and the "Grand Central Station" and other structures of a narrow-gauge railroad that circles the estate. The three-mile railroad was Mr. Gillette's hobby; he called it the Seventh Sister Shortline.

In the theater Mr. Gillette was known for his independence, inventiveness, precociousness and daring, and in developing his home he demonstrated all these traits. He had been married in 1882 to Helen Nickles of Detroit, but she died six years later. He never remarried, and he had a field day living as he wanted to. The local gendarmes remember him especially for his motorcycles and passion for speed. He occasionally was clocked at seventy miles an hour up the dusty roads to the Seventh Sister.

As the engineer of locomotives on his shortline he kept guests, including Dr. Albert Einstein, in nervous tension as the train plunged through tunnels, over high trestles and around curves with whistle screeching and bell clanging. It was perhaps fortunate for everyone that he could not nudge the locomotive into going more than twenty miles an hour, except downhill.

Although Mr. Gillette was not fond of most modern music he did enjoy George Gershwin's *Rhapsody in Blue*. He would relax on a lounge in the living room of the castle while guests played it over and over again on the piano, along with the music of his favorite composer, Chopin. Friends now think of the castle as something of a rhapsody in granite, created by the agile mind of a man who enjoyed off-beat harmonies.

The mansion resembles a medieval Rhenish fortress, with crenelated battlements and openings through which boiling oil could be poured on enemies. The structure has twenty-four main rooms strung together on four levels in a maze that is bewildering to many visitors. There are forty-seven massive doors of white oak, some weighing 300 pounds. They have hand-hewn bolts and latches of white oak that resemble Rube Goldberg contraptions. Some of the arms of the latches are three feet long and operate in unison with other arms. Even the light switches are made of massive chunks of wood.

The walls have panels of raffia matting, specially designed by Mr. Gillette and tinted in delicate colors. No paint has been used inside or outside the mansion; the native stone and the natural wood dominate the decorations, although Mr. Gillette often used red rugs to brighten the scene.

The living room is fifty feet long and nineteen feet high, with balconies off the bedrooms overlooking it. A large stone fireplace of the dining room was the gathering place at meal time. Tables on rollers faced the fireplace so that Mr. Gillette and his friends could sit facing the fire while dining.

Much of the furniture throughout the castle was made by local carpenters to specifications drawn by Mr. Gillette. In his study a large armchair on rollers and resting on a track enabled him to move easily back and forth. The drawers of the desk have a secret locking arrangement that requires no key. A large bar near the study, equipped with trick levers and panels, gave Mr. Gillette personal control of the bottled goods.

One thing common in all the bedrooms is the white iron bedstead, which was a fetish with Mr. Gillette. The bathrooms are numerous but secluded — another

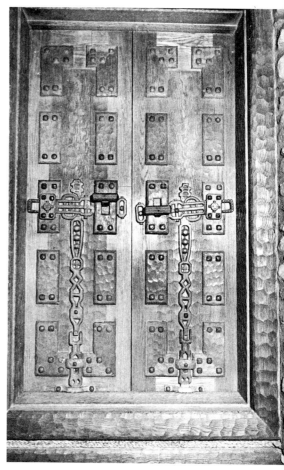

Grand Central Terminal beside Gillette Castle was the actor's train shed but now is a picnic shelter. (Right) Local carpenters, under Gillette's direction, made all the doors and their big wooden handles, latches and locks.

From his bedroom off the upper balcony, Gillette could look in mirrors and see what his guests were doing anywhere in the living room.

fetish of his. Mr. Gillette placed mirrors in his second-floor bedroom so that he could lie in bed and see over a balcony into the living room to watch guests there.

On one of the balconies is a long icicle-like handle of carved wood. One yank on it would put in use a fire-prevention apparatus containing 7,000 gallons of river water stored on the hilltop, separate from the supply of sanitary drinking water.

Electric fixtures are festooned with bits of colored glass from bottles that Mr. Gillette collected with the aid of friends. A conservatory was used not only for rare plants and goldfish but for Mr. Gillette's pet frogs, Lena and Mike. Mr. Gillette also was a cat fancier — whether live cats or those made of ceramics, concrete and granite. At one time he had seventy-seven cats at the castle, seventeen of them live. "The cat," Mr. Gillette said, "is the only critic of the human race with courage to act on his findings." He noted that dogs and other animals would lick the hand of a cruel person but that a cat, once deciding that a person was likeable or detestable, would display either affection or disapproval.

On the fourth floor was an art gallery containing 110 paintings Mr. Gillette had acquired; his tastes ran to rather academic landscapes and dramatic pictures of the sea.

Mr. Gillette's constant companion was Ozaki, a Japanese servant who began as a cabin boy on the *Aunt Polly*, then worked in the castle and its gardens and later was Mr. Gillette's valet in the theater. He was always courteous, quiet and efficient. One day Mr. Gillette was reading in a newspaper at the castle about a gift of Japanese cherry trees to Washington, D.C., by a high Japanese diplomat named Ozaki. He called the attention of his servant to the similarity of names.

"Excuse, please," the servant replied. "He my brother."

Mr. Gillette, who died in 1937, was so worried about the future of his castle that he left instructions to the executors of his estate "to see to it that the property does not fall into the hands of some blithering saphead who has no conception of where he is or with what surrounded."

The executors felt that the Seventh Sister Shortline, however, had outlived its usefulness as a hobby railroad. They sold the narrow-gauge track, locomotives and Pullman cars to an amusement park for the entertainment of children. It had cost Mr. Gillette $65,000 and was sold for $3,000.

Mr. Gillette's fondest wishes about the mansion were fulfilled in 1943 when the Connecticut State Park and Forest Commission acquired the building and 122 acres. The state paid $30,000 to buy the property and $20,000 more to repair the building and grounds. Friends of Mr. Gillette gave $10,000 additional. The state bought fifteen adjacent acres and built picnic areas and more than seven miles of trails. Now open to the public, the castle and grounds are visited by 100,000 persons a year.

✿ ✿ ✿ ✿ ✿ ✿ ✿ ✿

The Gillette castle is near the Hadlyme ferry slip, on the road linking State Route 9 on the west side of the Connecticut River with State Route 82 on the east side, where the castle is situated. The castle is open daily from 11 A.M. to 5 P.M. from Memorial Day to Columbus Day. The admission fee is 30 cents for adults. Children are admitted free.

Once a small farmhouse, this expanded mansion of stone and stucco was Franklin D. Roosevelt's home all his life. (Opposite page) The bookcase in the living room has books casually placed as they were when heavily used by the family.

From Birth to Burial

The Home of Franklin D. Roosevelt

HYDE PARK · NEW YORK

AT THE EDGE of a high escarpment beside the Hudson River eighty miles north of New York City there is a plateau of gently rolling fields and wooded hills. A red-brick mansion on the rim of the plateau dominates the countryside and has a panoramic view far across the river and into the mountains to the west. This residence, at Hyde Park, New York, was the home of the late President Franklin Delano Roosevelt all his life.

Near the dwelling is a newer stone building that Mr. Roosevelt built as an office and library six years before his death. The land and all the buildings now are a public shrine of the National Park Service.

Born in the mansion in 1882, Mr. Roosevelt throughout his life returned frequently to the ancestral surroundings there for relaxation from the turmoil of public life and to ponder domestic and international problems. He was buried in 1945 in the family rose garden beside the mansion, and his wife was buried there in 1962.

Built as an ordinary small clapboard farmhouse in 1826, the dwelling was bought in 1867 by Mr. Roosevelt's father, James Roosevelt, who took his bride, Sara, to it in 1880. James and Sara Roosevelt repeatedly enlarged and redeveloped the house until it approached being the mansion it is today. Their only child, Franklin, played in the fields and gardens, built tree houses and river rafts, learned the lore of the woods, the joy of freedom and the effects of collectivism. Then he went away to school. When he married his cousin and childhood playmate, Eleanor Roosevelt, the mansion became their home and the place where their five children were reared.

From the mansion Mr. Roosevelt embarked on his political career. Some biographers contend that the New Deal was born at the mansion, Mr. Roosevelt's concepts of social responsibility having taken root there. As early as 1917, he and his wife had a heated discussion about the home with his mother, who had been widowed in 1900. Sara asked Franklin and Eleanor to promise that the Hyde Park estate would be kept in the family after she died. She wanted it to be the private home of Roosevelts for many more generations. Franklin and Eleanor objected, Franklin entering into a vigorous exposition of his social and political philosophies and the rights of the poor to enjoy some of the properties and opportunities of the rich. Sara Roosevelt was shocked, and later correspondence between mother and son showed that he was already moving rapidly toward ideas that became the foundation of the New Deal.

It was from the Hyde Park mansion that Mr. Roosevelt first ran successfully for public office; from 1911 to 1913 he represented his neighbors as their New York State senator. He was Assistant Secretary of the Navy from 1913 to 1920 and then he set forth from Hyde Park to campaign unsuccessfully for Vice President.

Stricken with poliomyelitis in 1921 while at his summer home at Campobello, New Brunswick, he waged his long fight against the ailment at the home in Hyde Park. Here he greeted his friends in 1928 and in 1930, when elected and re-elected governor of New York. During his three successive terms as the thirty-second President of the United States and for part of the fourth term, until death intervened, the Hyde Park mansion remained his favorite home. In compliance with his wishes, his body was returned here after his sudden death in 1945 at Warm Springs, Georgia.

Now the public may visit his work rooms, trophy collections, personal bedrooms, recreation facilities and gardens to see in depth the intimate surroundings of the late President and evidence of the many social changes that now have become embedded in the American way of life.

The countless changes made in the mansion's design and contour since James Roosevelt bought it include the replacement of all the clapboards from the original farmhouse, which now is the central part of the dwelling, with gray stucco. A porch with a sweeping balustrade and a white colonnaded portico has been added on the front. Two-story wings of fieldstone on each end now give the whole structure an *H* shape. In 1916, under the guidance of Mr. Roosevelt, the final major changes, including the addition of an elevator, were made. All the members of the family agreed that the mansion was finally "just right" and in accordance with the late President's wishes. No further revisions were made or are likely ever to be made. It now is three stories high and has fifty rooms and nine baths.

Kings and queens of England and royalty of other nations who have been guests at the Hyde Park mansion have said they welcomed the opportunity to visit in a comfortable informal American home with all the treasures and knick-knacks dear to the hearts of family groups. The mansion today is just that. The interests and customs of the Roosevelt family are evident to visitors when they first step into the large front hall. The room is dominated by family antiques and pictures, chiefly naval prints. To the left of the front door are a massive oak ward-robe and an eighteenth-century grandfather clock. Both were purchased in the Netherlands by FDR's parents on their wedding trip in 1880. Against one wall is a sideboard bought by James Roosevelt in Italy in 1869. In a corner is a life-size bronze statue of the late President at the age of twenty-nine, done by Prince Paul Troubetzkoy in 1911. Behind the statue is a wall case of stuffed birds that Franklin collected as a boy.

The south hallway leads to the Roosevelt "snuggery" — a small, cozy sitting room — and on to the living room, which occupies the entire lower floor of the south wing. It is a cheerful and spacious room in which the family met, played, read and entertained. Two portraits over the fireplace are of Roosevelt ancestors. One is a Gilbert Stuart painting of Isaac Roosevelt, the late President's great-great-grandfather, a Revolutionary War leader and state senator. The other is a portrait of FDR's great-grandfather, James Roosevelt, a New York City merchant, state assemblyman and the first Roosevelt to come to the Hyde Park area — in 1819.

A large portrait of Franklin Roosevelt in this room was painted at the mansion in 1932 by Ellen Emmett Rand. Two high leather chairs were Mr. Roosevelt's in Albany, when he was governor of New York.

In this living room Mr. Roosevelt carried on the family tradition of trimming Christmas trees with real candles. It was here that he read Dickens' Christmas story of Old Scrooge and Tiny Tim, sitting at the fireside and making a three-evening event of the eloquent presentation.

And it was here that he concocted his celebrated dry Martinis. He started making them very mild, with more vermouth than gin, but his daughter Anna called them "awful" and induced him to have gin predominate, two to one. Then son James said "they aren't fit to drink" and induced him to switch to a three-to-one formula. Son Elliot later changed it to four to one, son Franklin five to one and son John six to one.

When the late President was in a jocular mood with guests he would sur-round himself with bottles and measuring devices and painstakingly measure the gin and vermouth into a cocktail shaker. When the awed guests were thoroughly convinced that they had seen the most carefully constructed Martinis in the world, Mr. Roosevelt would slosh into the shaker an extra wallop of gin.

In front of the living room fireplace on New Year's Eve the late President's custom was to silence all the relatives and guests just before midnight, count off the last seconds of the old year and then have everyone raise glasses high for a toast and repeat: "To the United States of America!"

The Dresden Room near the living room is a light and elaborately formal parlor, taking its name from a delicately wrought Dresden chandelier and mantel that James Roosevelt bought in Germany in 1866. The rug is an Aubusson and the floral drapes and upholstery were installed specially for visits of English royalty in 1939. Chinese ornaments were collected by all the Roosevelts.

The dining room is dominated by heavy, dark furniture. The oak dining table is now permanently set for two persons but can be extended to seat twenty or more. Antique sideboards were acquired by James Roosevelt in Italy and the Netherlands about 1880. In this room the late President took great pride in carving turkeys. He was exceptionally skilful and, although liberal in some things, carved the white meat so thin that people could read through it.

On the second floor is more evidence of the livable attributes of the mansion. On display are a small bedroom in which the late President was born, another one that he occupied as a boy and a large one at the end of a hall that he used in late years. After his poliomyelitis attack the large bedroom became a great favorite with him, since its windows provide a panoramic view of the Hudson and the mountain beyond. Here Mr. Roosevelt surrounded himself with his favorite oil

When the residence finally attained this size and received this amount of ornamentation, Roosevelt said it was just right.

The Franklin D. Roosevelt Library now adjoins the residence.

paintings, naval prints and family photographs. On the chair of Fala, his pet Scottie, are the dog's leash and blanket. Scattered about the room are the books and magazines that were here when Mr. Roosevelt was at Hyde Park just before his death.

Visitors wonder if the furniture and art treasures from many nations inspired the late President's comment to Daughters of the American Revolution and other august visitors: "Remember, please, that you and I are descended from immigrants and revolutionists."

Congress designated the mansion as a national historic site in 1939 when Mr. Roosevelt gave it to the nation, along with some thirty-three acres and subsidiary buildings. Members of the Roosevelt family at that time retained life interests of the property. In 1945 the Secretary of the Interior received full title to it when FDR's widow and children relinquished all claims to it after his death. In 1952 a tract of about sixty and a half acres between the house and the river was given to the government by the Franklin D. Roosevelt Foundation. Thus the shrine now has ninety-three acres.

The rose garden near the northeast corner of the mansion, almost surrounded by a century-old hemlock hedge, was chosen by Mr. Roosevelt as his burial place. A rose garden was traditional for the family because the surname Roosevelt was derived from the Dutch fields of roses in the ancestral land. The rose symbol is perpetuated in the family coat of arms, which has three roses on a shield, surmounted by a casque and three feathers.

Hyde Park 193

A white marble gravestone, with a slight trace of color highlighting its natural beauty, has been placed at the late President's grave. Known as Imperial Danby, the stone is from a Vermont quarry that produced the marble for the Thomas Jefferson Memorial in Washington. Plans for the stone were drawn by Mr. Roosevelt in a memorandum written the day after Christmas in 1937. He wrote:

"That a plain white marble monument — no carving or decoration — to be placed over my grave, east and west, as follows: Length, 8 feet; width, 4 feet; height, 3 feet. The whole to be set on marble base extending 2 feet out from the monument all around — but said base to be no more than 6 inches above the ground.

"It is my hope that my dear wife will on her death be buried there also, and that the monument contain no device or inscription except the following on the south side:

"Franklin Delano Roosevelt

"1882. 19—

"Anna Eleanor Roosevelt

"1884. 19—"

His instructions were followed precisely.

Adjacent to the mansion is the Franklin D. Roosevelt Library, administered by the Archivist of the United States. It contains the papers, books, letters and other historical materials of the late President. It was from his office in this building that he gave many of his radio addresses to the nation.

Recognizing the importance of the documents and other items he had collected, especially while in the White House, Mr. Roosevelt gave them and sixteen acres for the library to the nation. After Congress had built the library, Mr. Roosevelt spoke at the dedication in 1939. He said:

"To bring together the records of the past and to house them in buildings where they will be preserved for the use of men and women in the future, a nation must believe in three things:

"It must believe in the past. It must believe in the future. It must, above all, believe in the capacity of its own people so to learn from the past that they can gain in judgment in creating their own future."

The library has more than 28,000 volumes. From boyhood, Mr. Roosevelt had collected books on history, economics, government, public affairs, travel and other subjects. After he became President he received books as gifts from authors, publishers and friends. The library also purchased many books to complete its collections and has Mr. Roosevelt's accumulation of naval manuscripts and pictures, art objects, sound recordings, motion pictures and photographs.

From the time of George Washington the papers that accumulated in the White House during the tenure of a President have been his property when he left. Such papers have met varying fates. Some have been destroyed, many have been acquired by private buyers and others have been deposited in the Library of Congress. The establishment of the Roosevelt Library as a depository of papers set a new precedent.

The Roosevelt Library collections include gifts received by Mr. Roosevelt from heads of states and other notables throughout the world. There is a gold inkwell from King George VI of England, Chinese and Korean relics, a silver urn from Denmark, a gold-and-porcelain tea set from Norway, a gold filigree tiara and bracelets presented to Mrs. Roosevelt by the Sultan of Morocco, a large aquamarine given to Mrs. Roosevelt by the President of Brazil, a gold globe of the world from Emperor Haile Selassie of Ethiopia and a 200-year-old Torah manuscript rescued from a burning synagogue in Czechoslovakia.

Although Mr. Roosevelt's large stamp collection was sold at auction in 1946, some of the stamps and albums sent to him by heads of foreign nations are in the library here. On display also are foreign costumes from overseas and academic hoods and robes that Mr. Roosevelt received at college commencements. The library has more than thirty diplomas attesting to his honorary degrees.

The well-worn desk and chair used in the White House by Mr. Roosevelt and some of the curios that he liked to keep on the desk are now in the library. A cabinet contains china that had been used in the White House and two Arabian swords with sheaths of gold and diamonds given to Mr. Roosevelt by King Ibn Saud of Saudi Arabia. Four brocade wall hangings were sent by the Dalai Lama of Tibet.

There are cabinets filled with Mr. Roosevelt's rings, watches, cigarette cases, membership cards, medals, baptismal and marriage certificates and school essays. In some rooms are the ship models Mr. Roosevelt collected, ranging from Chinese junks to modern battleships. His favorite was a model of the U. S. S. *Constitution,* which was 100 years old when he bought it. He personally rerigged the model.

A large Persian rug in the library was given to Mr. Roosevelt by the Shah of Iran at the Teheran Conference in 1943. Some rooms are filled with clocks, urns and paintings from world notables. In the basement is a ceiling-high statue of Mr. Roosvelt as the Sphinx, inspired by his refusal in 1939 to say whether he would run for President again in 1940.

Other objects include carriages, iceboats and sleighs the late President had used. There also is the manually operated 1936 blue Ford convertible that he often drove on inspection trips around the Hyde Park estate and in which he often was shown in photographs.

❀   ❀   ❀   ❀   ❀   ❀   ❀   ❀

The Roosevelt shrine is on the Albany Post Road (U. S. Route 9) at Hyde Park and is accessible from the New York State Thruway and the Taconic State Parkway. The mansion, the other buildings and the grounds are open from 10 A.M. to 5 P.M. every day except Monday. The admission charge is 25 cents for adults at the mansion and also at the library. Children under twelve years old and groups of school children up to eighteen years old are admitted free.

Mrs. F. W. Vanderbilt's bed is a copy of one at Malmaison. A French custom was for servants to assemble at the railing for instructions.

The Mansion of the Hidden Nymphs

Frederick W. Vanderbilt's Hudson Valley Castle

HYDE PARK · NEW YORK

WORKMEN CLEANING A CEILING of the old Frederick W. Vanderbilt mansion beside the Hudson River at Hyde Park, New York, were astonished to find the blurred outline of a thirty-foot mural under layers of whitewash. They scrubbed deeper and finally exposed a detailed oil painting of bare-breasted nymphs gamboling around an old man sitting disconsolately with his head in his hands.

The discovery strengthened the posthumous appraisals of Mr. Vanderbilt as one of the least lusty descendants of Commodore Cornelius Vanderbilt, who built a multimillion-dollar empire of railroads and steamship lines and left the fortune for others to spend.

Frederick was one of four grandsons who vied with each other in building personal castles at Newport, Rhode Island; Asheville, North Carolina; Hyde Park; and on Long Island. But while some of the Vanderbilts were giving fantastic parties, hobnobbing with European royalty to marry off their daughters, traveling around the world on yachts and becoming involved with mistresses, Frederick was leading a quiet, sedate life as a squire of the Hudson Valley. His wife liked parties but he did not, so the childless couple had few. Their estate and the five centuries of art treasures they had acquired now belong to the National Park Service and are maintained for the public.

One thing at the mansion that is different under public ownership is the ceiling mural. The Vanderbilts obviously were shocked when they saw what decorators had put on the ceiling and they immediately ordered it covered over. The National Park Service feels less prudish about it and intends to keep the mural unwhitewashed for what government officials describe as "historical and interpretive reasons."

Mr. Vanderbilt owned a major interest in the then-prosperous New York Central Railroad. He was so wealthy that he kept $3,000,000 in his checking account "just in case I want to buy something." When he was forty years old and already had big homes at Fifth Avenue and Fortieth Street in New York City and at Newport, he jumped at a chance to buy acreage with several houses on it at Hyde Park. He had long admired the tract, on an escarpment 300 feet above the river and overlooking the mainline tracks of the New York Central on the east shore of the river, while beyond the far shore are the Shawangunk and Catskill Mountains.

Mr. Vanderbilt bought the vast tract in 1895, utilized 211 of the acres for his home and lived there for the following forty-three years — until his death in 1938. The mansion that he constructed on the site of an earlier house is one of the finest examples of Italian Renaissance architecture in the United States. It was designed by McKim, Meade and White and was built in 1896-98 while the Vanderbilts occupied another house on the property. Stanford White, whose name later was emblazoned in sensational headlines, shared in the planning and decorating of the mansion.

Decorated and furnished lavishly, the mansion conveys an impression of how the castles of Europe must have appeared centuries ago when royal families were immensely rich, servants were abundant and American millionaires had not yet stripped the palaces of furnishings and, as sometimes happened, entire ceilings, walls and floors. Likewise, the mansion testifies to the fact that Mr. Vanderbilt, despite his inhibitions and personal inclinations, adhered to the custom of the eighteen nineties for the rich to indulge in conspicuous consumption of worldly goods and ostentatious display of wealth to establish a public reputation.

Previous owners of the land at Hyde Park had long been lording it over their pecuniary inferiors. In 1705 Edward Hyde, governor of the Province of New York and Viscount of Cornbury, had given away 3,600 acres to friends and they named the area Hyde Park. A later owner, who obtained the property partly by inheritance and partly by purchase, was Dr. John Bard, a friend of Benjamin Franklin, personal physician to George Washington and the doctor who made medical his-

The F. W. Vanderbilt dining room is fifty feet long and has a 300-year-old Isfahan rug. The ceiling is from an Italian castle.

tory by conducting systematic anatomical dissection for purposes of instruction. Dr. Bard lived at Hyde Park and realized the Ciceronian ideal of old age — the planting of fine trees for future generations. His son, Dr. Samuel Bard, a distinguished physician in the early history of New York City and Columbia University, built a large house on the site now occupied by the Vanderbilt mansion and continued his father's hobby of developing the property with fine plantings.

Dr. Samuel Bard and his wife died a day apart in 1821 and the property became the home of one of their ten children, William Bard, the organizer and first president of the old New York Life Insurance and Trust Company. Dr. David Hosack, a Columbia professor and long-time friends of the Bards, bought the property in 1827 and planted more trees, shrubbery and flowers. Andre Parmentier, a Belgian designer, took charge of the work. The accomplishments of all these persons is evident today in the scenic vistas of the estate.

John Jacob Astor bought the estate in 1840 and gave it to his daughter, Mrs. Dorothea Langdon. One of her children, Walter, became the owner and it was just after his death that Mr. Vanderbilt bought the property in 1895.

Mr. Vanderbilt worked meticulously to conserve and improve the magnificent grounds of the estate and to build his Italian Renaissance mansion of fifty-four rooms and twenty baths on four levels. He built it of steel and concrete, with the outer walls faced with gray cut-stone — a radical departure from the dirty chocolate-colored stone of earlier mansions he had owned.

He also built carriage houses, stables, greenhouses, farm buildings, gatehouses and stone fences. The construction cost of the mansion alone was $660,000. More than $2,000,000 was spent on the decorations and furnishings. Just what Mr. Vanderbilt's total expenditures were on the estate has not been recorded but conservative estimates indicate that the estate could not be duplicated today for less than $10,000,000.

This house has a score of fine tapestries of French, Flemish and Brussels weaves, some dating back to the sixteenth century. The library, a masterpiece of the Swiss woodcarvers art, contains 700 volumes from the best presses and art binderies in the world; they are scholarly books that Mr. Vanderbilt actually read.

A forty-foot Isfahan rug that is 300 years old covers the floor of the dining room. This room has two carved Renaissance marble mantels: one bears the Medici insignia and the other has markings that indicate it was taken from a palace of Napoleon III. The room also contains two planetaria made in London in the eighteenth century. The dining table accommodates thirty persons.

Workmen scrubbing the ceiling of a reception room discovered this painting under layers of whitewash the Vanderbilts had applied.

A grand piano in the drawing room is an American Steinway decorated in Paris. It had been in the New York home of Mrs. Vanderbilt, who was Louise Anthony before her marriage. From her former home, too, came a Staffordshire candelabrum and a clock in the den. Other old clocks are in the French salon, which is a splendid example of the rococo style of the Louis XV period.

In the marble hallways and in the rooms of Santo Domingo and Russian mahogany are models of Vanderbilt yachts, Florentine tapestries, hand-carved French Renaissance cabinets, Venetian lanterns and Chinese bowls dating back 500 years to the Ming Dynasty. Italian and French busts occupy niches in the grand stairway.

The two chief master bedrooms on the second floor present a fascinating study in contrasts. The one Mrs. Vanderbilt occupied has a light-colored Aubusson carpet, specially woven to fit the area. The bed was copied from one at Malmaison, the château of the Empress Josephine. Richly colored wood panels are on the pastel green walls.

In front of the bed is a railing, customary for the beds of French queens. Courtiers and servants assembled outside the railing each morning to receive instructions from the queen.

Mr. Vanderbilt's bedroom, darker in tone, has woodwork of carved Circassian walnut from Russia and Flemish tapestries made in the seventeenth century. A marble mantel, deep red rugs from India and chairs upholstered in red velvet add masculinity to the décor.

Throughout the house there is evidence of Mr. Vanderbilt's tastes, which ran to delicate French paintings of subjects other than bare-breasted nymphs and included oddities such as Venetian torcheres and château guns.

The gardens, the walks and the drives along the escarpment overlooking the Hudson now have exceptional displays of European ash and beech; English elm; Norway spruce and maple; Japanese maple; South American maidenhair and the American sugar maple; flowering dogwood; coffeetree; hemlock; white, red, black and chestnut oak; white pine and blue spruce.

Mr. Vanderbilt bequeathed the estate in 1938 to Mrs. Vanderbilt's niece, Mrs. Margaret L. Van Alen, who later became Mrs. Louis Bruguiere. She gave the estate to the public as a memorial to Mr. and Mrs. Vanderbilt. It is owned and operated as a public shrine by the National Park Service. A few miles to the south of the Vanderbilt estate is another such shrine — the former home of Franklin D. Roosevelt.

* * * * * * * *

The Vanderbilt mansion is eighty-two miles north of New York City. It is on the Albany Post Road (U. S. Route 9) at the northern rim of Hyde Park. The mansion is open from 9 A.M. to 5 P.M. every day except Monday. The admission fee is 25 cents for adults. Children accompanied by adults are admitted free.

(Above) Kykuit was built by John D. Rockefeller and later was the home of John D. Rockefeller, Jr., whose widow now lives there. A colonial residence (below, right center) has been the home of Governor Nelson A. Rockefeller in recent years.

Besides a private golf course the Rockefeller estate has this million-dollar recreation center with indoor and outdoor pools.

A Mansion on the Road to the Poorhouse

John D. Rockefeller's Kykuit

POCANTICO HILLS · NEW YORK

THE PEOPLE in the Sleepy Hollow countryside of the lower Hudson Valley have a favorite saying that "the Rockefellers are on the road to the poorhouse." The 4,180-acre estate of the Rockefellers at Pocantico Hills is beside a highway, long known as County House Road, which leads to the near-by Westchester County Home for the Poor. The Rockefellers prefer the name Sleepy Hollow Road, as it is listed on some recent maps.

When not jesting, the neighbors speak almost reverently about the Rockefellers. They recall the friendliness of "Neighbor John" — the elder Mr. Rockefeller — when he was reaching from a buggy to give new dimes to everyone; the generosity of his son "Mr. Junior" in building local hospitals, monasteries, churches, roads and welfare centers; and the community services of Governor Nelson A. Rockefeller, which caused the villagers to honor him in 1960 as the "Man of the Year."

The villagers are proud that "rich as Rockefeller" has replaced in modern conversation the classic phrase "rich as Croesus." And many of the religious folk say that Kykuit, the main Rockefeller dwelling, symbolizes the American homes in which liquor, profanity, card playing, gambling and smoking are not allowed; the Rockefellers have traditionally frowned upon such "vices."

Parts of the Rockefeller property are open to the public for hiking, horseback riding and occasional deer hunting. However, all the property where members of the family have homes is as remote from the outside world as a fortified principality. Servants and certified guests are carefully scrutinized before being allowed through the gates.

The entire estate once was open to the public. Now high stone walls, massive iron gates, alert guards, police dogs and miles of barbed-wire fences make the homes a sanctuary. Stockade fences have been added to block the view wherever peeking through the wire barriers might be feasible.

The protections were begun by the elder Mr. Rockefeller after the Industrial Workers of the World had marched on the estate in 1914 with knives, clubs and firearms. On that occasion, squads of policemen and deputy sheriffs halted the invasion. There had been labor trouble in some of the Rockefeller companies in the West and the I. W. W. considered the elder Mr. Rockefeller a "robber baron," although he was to become the nation's greatest philanthropist.

After the I. W. W. incident, waves of cruel kidnappings throughout the nation caused consternation among wealthy families with small children; this led to a strengthening of the protections at the Rockefeller estate. Some of the safeguards at the home of Governor Rockefeller have been relaxed since he entered politics, but not at the homes on the estate of his brothers David and Laurence or of their stepmother, Mrs. John D., Jr.

John D., Sr., gained control of 95 per cent of all the oil refining business in the nation, in association with Henry M. Flagler and others, in the latter half of the nineteenth century. Leaving Ohio and the active control of the Standard Oil Company in 1893, he went to Pocantico Hills in search of a summer home near New York City. He was fifty-four years old, and he wanted to mold a small community to his own fancies and yet keep an eye on business and pursue a few hobbies.

He soon bought seventeen tracts of farmland for $168,705. The property is on a high ridge between the valleys of the Hudson and Saw Mill Rivers, with panoramic views for thirty miles. Known as Signal Hill, the ridge had been used by the Indians to send up smoke signals. Dutch settlers had called the hill Kykuit, and the English had translated this into Lookout Hill.

With a pick and shovel, John D., Sr., joined with workmen in planting trees and shrubs, moving stone walls and laying flagstones just as he wanted them. John D., Jr., after graduating from Brown University in 1897 and working for a few years in his father's corporations, took the same personal interest in Kykuit as his father.

On the hilltop was an old wooden mansion with broad verandas. It was the first Kykuit. The family moved into it and Mr. Rockefeller wrote to friends that "the fine views invite the soul" and that he and his wife, the former Laura Spelman, could "live simply and quietly here."

The old frame house burned in 1902 and the family moved to a smaller dwelling on the property for seven years while a fifty-room stone house — the present Kykuit — was constructed. Built largely of granite quarried on the property, the mansion is of modified Georgian design and has large windows that provide splendid views of the countryside.

Guest rooms are on the third floor. At first this floor had only dormer windows; because of inadequate light and air, the entire third floor was rebuilt and a fourth, with more guest rooms, was added. Rising above the treetops, a light-green copper roof of the mansion can be seen for many miles.

John D., Jr., who had turned from the business of earning money to the full-time task of giving away intelligently much of the fortune his father had amassed, helped enlarge the Pocantico Hills holdings. The New York Central Railroad was induced to close the Pocantico Hills station, move the tracks a mile to the east and raze an unsightly trestle and other structures that marred the appearance of Rockefeller properties.

Hotels, candy stores and shops were bought, closed and razed by the Rockefellers. Roads that bisected the estate were rebuilt at the Rockefellers' expense; bridges were built over, and tunnels dug under roads to link the various parts of the estate. The post office, gasoline stations and even public telephones were removed from the face of Pocantico Hills.

As they became the owners of 98 per cent of the property in Pocantico Hills, including scores of small private dwellings, the Rockefellers increased their benefactions. They contributed playgrounds, a school, a firehouse and churches. To the Union Church, which the Rockefellers attend, they gave a stained-glass window by Henri Matisse — the last art object the French master ever produced.

Inside their walled estate the Rockefellers built a private eighteen-hole golf course and a million-dollar family recreation center with bowling alleys, tennis courts and indoor and outdoor swimming pools.

Kykuit was the headquarters of the first business enterprise of Nelson and Laurence Rockefeller. While boys they formed a partnership to run errands, hoe gardens, shine shoes, raise rabbits and kill flies.

Events both gay and tragic have taken place at the estate. The Cinderella story of Anne Marie Rasmussen began there not long ago; she was a maid for the Nelson Rockefellers and married their son Steven. Michael, one of Steven's brothers, lived there until he went on an exploration in the South Pacific and was lost at sea. Winthrop, one of Nelson's brothers, lived there during his romance with Bobo Sears, whom he married and later gave $5,500,000 in a divorce settlement. The Nelson Rockefellers lived together there until their divorce.

Members of the family have built separate homes on the estate and Nelson Rockefeller has moved into a historic colonial house beside the golf course. On the woodwork of this dwelling are saber marks reputedly made in anger by British soldiers when they just missed capturing George Washington there.

Among recent additions to the estate are the 300 acres of Buttermilk Hill, where the Christian Brothers had a college; John D., Jr., made it possible for the religious order to build a better college elsewhere. The same thing happened when the family bought the buildings of the Convent of the Sisters of Mercy, just across County House Road from Governor Rockefeller's home. The old buildings were razed and a new convent built at Dobbs Ferry.

Conservative estimates are that the Rockefellers have spent $50,000,000 in Sleepy Hollow, about one-half of it for philanthropies. Because of the taxes they pay, the Rockefellers have been an added blessing to the community. They are the third largest taxpayers, with bills exceeded only by the local watersheds of New York City and the local facilities of the Consolidated Edison Company. The real-estate taxes of the Rockefellers have reached $263,678 a year.

Owen M. Quinn, once a golf caddy for the Rockefellers and recently the town supervisor, said of the family: "They check the tax list every year but never complain. And when they want a public road repaired they pay for it themselves."

The harmony has not always existed, however. For sixty years there were fights over assessed valuations on Rockefeller properties. The assessments of some other property owners were lowered but those of the Rockefellers constantly rose. Suits filed by the Rockefellers in State Supreme Court finally were settled by a compromise.

The taxes are still rising, due partly to new construction. On a remote corner of the estate Governor Rockefeller recently built an ultramodern lodge designed by Harrison and Abramovitz, architects of many spectacular skyscrapers in big cities.

On another part of the property, Mrs. John D. Rockefeller, Jr., has begun the construction of a $300,000 Georgian home of only ten bedrooms, into which she will move from the Victorian austerity and overwhelming spaciousness of Kykuit. She is the former Martha Baird Allen, whose first husband had been a classmate of John D., Jr., at Brown. She married Mr. Rockefeller in 1951, three years after the death of his first wife, Abby Aldrich Rockefeller, mother of his daughter and five sons.

John D., Jr., died in 1960. He had given $473,000,000 to philanthropies during his lifetime but he left an estate of $150,000,000, much of which went to his widow and the Rockefeller Brothers Fund.

*   *   *   *   *   *   *   *

Bedford Road (State Route 117), between North Tarrytown and Pleasantville, passes through Pocantico Hills and bisects the Rockefeller estate. From this highway and several intersecting roads the outlying parts of the estate can be seen.

Washington Irving's home was painted in water color by J. Henry Hills in 1878. The house now is the same after restoration by the Rockefellers.

The Sleepy Hollow Triptych

Washington Irving's Snuggery, Frederick Philipse's Castle and Stephanus Van Cortlandt's Manor House

TARRYTOWN, NORTH TARRYTOWN AND CROTON-ON-HUDSON • NEW YORK

THE RIP VAN WINKLE countryside of the Lower Hudson Valley has a folklore of romantic legends. It also has a political history that mirrors the birth of the nation.

The legends and the history date back to a warm September afternoon in 1609 when Henry Hudson sailed the *Half Moon* up the river in search of the Northwest Passage and dropped anchor in the Tappan Zee, a stretch of the river that is three miles wide, off the Tarrytowns. He had discovered a great harbor and a fertile countryside that were to play major roles in the development of America. The Dutch sailors called the paradise *Die Slapering Hafen*, which became known as The Sleeping Haven and, later, Sleepy Hollow.

Three mansions that rose in Sleepy Hollow in the seventeenth, eighteenth and nineteenth centuries were considered so interesting and significant in the twentieth century by John D. Rockefeller, Jr., that he spent $3,000,000 and gave twenty years of personal attention to restoring them and providing endowments that would guarantee their perpetual maintenance.

Although the houses are not exceptionally large in size they are mansions in literary, historical and architectural importance. Thousands of visitors every year are finding them as interesting as did Mr. Rockefeller, who lived near by, in Pocantico Hills. He loved to roam the fields, the paths and the buildings to re-live the past, and he demanded of his researchers and carpenters total authenticity in the redevelopment. The result is a small northern counterpart of Colonial Williamsburg.

The Sleepy Hollow homes that Mr. Rockefeller restored are those of Washington Irving, diplomat, folklorist, bon vivant and the most famous American author of his time; Frederick Philipse, who owned all the land from the Harlem River in New York City to the Croton River in northern Westchester County; and Stephanus Van Cortlandt, whose land reached twenty miles northward from the Croton River and eastward across Connecticut.

Washington Irving's study has a desk given to him by his publishers.

A guest room at Sunnyside has a low arch — a detail repeated throughout the house.

Washington Irving's home, Sunnyside, is on the site of a former Indian village beside the Hudson at Tarrytown. The fifteen-room structure began life as a simple four-room colonial salt-box in 1656. Part of the domain of Peter Stuyvesant, governor of New Netherlands, it was occupied by Wolfert Aker, a farmer, and his family until 1750.

Then it was owned by another farmer, Jacobus Van Tassel, who made the mistake of firing a rifle at a British warship in the river during the Revolutionary War. The British sailors climbed the hill and burned most of Mr. Van Tassel's house. It was rebuilt, however, and Washington Irving bought it, with twelve acres of land, in 1835.

Exercising his extraordinary imagination, Irving immediately added rooms and changed the entire appearance of the house. He built quaint crow-step gables, intricate chimneys and a Moorish tower. Although the house is commonly considered of Dutch-English design, it has obvious influences of the Italians, Spaniards and Chinese. Some architects say the design is Hudson Valley Gothic, others that it is just Yankee Ingenuity.

Washington Irving called it his "snuggery" and said, "I would not exchange it for any château in Christendom." Many of his literary friends felt the same way about it. Among the persons who trod the paths and joined in discussion groups there were William M. Thackeray, William Cullen Bryant and G. P. Putnam. European royalty also came, since Irving had lived in Europe for seventeen years before settling at Tarrytown.

Irving never married. When he was a young man he was engaged to Mathilda Hoffman but she died suddenly. There were many reports of later romances but the only women at Sunnyside were some of his sisters and nieces, whom he adored. He had ten older brothers and sisters, who lived with him from time to time.

When Irving returned to America to settle at Sleepy Hollow he had fond memories of the valley and of the Dutch legends that he had heard when he first spent a vacation there at the age of fifteen.

He sketched on paper the odd shape that he wanted his home to take. In executing the plans he had the assistance of George Harvey, a friend with some construction experience, and Calvin Pollard, a New York architect.

Off-white concrete and red bricks were used for the exterior walls, with roofs of red tile. Ivy from Sir Walter Scott's home was planted along the walls. Wisteria, trumpet creeper and honeysuckle that Washington Irving planted now have grown to huge size and have been carefully preserved. Parts of the ivy have been clipped for planting at other shrines throughout the United States.

The main corridor of the first floor has colorful Minton tiles. Off this corridor are Irving's study, with original books, papers and pens; a parlor; a dining room and a sitting room. The kitchen has a large Dutch oven that makes historians ogle and housewives shudder.

On the second floor are bedrooms, including the one in which Irving died in 1859. In this room are old medicine bottles as mute evidence of the famous author's illnesses. His shaving equipment also is there. He would occasionally arise in the middle of the night to shave; the soothing effect of the lather assuaged the attacks of asthma that bothered him.

The furniture in the house was largely Washington Irving's. Among the porcelains on display are some given to him by Prince Louis Napoleon when he was a house guest.

In 1847 the tracks of the New York Central Railroad were laid beside Sunnyside. Irving complained bitterly about the trains as "snorting monsters" that intruded on his solitude and interfered with boating on his Little Mediterranean — a pond that he had developed. His antipathy lessened somewhat when he became gravely ill one night and a train made a special stop at his doorstep to allow a doctor from New York to get off.

Relatives inherited Sunnyside and in 1896 Alexander Duer Irving added a baronial ballroom that would accommodate 200 persons. Sunnyside was transformed from a personal snuggery into a social mansion.

Historians induced Mr. Rockefeller to buy Sunnyside and twenty surrounding acres in 1945 from Louis du Pont Irving, a descendant of the author. Roland W. Robbins, the pick-and-shovel historian from Massachusetts, was retained to find the exact foundations of the buildings Washington Irving had developed, including an ice house, woodsheds and other structures that had vanished long ago. These were built anew by Mr. Rockefeller.

Determined to attain full authenticity, Mr. Rockefeller then reduced the mansion's size by 50 per cent, razing the wing that had been added in 1896. The removal cost $50,000, and that much more was spent in developing an old-fashioned kitchen garden on the site of the wing.

Philipsburg, Upper Mill, includes the stone Philipse Castle just beyond the mill pond on the Pocantico River.

Three miles up the river at North Tarrytown is Philipsburg Manor, with its old Philipse Castle and auxiliary buildings. Mr. Rockefeller barely saved the buildings from house wreckers in 1940 by buying them and twenty acres after the structures had become so dilapidated that owners would no longer pay taxes on them.

Built in 1683, the stone-and-timber castle had been the focal point of the 98,000-acre domain of Frederick Philipse, whose Dutch name had been Vredryck Flypsen. He was the son of a carpenter but he became one of the wealthiest men in America. From the docks and warehouses beside his castle he carried on an import-export business around the world. He dealt in building materials, foods and slaves; some historians say he traded on the side with pirates.

A grist mill was built on the Pocantico River, which empties into the Hudson at the castle. The tenant farmers of the manor brought grain there for grinding into flour for shipment overseas.

Frederick Philipse married the wealthy widow of Peter De Vries, who had inherited large shipping lines and other business interests. When she died, he married into the Van Cortlandt family, which had a manor almost as large as his own, farther up the river.

The castle that Frederick Philipse needed for all his commercial and family activities grew until it had more than twenty rooms. A grandson, Colonel Frederick Philipse, owned it and its vast acreage at the outbreak of the Revolutionary War. He remained loyal to the British. George Washington had him imprisoned in Connecticut and after the war he fled to England. His manor was confiscated by New York State and sold to tenant farmers.

Sleepy Hollow 211

Gerard G. Beekman bought the castle after the war. It passed through many other hands, each time being altered with "modern improvements" until it finally became just another country mansion on large grounds.

Elsie Janis, the noted actress, mimic and dancer, who was known as the Sweetheart of the American Expeditionary Force in World War I, took a fancy to the castle in 1935 and bought it to use in the lavish entertaining of her stage friends. She added theatrical effects and brought to the house her new husband, Gilbert Wilson, twenty-six years old to her forty-two.

Not long after getting the mansion to a peak of Hollywood perfection, however, Miss Janis and Mr. Wilson were seriously injured in an automobile crash. The mansion became vacant, dilapidated and in arrears on taxes. Reports spread that the land would be leveled for a housing development.

Mr. Rockefeller was induced by historians to buy the property when it was posted for sale at auction. He brought in researchers from Colonial Williamsburg. Old drawings of the castle, a picture made by Currier and Ives in 1880 and many documents concerning the old manor helped in planning a restoration. The first thing done was to strip away the Hollywood touches and other "improvements" that had been made inside and outside the mansion in the previous 200 years.

The old grist mill, smokehouse and related buildings were redeveloped. But not until Mr. Robbins, the pick-and-shovel historian, got on the job were the remnants of old piers and the original buildings found underground. Much of the restoration had to be done over again and this forced a closing of the buildings to visitors for several years.

The Little Dutch Parlor of Frederick Philipse contains objects the seventeenth-century settlers used.

The Van Cortlandt Manor House was saved from wreckers and was fully restored by John D. Rockefeller, Jr.

Nine miles up the Hudson from the castle, where the Croton River flows into the larger stream, the manor house that Stephanus Van Cortlandt began building in 1680 on his manor of 86,000 acres stands today, the oldest structure of its kind in America. It was occupied continuously for 260 years by seven generations of the same family — a record probably unequalled in this country. The last of the Van Cortlandts there was Miss Anne Stevenson Van Cortlandt, who died in 1940 at the age of ninety-three.

The house later was occupied by Chatfield Taylor, a newspaper publisher, until one night in 1945 he tried to drive his automobile between the stone gateposts. The driveway had been built for the passage of slow-moving carriages. Mr. Taylor was killed when his car struck one of the gateposts.

The house became a real-estate office and a headquarters for a drive-in theater. It was reportedly about to become an office for a smoked-turkey concern when Mr. Rockefeller was induced by historians in 1953 to buy and restore it. The 12 acres of land with it he increased to 175, to prevent encroachments by motels and hot-dog stands. Restored with the twenty-room manor house is a ferry house on the Croton River, a kitchen house, an ice house, barns, a coach-house, a quaint well and picturesque gardens.

Unlike the Philipses to the south, most of the Van Cortlandts fought with the American patriots. Overnight guests in the manor house included General Washington, Benjamin Franklin, John Jay, Marshal Jean Baptiste de Rochambeau, Governor DeWitt Clinton and Bishop Francis Asbury. Some of the most exciting revival meetings of the nation were conducted by preachers on the front steps.

For the restoration Mr. Rockefeller again brought researchers from Colonial Williamsburg. Wings that had been added to the house in 1812 and 1847 were removed. This exposed some of the original window frames and unusual colonial stone work that set a pattern for all the restoration.

New shingles, copies of the original ones, are red and thick and have rounded butts. Slit openings preserved in the walls, formerly thought to have been used as firing posts during Indian attacks, now are believed to have been merely for ventilation. The mansion had been used for the storage of raw furs bought from the Indians.

The kitchen contains a large Dutch oven. Also on the ground level are a dining room and a family sitting room. A handsome winding staircase leads to two upper floors. On the first are parlors, a formal dining room and bedrooms. On the top floor are more bedrooms. Some of the woodwork and floors are painted to resemble marble, as was fashionable two centuries ago. The furnishings are all authentic Van Cortlandt era, and some were owned by the family.

The Rockefeller researchers found that in 1733 the 86,000 acres of the Van Cortlandts had an official value of $25,062, which rose in 1829 to $2,048,829, and in 1875 to $9,167,037. A conservative estimate of the value today is close to a billion dollars.

Bargains were easy to get when the Van Cortlandts were there. One section of land as large as Manhattan was bought from the Indians for eight guns, nine blankets, fourteen kettles, fifty pounds of gunpowder, eighteen hatchets, two ankers of rum, five vats of beer, twelve knives and a few other items.

✿　✿　✿　✿　✿　✿

All the restorations are near the Albany Post Road (U. S. Route 9). Sunny-side and the Van Cortlandt Manor House are open from 9 A. M. to 5 P. M. every day except Thanksgiving, Christmas and New Year's Day. The admission fees at Sunnyside are $1 for adults and 60 cents for children and, at the manor house, $1.50 and 75 cents. Combination tickets and group tickets are available at reduced rates. Philipsburg Manor may be seen from the grounds without charge while restoration work continues.

The Van Cortlandt parlor has marbleized floors and furnishings used by Benjamin Franklin, John Jay and other famous visitors.

The House with Nine Lives

Boscobel, the Manorial Mansion of States Morris Dyckman

GARRISON • NEW YORK

Boscobel has experienced as many lives as the proverbial cat. It has even been resurrected from the grave. After being sold to a housewrecker for thirty-five dollars and then reduced to small parts for storage, the twenty-room structure was reborn, through gifts exceeding $1,000,000 that enabled it to rise again on a new site fifteen miles north of its original one.

The public's enthusiasm for Boscobel stems largely from its classic Adam architecture. Historians call it one of the first and finest examples in the United States of the sophisticated type of eighteenth-century English residence. Architects rate it as one of the outstanding houses of the period. To scholars it is a jackpot for the study of the customs and culture of the past. For generations to come it will be a public exhibit, showing how families of affluence lived in the era of elegance after the Revolutionary War.

Restored to its original beauty and furnished with eighteenth-century rugs, paintings, furniture, chandeliers and bric-a-brac, Boscobel stands tall and stately on a knoll 200 feet above the east side of the Hudson River near Garrison, in Putnam County, New York. It occupies a tract of thirty-five acres. Originally it occupied one of several hundred acres at Crugers, in Westchester County.

States Morris Dyckman, whose Dutch given-name had been Staats until he Americanized it, built the mansion in 1805. The resurrection of Boscobel on its present site was completed in 1961.

Mr. Dyckman, a determined Tory, fled to England during the Revolution. Later he returned to this country to regain stature, marry Elizabeth Corne, who was a member of a distinguished Mohawk Valley family, and build Boscobel.

The Wedgwood pottery, the glass and all the other ornamentations typify the classical revival in the arts initiated by Robert Adam, the Scottish designer. The mansion invites contemporary Americans to imagine themselves living in the eighteenth century, when man believed that good taste and elegant manners were the marks of a true gentleman's home.

At its new site, Boscobel commands a panoramic view across the river to the massive towers of the United States Military Academy at West Point, of Constitution Island and of Bear Mountain Bridge. For motorists on mansion safaris, Boscobel is less than an hour from the Sleepy Hollow Restorations at Tarrytown and Croton-on-Hudson.

Boscobel Restoration, Inc., a philanthropic and educational organization, redeveloped the mansion on its new site and operates it as a museum of the Hudson Valley, a community meeting center and a mecca for architects and historians.

The chief benefactor of Boscobel is Lila Acheson Wallace of Mount Kisco, New York, who shares with her husband, DeWitt Wallace, ownership and editorial direction of the *Reader's Digest* magazine. Declaring that Boscobel is a "rare work of art" that should be preserved forever, she gave $500,000 for the restoration. The Reader's Digest Foundation, headed by Mr. and Mrs. Wallace, then gave another $500,000 as an endowment for the perpetual operation of Boscobel. Other contributions have been made by seventeen national and regional organizations and by many individuals.

The name Boscobel (the Italian *bosco bello* means "fair wood") was taken by Mr. Dyckman from an estate in Shropshire, England, where King Charles II hid in a giant hollow oak while evading the Roundhead pursuers after his defeat by Cromwell in the Battle of Worcester.

Mr. Dyckman, frail and arthritic but with a will of iron, dreamed most of his life that some day he would build a beautiful home overlooking the river he loved. An ancestor, Jan Dyckman, had been one of thirty Dutch freeholders on Manhattan who received large grants of land in 1666. States grew up in an inn that his father operated at the Manhattan end of the old Farmers' Bridge over the Harlem River. There he experienced the turbulent days before the Revolu-

(Left) Elegantly refurnished with period art objects, Sheraton and Hepplewhite chairs and an Aubusson rug, Boscobel's parlor is light and airy. (Right) The spacious entrance hall of Boscobel was flooded and used for ice skating by boys before the recent restoration.

tion. He was twenty-one years old when the Declaration of Independence was signed in 1776.

States, a Tory by conviction, worked as a clerk for Sir William Erskine, a British Army commander in New York. In 1779 he went to England with Sir William and lived there for nine years, exposed to the elite living standards and luxuries of Sir William's friends. Returning to New York in 1788, Dyckman had an annuity of 100 pounds from Sir William but found it to be scant security. His kinsfolk had been ruined financially and socially by the war and he undertook to help them. In 1794 he married Elizabeth Corne, who had recently left her Mohawk Valley family, and wrote to a friend: "Late in life my happiness has begun." He was thirty-nine and his bride was eighteen. They had two children, Peter and Letitia.

In a struggle to continue collecting his annuity, Dyckman went to England in 1800 and remained for four years, arguing with the arbitrators and, later, planning Boscobel and buying furnishings for it. One of his legal advisers was William Adam, a nephew of the architect Robert Adam, and together they became experts on Adam-style houses.

Dyckman returned to his country in 1804, having won a big financial settlement on his claim. His daughter Letitia had died during his absence, but there was a joyous reunion for him with his wife and son. Then he unfolded the plans for Boscobel and in 1805 started building the house of his dreams. He died in 1806 before it was finished. His widow and his son Peter continued to live at Boscobel and operate a farm, sawmill and brick kiln to pay the expenses until Mrs. Dyckman died seventeen years later.

Boscobel, still unfinished, fell into disrepair until a granddaughter of Mr. Dyckman, Eliza Letitia, married John Peach Cruger. After that the house was restored, completed and given new life as the Dyckman-Cruger mansion. It was a social center of the Hudson Valley, with women in party gowns, men riding up to the door on smart horses and later the leaders of the valley driving up in some of the first horseless carriages. The Crugers were the last family to live in Boscobel while it was a private residence.

The Westchester County Park Commission bought the house and its large acreage in 1923 for Crugers Park. The county planned to raze the building but a storm of protest rose from the Westchester Historical Society, the Hudson River Conservation Society and other groups. A group headed by Harvey Stephenson saved the house by leasing it and making essential repairs that would protect it from the elements. Nobody knew quite what to do permanently with it, however.

After World War II the park commission sold the house and acreage to the federal government for the new Franklin Delano Roosevelt Hospital for neuropsychiatric veterans. The red-brick buildings of the hospital soon towered beside Boscobel. The Veterans' Administration promised to preserve the mansion but soon discovered it was not suitable as a reception center. Mentally disturbed patients considered its cellar a good place to hide from doctors. Boys found that the ballroom could be flooded with water in winter to produce ice for skating; Boscobel became a popular indoor rink for children.

Then the federal government declared Boscobel surplus property and signed its death warrant. Not even the National Trust, chartered by Congress for historic preservations, could save Boscobel from imminent destruction. The mansion was sold to a housewrecker for thirty-five dollars. Some of the choicest woodwork and exterior trim were carted off to a mansion that was being built on Long Island, although these parts soon were retrieved.

Historians were highly indignant when they heard of the sale. They said the thirty-five-dollar price was an absurdity matched only by Peter Minuit's purchase of Manhattan for twenty-four. A group headed by Benjamin Frazier, under the aegis of the Putnam County Historical Society, literally defended the mansion with force to halt the swinging axes and wrecking bars of wreckers. The State Police were alerted to be ready for trouble.

The bizarre battle was abruptly halted for a month by a government order. Just as the month was running out the historians collected $10,000 to move Boscobel, but they had no property to put it on. Undaunted, 125 organizations and friends of Boscobel, including Mrs. Wallace, planned to dismantle the crumbling structure and store the parts rather than attempt to move it intact.

For one thing, it was sixty feet wide and few roads in the area would have accommodated it in transit.

John McNally, a housemover, devised an orderly system of numbering all the studs, beams, sills, baseboards, moldings and even the stones of the foundation as they were removed. Sections of the plaster cornices and ceiling medallions were carefully cut out so they could be accurately reproduced later.

Unusual things were found behind the plaster. There were sixty-foot beams running the entire length of the house, hand-split lathing and a huge main beam spanning the arches of the entrance hall. Old-time carpenters of the Hudson Valley had never before seen such timbers. The parts of the great jigsaw puzzle were stored in many widely separated buildings, including an icehouse, sheds, warehouses and uninhabited castles of the valley.

The dismantling of the house had required five months but its reconstruction on the new site took several years and was not finished until 1961. The reconstruction would have taken much longer if three architects on a federal project in 1932 had not made detailed drawings of the entire house.

Normal building procedures were not followed in much of the reconstruction. Instead of putting up the walls first, the workman installed Boscobel's decorative doorways and windows on temporary supports and then built the walls of proper thickness and design around them. Discrepancies were found between the 1932 drawings and the parts of the house. The segments of the front of the building fitted together until the men got to the swags at the top, then some swags were too long and others too short. This was remedied by making new ones. A tedious job was the cleaning and patching of all the interior trim. Five men worked six months removing multiple layers of paint and patching the scars.

While the house was being restored, a search for furnishings that the Dyckmans had actually used or would have used in that period was made by William Kennedy and Ben Garber. They spent years on the hunt in this country and Europe, covering many of the routes in London that Mr. Dyckman had traversed on his shopping trips while he was planning Boscobel.

In this country, many of the objects originally in Boscobel were retrieved from collectors. Pieces of old Wedgwood ware, found when the building was razed at Crugers, were sent to the Wedgwood Company to have new china and crockery made that would be identical with that originally bought for Boscobel.

Robert Adam, who perfected his architectural style after study of classical buildings in Greece and Italy, was also a designer of furnishings for houses, from carpet to chandelier. The Adam touch is recognizable everywhere in Boscobel.

On the front of the mansion the classic Doric columns have lengthened capitals. The frieze and pediment are softened and lightened by the unusual wooden swags across the upper portico. The proportions of the windows, the spacious interior, the decorative motifs and the fireplaces achieve a harmonious relationship typical of the Adam design.

Lila Acheson Wallace and her husband, DeWitt Wallace, owners and editors of the Reader's Digest, *saved Boscobel.*

One of the most startling innovations of the period in which Boscobel was built is the vast area given to windows. Persons are accustomed today to see walls of glass but in 1805, when homes relied on fireplaces for heat, such natural illumination was rare in this country. More than one-third of the south façade of Boscobel is glass.

The wide entrance hall seems to be flooded with sunlight on bright days. The height of all the ceilings produces an effect of spaciousness seldom found in early American houses.

Beyond a triple arch of the entrance hall the great staircase rises toward a ten-foot Palladian window centered above a landing. Here, again, natural illumination plays upon exquisite ornamentation to produce an unusual effect of light and shadow.

The interior exemplifies the attention that Adam gave to detailed decorations. The woodwork, the mantels, the framing of windows and doors, the ceiling medallions and the cornices were individually designed for each room. In the dining room, an oval sunburst at the mantel is repeated over windows, doors and arches.

The front parlor has a melding of patterns. Corinthian columns frame the fireplace; two types of fretwork adorn the mantel; oval and round medallions are blended to complete an impression of unity in the room.

The focal point of the back parlor, which joined with the front parlor to form a ballroom for parties, is the delicate and elegant ornamentation on the mantel. Robert Adam and his brothers had patented a composition that they used for molding fragile decorations such as these. They often sold them in separate pieces to be glued into place according to a pattern, and the indications are that such pieces were used in Boscobel. The rest of the back parlor was left plain to accentuate the effect of the mantel's ornamentation.

The majestic stairway leads to a second floor that is less elegant. The library, twenty-two feet square, is at the head of the stairs, and commands a spectacular view of the river valley below. Mr. Dyckman had a large collection of books and he put the library next to the bedroom in which he had intended to sleep.

Boscobel was painted white at Crugers. It was painted white when reconstructed at its new site but research indicated that this may not have been the way Mr. Dyckman would have painted it. So now it is gray, with the abundant trim in white.

The enthusiasms generated by the restoration are exemplified by this comment of the Society of Architectural Historians: "The house was one of those rare monuments which casts its shadow forward to influence the architecture of the next several decades. It possesses a charm and grace seldom equalled."

While participating in the dedication of the restored Boscobel as Governor of New York State, Nelson A. Rockefeller added his own thought: "The rebuilding of Boscobel restores to our Hudson Valley one of the most beautiful homes ever built in America."

❋   ❋   ❋   ❋   ❋   ❋   ❋   ❋

Boscobel is beside State Route 9-D north of Garrison, about fifty miles from New York City. It is open to the public all year, every day except Tuesdays, Christmas and New Year's Day. The tours begin at 9:30 A. M. and continue until 4 P. M. in the winter and 5:30 P. M. in the summer. The fees are $1.50 for adults and 75 cents for children.

The King and Queen of Siam lived at Ophir Hall.

The Mansion a King Chose and the United Nations Wanted

Ben Holladay's Ophir Hall

PURCHASE · NEW YORK

ALMOST EVERY BIG METROPOLIS has a fine old residential area just outside its hub-bub — an area of greenery, where it is fashionable to have spacious homes, elabo-rate gardens, acres of fields, elegant country clubs and constant rounds of parties.

Westchester County, on the north rim of New York City, is such a place and the community in it that typifies the ultimate in wealthy suburban living is Pur-chase. There are about as many millionaires to the square mile in Westchester as any place on earth, with a heavy concentration in Purchase.

The "first families" in the county have included the Van Cortlandts, the Philipses, the Wainwrights and the Rockefellers. When the King of Siam, as Thailand was then known, wanted a place in the United States to spend the summer of 1931 he chose as his castle Ophir Hall, an eighty-four-room granite mansion in Purchase. After a nationwide search in 1946 for a site for a permanent headquarters, the United Nations was about to acquire Ophir Hall and neighboring estates when John D. Rockefeller, Jr. donated acreage in Manhattan for the U. N. enclave.

In the era between the first of the "first families" and those of today there arrived in Westchester a strange man who had as much to do with the genesis of elegant country estates there as any person in history. He was Ben Holladay, a boisterous, flamboyant Westerner who shot from the hip and cussed with rare eloquence.

Through his exploits in the West, Ben Holladay had been dubbed America's King of Transportation. Among businessmen, a move from the West to New York is supposed to be ten times more difficult than one in the opposite direction. Ben Holladay made it in one leap, and to solidify his bridgehead he built Ophir Hall and eighteen auxiliary buildings on 900 acres at Purchase.

For many years his Ophir Hall home was considered one of the finest gentlemen's country estates in the nation. Ironically, Holladay was not a gentleman; he was an illiterate, uncouth roughneck who believed that everything was fair in love, war, business and politics. But he could spend $1,000,000 for a new ballroom or $10,000 for a party so easily that his wife Ann had him do it quite often. She was a social climber, skilled in the social graces that her husband lacked.

After getting Mr. Holladay to build mansions for her in Weston, Missouri; San Francisco; Portland, Oregon; and Washington, D. C., she induced him to build Ophir Hall so she would be in the New York social whirl and also be close to the steamship lines to Europe. She doted on European culture and royal personages.

Ben Holladay was born in 1819 in a log cabin on the Kentucky frontier. Twenty years later in a log cabin on the Missouri frontier he married Notley Ann Calvert. They eloped, since her parents considered him a barbarian; the Calverts could not abide his vulgarity or the odorous stogies he smoked. (Ann had gone to finishing school and been introduced in society.) But she was overwhelmed by Ben's ardor, and he promised that someday he'd build her one of the biggest castles in the nation.

For years he made fortunes from every business he touched. He traded with Indians, organized wagon trains, dealt in cattle, transported merchandise for Brigham Young, developed the Holladay Overland Mail and Express Company, received multimillion-dollar mail contracts and operated steamship lines to Alaska, Mexico and the Orient.

In his spare time he bought newspapers, acquired mines and built railroads. One night in a poker game he won part of the Ophir silver mine in Nevada. He had not wanted it particularly, but it soon was producing more money than Ann could spend in the West. It was then that Ben Holladay decided to grant Ann's wish to enter New York society. He bought a score of farms totaling 900 acres in Purchase to unite into what he first called Ophir Farm and later Ophir Place and Ophir Palace. It finally became Ophir Hall.

The Holladays had been to Europe several times and Ben ordered an Ophir mansion that would enable him to live like a monarch. He wanted to fulfill his promise to Ann and also to impress business rivals and politicians with his success.

There rose on a hilltop, so lofty that it overlooks Long Island Sound and the edges of New York City and Connecticut, a six-story granite mansion with balustraded turrets and crenelated towers. In addition to the mansion of eighty-four king-size rooms, the Holladays built a Norman Gothic chapel, a coach house, stables, a root cellar and employees' houses. Sixty servants worked on the property.

The Holladays became famous for $10,000 romps and for week-long house-parties that cost twice as much. Along the wooded drives to the mansion came congressmen, cabinet officers, Wall Street millionaires, foreign diplomats and the social elite. Beautiful women always were present, some of them for the benefit of men who had "forgotten" to bring their wives.

Ann enjoyed the parties until she noticed that roughshod miners and stagecoach drivers were becoming more and more numerous among the guests. She found the frontiersmen offensive and she showed it first by apologizing to the other guests and then by heaping abuse on Ben. A devout Roman Catholic, she spent more time in the chapel.

On the grounds of Ophir Hall, Holladay developed a museum of the West. He also stocked the streams with trout, brought herds of buffalo and elk to roam the fields and imported wild ducks from the Middle West for the lakes. He often led hunting and fishing parties across his estate.

The Holladays had seven children but Ben saw little of them. Three died in childhood and were buried beside the Ophir Hall chapel. Two married into titled families of Europe; Holladay tried to make his new sons-in-law acquainted with the work of frontiersmen but he quit when he decided that "they can't tell a horse from a jackass."

One of Holladay's sons kept a pet parrot that would remain silent until Ben began to speak, then it would shriek: "Shut up you sonofabitch." Everybody thought it was exceedingly funny.

The financial panic of 1873 stripped Holladay of most of his wealth and on the Black Friday of that financial debacle Ann died at Ophir Hall. She was buried at the chapel next to the mansion. Her last will bequeathed Ophir Hall to her remaining children and grandchildren but Holladay contended she had been of unsound mind and had the will set aside so that he could inherit the estate. The inheritance kept the creditors away from his doorstep briefly, and in the following year he married Lydia Esther Campbell in Oregon. But he soon lost Ophir Hall and when he died he had an income of less than $5,000 a year.

John Roach, a builder of large ships, bought Ophir Hall in 1876 and lived there until 1887, when the property was bought by Whitelaw Reid, diplomat, social leader, ambassador to England and publisher of the old *New York Tribune*.

While Mr. Reid was having the mansion altered in 1888 it caught fire from

Ophir Hall's entrance room is decorated almost entirely in pink marble.

a workman's torch and burned, leaving only the foundations and thick stone walls. He rebuilt the house and in 1912 added a wing that has an elaborate library eighty-eight feet long with ceilings of ornamental plaster and armorial windows. McKim, Mead and White of New York were the architects.

The mansion has a pink marble entrance hall and stairs, carved woodwork with many inlays of contrasting woods and lustrous mother-of-pearl. Ceilings are twenty feet high, with ornate cornices. Every major room has a marble fireplace; many are ornate but some are delightfully simple. Secret staircases are concealed by massive panels. Fixtures are of sterling silver and crystal, and on some ceilings there are allegorical paintings typical of those found in French palaces. The library has thirteenth-century stained-glass windows from the clerestory of the Salisbury Cathedral in England. Several other windows are Flemish.

Architects who try to define the style of the mansion are baffled. It has the feeling of a castle in the Scottish highlands but many of its details show English, French and Italian influences. The library is Jacobean and a piazza is Spanish.

Mr. Reid's wife, who had been Elisabeth Mills of California and New York, added to the puzzle by installing in one of the rooms the entire interior of the study of the Fifth Avenue, New York, home of her father, Darius Ogden Mills. Of 1840 vintage, it is so ornate and has so many carved mahogany figures that some visitors find it dreadful — so dreadful it is interesting as an example of the acceptable style of interior decoration of 1840.

When King Prajadhipok and Queen Rambai-Barni of Siam came to this country in 1931 to spend several months while the King underwent treatment for an eye ailment, they lived at Ophir Hall. The fame of the mansion had reached Bangkok; our State Department thought it would be a suitable and safe place for the royal family and Mrs. Reid, then a widow, offered the use of her home.

One bedroom of the mansion was converted into an operating room and it was there that New York specialists performed delicate surgery on the King. As a "thank you" gift, the Siamese royal party gave a new marble mantel for a dining-room fireplace. It is elaborately carved with figures of water buffalo, fields of rice and other symbols of Siam.

Mrs. Reid died later in the same year and the property was inherited by her son, Ogden Mills Reid, the then publisher of the *New York Herald Tribune*. But Mr. Reid and his wife, Helen Rogers Reid, preferred a smaller home for themselves and their two sons, and Ophir Hall remained vacant.

In 1946 a team of United Nations diplomats decided that of all the properties they had inspected in the United States for the projected U. N. headquarters, the best was in Purchase, centered on Ophir Hall. Neighbors protested vehemently. The discussion ended abruptly when John D. Rockefeller, Jr., offered a tract in New York City and it was accepted.

After Ogden Reid died his widow undertook to sell 220 of the remaining 677 acres of the estate to a group of Massachusetts investors for a $7,000,000 shopping center. The neighbors again rose in stormy protest and the plan was defeated.

Mrs. Reid noted that in 1949 the property was assessed at $1,691,000 and paid an annual tax of $37,980. She said that because of the desire of people for smaller homes Ophir Hall was suitable only for business use — or for an educational institution, which would pay no taxes. The neighbors welcomed the idea of having a college there, even though their own taxes would rise.

Manhattanville College of the Sacred Heart, a Roman Catholic institution, which had outgrown its campus in Manhattan, bought the mansion, a dozen auxiliary buildings and 250 of the acres in 1949. The college paid $500,000 for the property and spent another $500,000 in repairing the mansion and altering it for college use. A first step was to install a modern heating system. One of the worst problems was correcting buckled floors, warped paneling and fallen ceilings. One corridor became known as the Hall of the Missing Teeth, so many parts of cornice were missing. Vandals had mutilated much of the woodwork.

The large Jacobean library was converted into a temporary chapel. Other downstairs rooms, including a Louis XV salon with ceiling paintings, became reception and conference centers. The second-floor bedrooms were converted into offices. A marble bathroom became two offices. Shallow drawers built into the house for Mr. Reid's shirts made a perfect filing cabinet for the records of college-entrance applicants.

The four top floors, once occupied by servants, were converted into bedrooms for nuns, with a roof garden for watching the stars at night and seeing the boats on Long Island Sound. A modern elevator serves all the floors.

The old coach house, which had bowling alleys and squash courts, was converted into an alumnae house and dormitory for thirty students. It was here that male guests at the Holladay and Reid affairs spent three hours every afternoon at cocktail parties they originated, until the hostesses contrived to get them back to mixed parties in the main lounges.

Manhattanville built dormitories, a dining hall, a chapel, a music building and other structures that harmonize surprisingly well with the old castle. Eggers and Higgins of New York kept the designs modern and functional, yet not incongruous with the granite mansion of yesteryear.

The dining room of Ophir Hall has oak and walnut paneling. The tapestries are French; the rugs, Oriental; and the chandeliers, English.

Even the new chapel has a stained-glass window that is a nonobjective cyclone of color, yet it does not conflict with the stained glass of the adjacent mansion.

Whitelaw Reid's fifteen-foot desk is in the entrance hall of the mansion but most of the furnishings today are gifts assembled by the nuns. Modern Cantonese rugs that were in the lounges of the steamship *United States* when it was converted into a troop ship in World War II are in the fifty-foot dining room. Rare antique chairs, tables, cabinets and paintings have been donated by Joseph P. Kennedy and other noted Catholic laymen.

A number of corporations have found other parts of the old Ophir Hall property useful. Companies with new headquarters on it include International Business Machines, Ford Motors, Allstate Insurance and Von Kohorn International.

❀ ❀ ❀ ❀ ❀ ❀ ❀ ❀

Manhattanville College of the Sacred Heart is on Anderson Hill Road and Purchase Street in Purchase, which is in the Town of Harrison, adjacent to White Plains. The mansion is open to visitors from 9 A.M. to 5 P.M. every day in the year.

The Jacobean library of Ophir Hall has large windows and doors opening onto lawns.

Beauport grew room-by-room to meet the whims of an indefatigable collector of antiques.

The Cottage that Grew and Grew and Grew

Harry Davis Sleeper's Beauport

GLOUCESTER · MASSACHUSETTS

A THREE-ROOM SHINGLE COTTAGE on the rocky shore of Gloucester Harbor has grown into a fifty-six-room crazy-quilt mansion. Every room has been developed differently to recapture some specific mood or era of American culture from the time of the Plymouth Colony to the early years of the Republic. The mingled skeins, often incongruous and confusing, have been merged into a glowing tapestry of bricks, timbers and antiques.

The mansion now has wings, towers, gabled roofs, galleries and broad terraces resembling those of old ivy-covered dwellings in the Shakespeare and Brittany countrysides. It has been called the "House of Mystery" and the "Most Fascinating House in America." It could be labeled more precisely "The House that Harry Built — A Mansion of a Thousand Dreams."

Henry Davis Sleeper, known as Harry to close friends, was an architect, interior decorator and antique collector. He frequently had extravagant dreams of how to add to the interest and charm of his home and he possessed the energy and the funds to fulfill the dreams. A bachelor all his life, he created a home to meet the discriminating taste of one strong-willed person — himself.

Mr. Sleeper and Robert L. (Believe It or Not) Ripley had much in common in the collecting of uncommon furnishings for their own homes. At his Gothic manse, staffed with Chinese, on the shore of Long Island Sound in Mamaroneck, New York, Ripley installed the curiosities with deliberate intent to startle and overwhelm visitors. Mr. Sleeper merged oddities into the decorative web of his rooms to make every object an unobtrusive part of a pleasing total scene.

"Where can I hide it?" Mr. Sleeper asked himself when he returned home with a seven-foot wooden eagle or the paneling of a pre-Revolutionary house. What he meant was: "Where can I install this acquisition so it will not dominate the room or command the immediate attention of a stranger and yet be a point of interest to cultured people with searching eyes?"

The fame of Beauport gradually spread and the influence of Mr. Sleeper was felt widely as he lectured throughout the nation. He played a major role in decorating and furnishing homes of the Hollywood motion-picture stars of yesteryear. Some people credit him with fathering the modern vogue of antique collecting and the art of merging old items in ultramodern settings to generate dynamic interest. His disciples include millionaire hobbyists who have developed virtual castles from Sleeper blueprints.

Mr. Sleeper was a grandson of Jacob Sleeper, one of the founders of Boston University. His father, Major J. Henry Sleeper, gained some fame on Civil War battlegrounds. Inheritances from the family enabled Mr. Sleeper to travel in Europe as a student in the eighteen nineties. He had a craving for color and composition; some friends said he was a frustrated painter. After studying architecture extensively in Paris, he returned to New England and entered the publishing business. He soon turned to the practice of architecture, although he disliked the drudgery of routine work at the drafting board.

In 1604 Samuel de Champlain had explored the Gloucester area and called it Beau Port, or Handsome Harbor, so when Mr. Sleeper built for himself in 1903 a tiny summer cottage near the tip of Eastern Point on Cape Ann he called it Beauport. It resembled scores of other vacation retreats in this fishing region, but since it had less than two acres of grounds and big estates grew up in the neighborhood it became an architectural wallflower.

However, the cottage had a 180-degree view of the harbor, of Five-Pound and Ten-Pound Islands and the Reef of Norman's Woes, the treacherous 200-foot ledge of rock immortalized by Longfellow in the "Wreck of the Hesperus." While watching the lobstermen at work in the harbor and the gulls wheeling lazily overhead, Mr. Sleeper decided to make Beauport a show place and he devoted thirty-one years to the job.

The metamorphosis began one day when Mr. Sleeper was driving through the near-by shipbuilding village of Essex and noticed that the dilapidated William

Beauport's breakfast room contains many of the odd items that Sleeper acquired at auctions.

Cogswell house was for sale. Bidding was high for the 200-year-old colonial paneling, which prospective buyers wanted to install in New York City mansions. Mr. Sleeper bid low but obtained the woodwork by promising to "preserve it in dignity among its own people." So a pine-paneled room became the front hall of Beauport, with the roofs and grounds rearranged to accommodate it.

Other rooms were likewise added. Mr. Sleeper was in a Boston junkshop one day and to the dismay of friends bought for twelve dollars three carved wooden curtains from an old hearse. The curtains had been on curved windows and were semi-elliptical. The next day Mr. Sleeper decided that curved curtains called for a round room, which in turn would call for a Norman tower with a tile cap. So the tower room was built and today it is a comfortable, functional library — with carved wooden curtains.

"Beauport is an assembled house of integration and adaptation rather than restoration," commented Mrs. William Blanford, the resident director who is a lineal descendant of Henry Clay. "It was assembled for the modern enjoyment of old treasures and the design is Sleeper, not colonial."

By 1909 Beauport had twenty-six rooms and at the outbreak of World War I it had thirty. Then an interruption in its growth occurred when Mr. Sleeper became a founder of the American Field Service. He operated ambulances behind the battle lines in France for four years and was decorated with a medal of the French Legion of Honor. After the war he returned to Beauport. He was in financial straits because of his war work but his skills as an architect and decorator soon brought in more funds to resume the expansion of Beauport, which continued until his death in 1934.

The people who visited Mr. Sleeper to admire his decorative techniques and later go home to emulate them included Henry James, Alma Gluck, Helen Hayes, Paul Robson, Booth Tarkington, John P. Marquand, Owen Wister, Leopold Stokowski, the Astors, the du Ponts and the Newport social set. Other visitors were museum directors, including those setting up an American wing in the Metropolitan Museum of Art in New York, since Mr. Sleeper had demonstrated that white did not have to predominate in colonial color schemes. He had found that in their generally drab surroundings the early settlers had delighted in using splashes of color whenever they had the chance.

At the front gate of Beauport there is a sheet-iron Indian beckoning to visitors and pointing the way along short garden paths to the front door. Terraces, low walls and quaint shrines flank the paths.

The mansion, on a ledge of granite close to the ocean, seems at first to be a confusion of wings laid out in a cockeyed domino fashion, but visitors soon detect rhythms of line and mass in the offbeat architecture, as in some abstract expressionist paintings. The rumpled roofs, half-timbered and brick walls and the eight chimneys, all different, have syncopated harmonies of shapes, textures and colors. If a nook on a roof lacked a point of interest, Mr. Sleeper placed a statue of St. Barbara there and it seemed just right.

The entrance hall is the Cogswell Room, with the old paneling painted a dull ivory. The floor is of red brick with a glossy wax finish, as are many other floors in the mansion. The visitor finds himself immediately in a maze of antiques — colonial, English, Chinese, French and Portuguese. A tall goblet of mercury glass holds a single pineapple as a colonial symbol of welcome. In rooms off the hall are ledges laden with copper and pewter antiques, collections of early glass in kaleidoscopic colors, bull's-eye windows artificially illuminated and enough old furniture for an armory show.

Near the hall is a statue of George Washington wrapped in an iron sheet, as a Roman emperor might wear a toga. In cold weather a stove under the statue turns Washington a rozy red.

The Golden Step Room has a rare Chinese funeral bench that supports a large model of a square-rigged ship. It is one of five rooms for dining, all opening onto a kitchen. Another of these rooms is octagonal; twenty feet wide it is decorated strikingly in red, black, gold and pink, with each alternate wall bearing a pediment suitable for the front door of a post office.

The Chinese Parlor, said to resemble one in a royal palace in Peking, is thirty-five feet long, has a pagoda-type ceiling twenty-five feet high, a serpentine chandelier of Waterford glass and cluttered Oriental antiques. The hand-painted Chinese wallpaper was imported early in the nineteenth century but was never used until Mr. Sleeper found it in storage at Marblehead. According to one's taste, the Chinese Parlor may be either the most horrible or the most interesting room in the house.

One of the rooms has a tomahawk door from an old house in the Indian country. This door has layers of wood with the grains running in varying directions and sheets of leather between the layers, so no hatchet could pierce it.

The Franklin Room has an authentic Franklin stove and other items associated with Benjamin Franklin, and the Paul Revere Room has furniture, decorations and silver of the Revere era. Lord Byron's bed is in an upstairs room, with the roof of the house enlarged to accommodate the posts of the bed.

A secret staircase leads from the Jacobean Room. Mr. Sleeper's bedroom has a door and pediments salvaged from the exterior of an old house, and next to this is the gay Strawberry Hill Room that wins the hearts of many visitors.

One of the surprises not in harmony with the general Sleeper philosophies are doors that seemingly lead into closets but actually open onto large plate-glass mirrors immediately behind the doors. Some visitors and new caretakers, opening the doors in semi-darkness, have been scared out of their wits when confronted by staring faces.

The future of Beauport was in doubt after Mr. Sleeper's death but a Woolworth chain-store fortune finally came to its rescue. Mrs. Helena Woolworth McCann, a daughter of F. W. Woolworth and the aunt of Countess Barbara Hutton Mdivani Haugwitz Reventlow Grant Troubetzkoy, bought it. After her death her children, Constance, Frazier and Helena, transferred Beauport in 1942 to the Society for the Preservation of New England Antiquities. They provided a grant for maintenance through the Winfield Foundation, directing that Beauport be permanently available to the public as a memorial to their mother.

An authentic colonial kitchen was installed in Beauport.

On a hilltop across the harbor from Beauport is Stillington Hall, a mansion based on Sleeper ideas but developed lavishly on a tract of 110 acres. It is the private home of Colonel Leslie Buswell, a disciple and close friend of Mr. Sleeper.

"Everything I know I learned from Harry," Colonel Buswell says. "A decorator builds a home from the inside out. An architect builds from the outside in. Harry did both, and so have I."

The Colonel's house, assembled one room at a time since 1922 and still expanding, now has fourteen private suites with baths and a great hall with a vaulted ceiling, a stage, space for 250 persons and so many decorative treasures that even an eight-foot wooden eagle on one wall does not command immediate attention. If too many visitors pay too much attention to any particular chair or picture, the Colonel has it moved. A valuable Gainsborough painting and other art works have no special lighting, for the Colonel considers it "sinful" to accent any item.

"Harry was perfectly unscrupulous in using colors, forms and shapes adventurously and imaginatively," the Colonel recalls. Giving the technique his own twist, the Colonel has installed in Stillington Hall the Sleeper Room, with Dutch furniture merged with items of many other national origins.

The Colonel recalls that Mr. Sleeper always carried a small notebook containing the dimensions of spaces at Beauport he would like to fill; he wanted to be prepared whenever an unusual item came to his attention. The Colonel also keeps himself prepared. It took him eleven years to find the "right" statue for a certain niche.

Colonel Buswell opens Stillington Hall to the public periodically as a benefit for local charities. The admission fee is apt to be five dollars, but it is worth it, especially to persons infected with Sleepermania. The Gloucester Chamber of Commerce can provide information about open house at the hall.

On the rim of the harbor near the hall and with an open view across the water to Beauport is a medieval-type stone castle that has turrets and drawbridge. It was the home of John Hays Hammond, Jr., and was built of stones and architectural parts of castles and churches overseas. Now open as a museum, it contains Mr. Hammond's sculpture, furniture, paintings and other art. The great hall has an organ with 10,000 pipes. If Mr. Sleeper were still alive he would be roaming the castle with a yardstick and covetous eyes.

✦   ✦   ✦   ✦   ✦   ✦   ✦   ✦

Beauport is on Eastern Point Boulevard at Gloucester. Accessible only by way of a private road through neighboring estates, it is open to the public only from Monday through Friday, June 1 to September 30, and never on holidays. The hours for visitors are 2:30 to 4:30 P.M. and the guided tours cost $1 for adults and 50 cents for children.

An Incubator for Statesmen

John Adams's Peacefield

QUINCY · MASSACHUSETTS

A SIMPLE FRAME HOUSE on Adams Street in Quincy has a unique distinction among the mansions of America: it is the only one that has been the private residence of two Presidents of the United States and of a woman who was the wife of one President and the mother of another. For four generations, covering a span of 139 years, it was the residence of a family distinguished in public service and in the intellectual life of the nation, and it grew steadily, just as the family did.

John Adams, President from 1797 to 1801, made it a citadel for calm reflection and lively discussions of national problems. His son, John Quincy Adams, President from 1825 to 1829, spent his youth there, worked in the gardens and studied politics. The father and the son each made the residence a summer White House and finally retired to it. A wing chair is still in the study, just as it was on the day in 1826 when John Adams slumped over in it and died at the very moment Thomas Jefferson was dying at Monticello.

John Quincy Adams's son, Charles Francis Adams, lived in the house when not overseas as Ambassador to the Court of St. James and in other diplomatic posts. After that it was the home of his sons: John, a Civil War leader; Charles, a Civil War general and president of the Union Pacific Railroad; Henry, a statesman; and Brooks, an author.

A procession of world dignitaries passed through the house. Dignitaries such as the Marquis de Lafayette stopped for constructive discussions with the Adamses, shared in the family custom of daily Bible reading and observed the children being taught to be "on guard against the airs of superiority" common among some scholars.

Even as the Quincy residence witnessed gracious manners, it sometimes heard salty, muleskinning talk from the Adamses just back from trips to Washington. Hearing a member of a recent generation of the family shouting caustic comments at the players in a Harvard football game, Charles W. Eliot, then president of Harvard, turned to him and said, "Spoken as a true Adams!"

The residence has twenty-two rooms on three floors, with a gabled mansard roof, gray clapboard, white trim and green shutters. The structure is generally colonial in design. Although not a clear example of any architectural period, owing to the long years of development, it does have an element of unity that in a way symbolizes the family.

In its furnishings, too, the residence shows a continuity of ever-changing styles and tastes of the Adamses, from their first occupancy of the building in 1788 until the death of Brooks Adams in 1927.

John Adams called the home Peacefield in memory of his work in Europe in negotiating peace treaties. It also became known to the family as the Old House. All the Adamses often expressed their deep fondness for the mansion and the farms around it.

The oldest part of the house was built in 1731 by Major Leonard Vassall, a prosperous West Indian sugar planter who had chosen Quincy for retirement. He planted elaborate gardens rimmed with boxwood hedges and farmed many of the seventy-five acres of his estate. The gardens and the hedges are still there but most of the acreage has been absorbed by commerce and small homes.

While in foreign service in 1787, John Adams bought all the property from the Major's grandson, Leonard V. Borland, and the next year moved into the house. The building had only seven small rooms. John's wife Abigail called it a wren's house in height and width. The back door was only five feet high, and Abigail wrote to a daughter not to wear feathers in her hat when she came to visit or to bring guests with high heels since they would not be able to stand upright.

In 1800 John Adams satisfied his wife's demand for more space by adding a large gabled ell that contains a spacious entry, the Long Room for entertaining and a study on the second floor. The gardens were expanded and some of the trees planted then are still standing.

Peacefield's living-room furniture formerly was used in the White House. Most of it was made in France.

In 1836 John Quincy Adams added a passageway along the north side of the house to connect two ells. After serving as President he was a representative for seventeen years, with the house in Quincy as his residence.

The first substantial wealth came into the Adams family when Charles Francis Adams married the daughter of a prosperous Boston merchant. In 1869 he added thirty feet to a kitchen ell to enlarge the servants' quarters, and in the following year he built a massive granite library close to the house and overlooking the gardens.

The library contains today 11,000 books that John Quincy Adams had collected, plus 3,000 more that descendants added to the shelves. Three stories high, the building is fireproof and has galleries for the bookshelves. Wisteria now covers much of its exterior. On the roof is a 1666 weathervane taken from a church at Braintree, Massachusetts, when it was razed.

The interior of the residence has mahogany paneling from South America. The paneling was painted white by John Quincy Adams but his son had it scraped and restored to natural color in 1852. Charles Francis Adams also removed a tile fireplace and built a new one of brick.

Abigail Adams installed in the Quincy residence some of the furniture that she had used in the White House as its first mistress. Most of this is of Louis XV design and was purchased in France. Peacefield also has an abundance of portraits by Gilbert Stuart, Charles Wilson Peale and other early painters. Some of the pictures are of three couples who celebrated golden wedding anniversaries in the house.

The residence has a bed that belonged to Daniel Webster, the dumbbells that Brooks Adams took with him for exercise wherever he traveled, Oriental rugs, a 1715 silver tankard and rare china and glass that the Adamses had imported from Europe and Asia. The oldest item in the house is a clock made in London in 1680. Most of the furnishings reflect the family's diplomatic background and extensive travel in France and England. One of the latest changes in the residence consists of entrance gates added by Brooks Adams.

After the death of Brooks Adams in 1927, descendants of the family organized the Adams Memorial Society to perpetuate the home, the library, the gardens and the stables. The project was continued privately until 1946, when the property was given to the United States and became the Adams National Historic Site, administered by the National Park Service. The site comprises almost five acres.

❄   ❄   ❄   ❄   ❄   ❄   ❄   ❄

The Adams National Historic Site is bounded by Adams Street, Newport Avenue and Furnace Brook Parkway. It is eight miles south of Boston, on State Route 135 near State Route 3. The buildings are open from 9 A. M. to 5 P. M. every day from April 19 to November 10. Admission charges are nominal and they are waived for children under twelve and for organized groups of older children.

The Three Bricks

Joseph Starbuck's Houses

NANTUCKET · MASSACHUSETTS

THE LITTLE ISLAND of Nantucket, the "faraway land" to the Indians, is an unspoiled hallmark of a faraway era of American life. Its remoteness from thruways, factories and other mundane components of modernity protects it from change.

Another protective force is the determination of the islanders to preserve Nantucket's quaintness. The determination is shared by the thousands of its summer residents who travel from many states to ferry across the thirty miles of sea from Cape Cod to the island.

The Nantucket Historic Trust now has more than $1,000,000 to buy and preserve the finer houses when they are in danger of destruction or alteration. The trust acquired one house for $30,000 recently, then found a prospective buyer who believed the structure should be preserved. "But I can't afford to pay more than $25,000," he said. The trust replied that the house was his at that price.

Among the houses most talked about, photographed, painted and revered are East Brick, Middle Brick and West Brick that Joseph Starbuck built at the top of the hill on Main Street from 1837 to 1840 for his three sons. Designed personally by Mr. Starbuck to include Federal and Georgian features he admired, they are identical except for a few variations in stairways and rooms to gain sunlight.

William, the youngest son, received East Brick at 93 Main Street; he and his wife had two children. Matthew, the middle son, received Middle Brick at No. 95; his first wife had died and he remarried in 1840 to bring a bride to his house. George, the oldest son, received West Brick at No. 97; he and his wife had six children.

Joseph Starbuck hired Christopher Capen as master mason and James Childs as master carpenter for the construction and kept such a close watch on costs that the spending ran only to $40,124. In accordance with the custom of the time, a lot 60 feet wide and 300 feet deep was used for each house, with the structures built close to the street.

A devout Quaker who shunned liquor, big parties and ostentation, Mr. Starbuck shocked other members of the religious clan who preferred the more common saltbox cottages of weathered-gray shingles and simple rooms.

But Nantucket, a foremost whaling center, was a community of contradictions. With their newly gained wealth some of the Quaker sea captains were even constructing Greek Revival mansions for their families. And when the captains were away at sea, some of the wives adopted the Asiatic custom of taking a taste of opium every morning before performing household chores. One of the sheriffs, a Quaker who did not touch liquor, even indulged in this custom.

Joseph Starbuck was the son of a cattle trader, whale-oil merchant, ship owner and proprietor of rope, candle and barrel shops. Shunning jobs on whaling ships, which caused island traditionists to view him with alarm, Joseph became a partner and then the owner of all his father's businesses. He was married when twenty-three years old and built a home near Main Street.

Years later, after sharing his business prosperity with his sons, Joseph Starbuck built the three Bricks in recognition of the loyalty and affection they had shown him. He also named one of his ships *The Three Brothers* in their honor.

The tract of land he acquired on upper Main Street was in the most fashionable area in town, he believed. He paved the street in front of the property with cobblestones, just as all of the street is paved today. There are periodic disputes among residents over whether a smooth pavement should be laid, with the advocates of modernization always in the minority.

Mr. Starbuck built the houses of red brick and added white trim and green shutters, with additional shutters also on the inside of some windows. Built on high foundations, the houses have two main floors. Large white cupolas, white balustrades and five chimneys rise from each roof.

East Brick, on the right in viewing the houses from the street, has this entrance hall and cantilevered staircase.

Ordinarily, houses of that era in Nantucket would have had high landings on the front, with stairs extending in two directions close to the house. Mr. Starbuck deviated from custom; declaring he wanted "stylish entrances" he built white, pillared porticos, with steps leading straight up to the front doors.

The eighteen rooms of each house are moderately small. Mantels are of black marble and carved woods; some cornices are ornately carved and decorated; and each house has a curved, cantilevered staircase built without use of steel.

At first the houses had no bathrooms, relying instead on outbuildings in the rear. Neither did they have central heating systems. No doorways linked kitchens and dining rooms; there were elevated openings through which kitchen servants passed food to the dining-room servants. Bathrooms, heating plants and kitchen-to-dining-room doors now have been added.

Other things, too, have been altered. Some of the original iron fencing has vanished and been replaced with a wooden replica. Vines have crept up some of the walls and loosened the bricks. The houses have changed owners many times, but the Starbuck nameplates still glisten at the front doors.

Mr. and Mrs. Gwynne Evans bought East Brick in 1955 and have four generations of their family living there in the summer. Mr. Evans is a retired tea and coffee merchant from St. Louis. Mrs. Evans Melville, a daughter of the Evanses, likes modern ranch houses well enough to own one at Delray, Florida, but she has said that East Brick is "a wonderful house" she would not hesitate to duplicate today. She spoke especially of the coolness the fourteen-foot ceilings provide in hot summers.

The Bricks receive so many visitors, however, that Mr. Evans is sometimes annoyed — especially when the visitors arrive uninvited and unannounced. One day a group of them rang the doorbell of East Brick and he, wearing old clothes and a torn fishing hat, answered it.

"Are you Mr. Starbuck?" one of the visitors asked.

"They tell me that I am, and they won't let me out of here," he replied, making an ugly grimace. The visitors turned and fled, and Mr. Evans was delighted, having finally discovered how to protect his privacy.

The resident of Middle Brick until her recent death was Mrs. Pauline Mackay Johnson, a descendant of the Starbucks. She was the fiery matriarch of Main Street and friends recall the salty language she delighted in using, particularly when talking to clergymen. She left Middle Brick to a daughter, Mrs. H. Crowell Freeman of Farmington, Connecticut.

West Brick is owned by Mr. and Mrs. Winthrop Williams, who retired to the island with more wealth than most of the islanders. They bought the rear yards of Middle and East Brick to add to West Brick's and they built terraced gardens, laid red-brick walks and planted boxwood hedges.

Next door to West Brick is the old Thomas Macy house, a splendid white colonial. One of the Macy clan failed at operating a general store, had little success on whaling ships and missed winning a fortune when he joined the California gold rush in 1849. Returning to the East, he did make a success operating a department store. He was R. H. Macy.

Across Main Street from the Bricks are two Greek Revival houses of importance. They were built in 1845-46 by William Hadwen, a wealthy oil merchant. His wife was the former Eunice Starbuck, sister of the three brothers in the three Bricks.

✿   ✿   ✿   ✿   ✿   ✿   ✿   ✿

The three Bricks on Main Street and other Nantucket houses are easily viewed from the highways but the interiors may be seen only by arrangement with the owners or on special tours set up by organizations. Information may be obtained from the Nantucket Historical Association, Civic League and Public Relations Center.

Across Main Street from the Three Bricks, Greek Revival houses were built by William Hadwen, whose wife was a Starbuck.

The Elms is one of the newest attractions of the Newport Preservation Society.

They Paid Half the Taxes

"Cottages" of the Elite

NEWPORT · RHODE ISLAND

SINCE THE WITHERING of the big fortunes in the depression of the nineteen thirties, the Newport "cottages" that begin at the top of the hill on Bellevue Avenue have undergone drastic changes. Most of these changes have benefited ordinary citizens who have more and more leisure time to go touring.

Many of the mansions still standing in original monumental dignity are open to the public. Others have been converted into clubs, jazz centers, luxury apartment houses, museums and motels. Still others remain as private homes, their original splendor somewhat tarnished. The giant parties and other social extravaganzas are only memories, as are the footmen in knee breeches and in powdered wigs holding candelabra aloft on glittering marble-and-gold grand staircases.

In 1962 the Newport Preservation Society rescued from total destruction a fifty-six-room mansion on Bellevue Avenue known as the Elms. It had been a house of mystery for two generations, protected from the outside world by a palace guard. High stone walls punctuated with occasional iron grills permitted strangers to get only glimpses of the elegance inside.

The Elms had been built in 1901 by E. J. Berwind, a coal baron from Pennsylvania. The architect, Horace Trumbauer of Philadelphia, modeled the structure after the Château d'Ansnières, near Paris. The grounds were laid out by Jacques Gréber of Paris. Statues, fountains and marble gazebos line the walks to the gardens, terraces and balustraded stone stables.

After Mr. Berwind and his wife died, his sister, Miss Julia Berwind, lived at the Elms until her death in 1961. She occasionally slept in the stables, which Newporters explain today by noting that the building resembles a cozy private home.

A nephew of Miss Berwind sold the Elms in 1962 to a real estate syndicate that planned to raze the mansion and subdivide the land. After a sharp decline in the stock market, the syndicate wanted quick cash and it accepted an offer of the Newport Preservation Society to buy the estate for public display.

The contents of the mansion, however, were sold at auction at prices the society could not match. Television and motion-picture producers bought much of the ornate furniture for future spectaculars. However, by borrowing from museums and rummaging through attics and warehouses of its own, the society quickly furnished the mansion with items such as those the Berwinds had collected, and the estate was opened.

The Hunter House is an architectural treasure of early Newport.

"Cottages" such as the Elms once paid half the real estate taxes in Newport. Because of their new uses and a general broadening of the tax base by the inclusion of many new small structures, the mansions now contribute less than 20 per cent. The assessed valuation of ten large ones fell from $2,800,000 to $850,000 in a few years. The decline in values was partly due to the evolution in public taste in matter of home ownership, also to the short supply of servants. Indicative of the change was the recent sale for $18,000 of a forty-bedroom mansion that had cost $2,000,000 in 1925, while a neighboring four-bedroom house had increased in value from $16,000 to $28,000 in the same period of time.

When James B. Duke, Robert R. Young, Mrs. Perle Mesta, Oliver H. P. Belmont, Mrs. Stuyvesant Fish, the Vanderbilts, the Firestones, the Jelkes, the Van Rensselaers, the Havemeyers and others in the social whirl spoke of their "cottages" they meant just the reverse. Similar "logic" seems to have governed the choice of names for some of their estates. Champ Soleil is in the shade of huge trees. Land Fall was built by an admiral. Château Sur Mer is not on the sea. Exceptions are the Waves, at the edge of the surf; the Marble Palace, built largely of marble; and Shamrock Cliff, rising on an escarpment reminiscent of the Irish coast.

The Cliff Walk, which skirts the seashore near Bellevue and Ochre Point Avenues, provides a good opportunity for visitors to observe the fronts of many of the mansions. Estate owners once were so irked by the curious tourists that they built stone walls across the walk. Newport residents who did not have ocean views tore down the walls and flung the rocks into the sea. The walls were rebuilt, with jagged broken bottles embedded in the concrete, but again they were torn down. After long litigation the courts decided that the public had a right to use the Cliff Walk, so today it is open. Part of it passes through a tunnel, and it twists and has many steps, but the views from it are rewarding.

Newport was settled in 1639 by persons fleeing from the Massachusetts Bay Colony. One of the finest surviving houses from Newport's era of great prosperity before the American Revolution is the Hunter House, in the center of the city. Built in 1748 and far from being a mansion, it is considered one of the finest colonial structures remaining in America and is included in this discussion because of its sharp contrast with the Greek Revival, Georgian, Federal, American Tudor, Carpenter Gothic and Florentine buildings of the comparatively recent social era of Newport. The early cottages, which really were cottages, explain why Newport once attracted such residents as Edgar Allan Poe, Oliver Wendell Holmes, Henry James and Henry Wadsworth Longfellow.

The Hunter House was built at a time when Newport was a greater seaport than either New York or Boston. Washington Street, where it stands, was lined with the homes of merchant princes. The house was occupied successively by Jonathan Nichols, deputy governor of Rhode Island and the owner of a fleet of ships; Colonel Joseph Wanton, a son of Governor Joseph Wanton; and William

The Hunter House's parlor has authentic period furnishings.

Hunter, a United States Senator from Rhode Island and Minister to Brazil. Completely restored to its eighteenth-century appearance, it is furnished with antiques of that period. It is one of several of the shinglehouse era in Newport that are operated as public shrines by the Newport Preservation Society.

In sharp contrast with the Hunter House are some designed by Stanford White; among these is one that he built for Harry K. Thaw, later the slayer of Mr. White in a feud. Perhaps in the sharpest contrast, however, is the Waves. This is a modern, rambling, organic structure that could almost have come from the drawing board of Frank Lloyd Wright. It was built in 1927 by John Russell Pope, the revered architect of many such houses throughout the country, and was his home until he died.

On Ledge Road, the Waves occupies a rocky point of land projecting into the sea. After Mr. Pope's occupancy it was brought by Louis Chartier, a real estate developer who specializes in bringing new life into old structures. He converted the Waves into a luxury apartment house for families with comfortable incomes who seldom move. One prospective tenant reports that when he sought one of the apartments he was told that if he would sign a ten-year lease he could have one for $5,000 a year.

The Waves spreads out on the rocky promontory as though it had grown there. Of Tudor design, it has very steep roofs at varied angles. The gray slate of the roofs sometimes extends down the sides of the house, adding to the blending with the rocks, the sky and the sea. The exterior walls have accents of timber inlays and heavily beamed entrances, with leaded-glass windows, abundant woodbine and a weathervane patterned after a Spanish galleon.

The Marble Palace on Bellevue Avenue is another of the mansions designed by Richard Morris Hunt, who planned The Breakers, Belcourt and others. Its elegant, spectacular splendor is worthy of the Arabian Nights. Visitors approach it through massive wrought-iron gates, which open onto a white marble ramp. The mansion is a temple of white marble, with pilasters and capitals modeled after those of the Temple of the Sun at Baalbek — although considerably larger.

The hallway of the Hunter House has paneling and a low arch that marked the early colonial homes of distinction.

The mansion was built in the early eighteen nineties by William K. Vander-bilt, a brother of Cornelius Vanderbilt, who built the near-by Breakers, and a grandson of Commodore Cornelius Vanderbilt, founder of the clan in America. William Vanderbilt's wife when he built the Marble Palace was the former Alva Smith of Mobile, who divorced him in 1895. She then married Oliver H. P. Belmont, who had built Belcourt a few blocks away.

The Marble Palace cost $2,000,000 to construct and $9,000,000 to decorate and furnish. Alva Vanderbilt, known to her friends as "always being knee-deep in mortar," had a red-and-gold lacquered teahouse built on the lawn, importing craftsmen from China for the purpose. The teahouse is in front of the mansion, near the Cliff Walk.

Mrs. Vanderbilt made certain that the teahouse had a wonderful view of the sea and the gardens and that its comforts were luxurious. It was perfect except for one thing. It had no facilities for making tea. So a miniature railway was built from the Greek pantry of the mansion to the Chinese temple on the lawn. Visitors were treated to the spectacle of footmen in full livery riding to the teahouse in the open cars of the small train, holding silver tea services aloft as they emerged from the hedges of evergreens and hydrangeas.

Supplementing the luxury of the Marble Palace, the Vanderbilts had the yacht *Alva* anchored in the cove. They went on Mediterranean cruises and on their last one took along Mr. Belmont as a guest. The Marble Palace was completed in time for the debut of the Vanderbilts' daughter Consuelo, and Mr. Belmont was one of the guests at the lavish party. In the divorce settlement, Alva Vanderbilt received custody of the three children and the ownership of the Marble Palace. When she married Mr. Belmont, he revolted at the "showiness" of the Marble Palace and took his bride to live at Belcourt.

Shamrock Cliff, on the outer rim of Newport and facing Narragansett Bay, near Ridge Road, is one of the mansions that has been converted into a hotel, motel and restaurant. It was built by Guan Hutton, an Irishman from Belfast, but it is no Irish castle. Of Italian design, with red granite walls, a red roof and a boat pier on the bay, it could be mistaken for a villa on the Italian Riviera. The Hutton family was one of the last in Newport to retain horses and carriages, shunning automobiles until 1925, although they did have a sixty-foot power yacht, the *Oriole*.

The mansion has thirty-five rooms, including sixteen original guest bedrooms. Mr. Hutton, who had been in the American consular service, married Celeste Winans of Baltimore, the daughter of a wealthy engineer; her money largely paid for Shamrock Cliff. They and their four children used Shamrock Cliff as a summer home, spending the winters in Baltimore. Mrs. Hutton encouraged the children to entertain friends at the mansion but shunned Newport society herself and joined in none of the big Bellevue Avenue fiestas.

Miss Elsie C. Hutton, one of the daughters, remained in the mansion until 1958. Ten contractors then bought Shamrock Cliff, along with forty acres, and converted it into a hotel. They added modern bedrooms, a large dining room and a bar, harmonizing them with the Florentine gingerbread and other old-fashioned features. Besides the swimming pool they built a series of motel units. Tennis courts and gardens were retained.

Miramar, one of the "palaces" on Bellevue Avenue, now is a Protestant Episcopal conference center and much of it can be seen by the public — especially its garden area, which once was a main attraction at Newport. Miramar was built in 1912-14 by Mrs. George D. Widener. The contractor started building the mansion on the day that Mr. Widener died in the sinking of the *Titanic* in April, 1912.

After completing Miramar, Mrs. Widener married Dr. Alexander Hamilton Rice, a physician and explorer who was one of the first white men to go up the Amazon. When his wife died, life tenancy of Miramar was left to him and on his death in 1957 the ownership went to the Widener children. They gave it to the Protestant Episcopal Diocese of Rhode Island. They also gave $150,000 for maintenance.

The stone mansion is of Louis XV design. It is said to be a "blown-up version" of the Petite Trianon in Versailles. Among the fifty rooms are twenty-eight bedrooms. The construction cost $1,500,000 and the original furnishings, few of which remain, $2,000,000.

✿ ✿ ✿ ✿ ✿ ✿ ✿ ✿

The Newport mansions are always a spectacle from the public Cliff Walk, although many are closed to the public. Those converted to public uses and others operated as shrines of the Newport Preservation Society may be entered. Admission to some is free and the fees of others average $1 each. The hours for visits generally are 10 A.M. to 5 P.M. all year.

The Marble Palace, built by William K. Vanderbilt, has an elegant splendor.

A Seventy-Room "Cottage"

The Breakers of Cornelius Vanderbilt

NEWPORT · RHODE ISLAND

THE MAGNITUDE and the extravagances of Newport as a summer citadel of high society have seldom been approached elsewhere. The fame of the watering place began to grow in 1880 and continued to expand into the nineteen twenties. Mansions of extraordinary size were built, some with the dimensions of railroad terminals, Florentine palaces, English castles and French châteaux. All of them were called "cottages" and were occupied only two months a year.

Architectural extravagance and reckless spending for luxuries were characteristic of this Golden Era, when income taxes either had not been imposed or were comparatively low. Big family fortunes continued to grow faster than they could be spent. Prevailing at Newport was a feeling of "Let's have a good time with the money while we're young."

If one "cottage" dweller imported the Boston Symphony Orchestra for a concert on the terrace, a neighbor would bring the company of a New York

Cornelius Vanderbilt 251

musical show to his outdoor amphitheatre the next week. Some estates had parties for 3,000 guests, and $200,000 might be spent for one ball. Powdered-haired English butlers in knee breeches would serve ten-course dinners on ornate solid-gold service. A jeweler's books showed that $10,000 was spent for favors at one party. At another, each guest received a sterling-silver bucket and shovel to use for digging in a pile of sand in the ballroom where hundreds of emeralds, sapphires, rubies and diamonds were buried.

Southern planters started the social rush to Newport, followed by wealthy Bostonians. Then came the Wall Street tycoons and Mrs. John Jacob Astor's famous "four hundred" — that being the number of guests she could get comfortably into the reception rooms of her New York home. She could handle more at Newport.

Among the vanguard of the wealthy elite arriving in Newport were several of the Vanderbilts. They included Cornelius, a grandson of the Commodore, who had founded the family's railroad and steamship fortune in America; he was a son of William, who had greatly enhanced the fortune. Cornelius built The Breakers, the largest of the mansions on the golden five miles of Bellevue Avenue here. His brother, William K., built near by.

In 1885 Cornelius Vanderbilt bought a previous Breakers mansion on the same site from Pierre Lorillard, the tobacco tycoon. Mr. Vanderbilt paid $400,000 for the huge brick-and-wood structure, on a plateau overlooking the Atlantic Ocean. The mansion burned in 1892 and Mr. Vanderbilt quickly determined to build a new Breakers that would "put to shame" a magnificent fifty-two-room French château which Ogden Goelet had completed next door and which everyone was admiring.

As his architect, Mr. Vanderbilt hired Richard Morris Hunt, who had designed the Goelet mansion and several others here. After extensive study in Europe, Hunt had come to Newport to visit a brother and had become so fascinated that he remained to play a chief role in replacing wooden mansions with marble and granite palaces. Hunt conceived of a new Breakers resembling a Roman villa of the Italian Renaissance period; as models he chose villas near Genoa and Turin.

Importing marbles and alabasters from Italy and Africa, Caen stone from France and rare woods and mosaics from five continents, he completed the present Breakers in two years at a cost of $7,000,000. It was opened in 1895 in time for the debut of Gertrude Vanderbilt. The gold cigarette cases and other "trinkets" given to guests at this party cost more than a de luxe Rolls Royce does today, and Mrs. Vanderbilt wore jewels that had cost $1,000,000 in an era of uninflated prices.

There was ample room for all the guests at all the Vanderbilt parties. The mansion is 250 feet by 150 feet and it has seventy rooms and thirty baths. It has eleven acres of lawns and gardens inside the massive wrought-iron fence that surrounds the estate.

The dining room of The Breakers has abundant marble and hand-loomed Italian drapery.

The Breakers, its stables and gardens are operated as a public shrine by the Preservation Society of Newport County, which leases it for one dollar a year from a Vanderbilt daughter. The mansion still is furnished with art treasures of seven centuries that the Vanderbilts acquired throughout the world.

The four-story mansion is one of superlatives but it appeals more to men than it does to women. Men can imagine themselves living it up there as kings of the realm, ringing for the elevators and enjoying luxuries such as the billiard room, paneled with twenty varieties of marble, the palatial great hall three stories high and the sumptuous bedrooms, equipped with sliding grills that serve as anti-kidnaping devices. Women are more apt to prefer the French château that the Goelets built, with its intimate splendors and relaxed comforts.

Not a stick of timber was used in the main structure of The Breakers, since Mr. Vanderbilt wanted a house that would not burn as the previous one had. The walls are of brick, stone and tile. Steel beams form a great latticed network to support vaulted arches and slabs of marble, mosaic, terrazo and tile. The heating plant is under the caretaker's lodge; pipes lead from it to the mansion through a tunnel large enough for a team of horses, with steel fire doors at each end of the tunnel. Engineers say that even today the house could not have been made more effectively fireproof.

After passing through the ivy-covered porte-cochère, visitors come to massive carved oak front doors that are so carefully balanced that a touch of the finger will move them. Hand-wrought iron doors with glass panels are just inside, giving to visitors a hint of the lavish scale and sumptuous ornamentation of the interior.

Off the entrance hall is a pleasant room paneled in quartered-oak that was Mr. Vanderbilt's study. Just beyond is the galleried great hall, rising forty-five feet to a decorated ceiling that appears to be a distant, cloud-swept sky. Across the hall is a wall of glass providing an unobstructed view of gardens and the Atlantic. The walls of the other three sides are faced with Caen stone, carved and ornamented with plaques of marble. Huge fluted pilasters, supporting an ornate cornice, are decorated with oak leaves and acorns in stone, a symbol of the Vanderbilt family found in decorations throughout the estate.

A grand staircase leads to a series of balconies. Wrought-iron and bronze railings, marble columns, fountains and tapestries add to the spectacle. A rare Flemish tapestry, twenty-four by eighteen feet, is 300 years old. Eight great bronze candelabra are patterned after Italian sixteenth-century originals.

The library in a south wing has panels of Circassian walnut and bas-relief carvings in the style of the High Renaissance. The coffered ceiling and embossed green Spanish leather panels add to the setting for the Vanderbilts' collection of hundreds of the most beautiful and important books of the past century. An antique French fireplace is from the Château d'Arnay-le-Duc and dates from the sixteenth century. Engraved on it is an inscription which is freely translated as "Little do I care for riches, since only cleverness prevails in the end."

A French motif is followed in the gold-and-white music room of The Breakers.

The grand salon, used for recitals and dancing, was designed by the French architect Richard Bouwens Van der Boyen and executed by Allard and Sons, French cabinetmakers. The paneling, columns and ornamentations were made in France and shipped to this country, with French craftsmen accompanying them for the installation. The decorations of the morning room were similarly produced and installed.

The dining room is generally considered the most magnificent of the rooms. Said by architects to be as ornate as any in the palaces of Italy and France, it is fifty-eight feet long and rises two stories to a ceiling painting of Aurora at Dawn. Twelve monolithic shafts of red alabaster, topped with gilded bronze Corinthian capitals, support a gold cornice decorated with garlands and masks, which provide a setting for life-size figures carved in the arches of the ceiling. Lighting is provided by two crystal chandeliers and twelve crystal wall sconces.

The mansion was built at a time when electricity was unreliable, so the fixtures are not only wired for electricity but also piped for gas.

Adjacent to the mansion is a genuine cottage. Large enough to live in, it was built as a playhouse for the Vanderbilt children.

The wrought-iron fence surrounding the grounds is one of the most beautiful examples of ornamental ironwork anywhere. Each of the main panels of the fence is thirty-one feet wide and eight feet high. The panels are atop a tooled limestone wall four feet high, and between the panels are large limestone pillars. Outstanding features of the fence are iron gates twelve feet high, ornamented with forged clusters of oak leaves and acorns and the monogram *CV*. The gates were inspired by earlier ones in Italy.

Near the mansion are the Vanderbilt stables, which are two stories high and 150 feet wide. They still are maintained as in the nineteenth century, except for the horses. A carriage hall has sleighs, victorias, broughams, cabriolets, phaetons and an omnibus. There are twenty-eight luxury stalls, some monogramed, and displays of coachmen's liveries, silver-trimmed harness and garments for horses.

It was perhaps the irony of life that Mr. Vanderbilt, who was a handsome man and full of vitality, could not fully enjoy all that he had created. He suffered a severe stroke a year after The Breakers was completed and died in 1899. Other tragedies also overtook the family. His son William died while a junior at Yale University. His daughter Alice died in childhood. His son Cornelius displeased Mr. Vanderbilt and received a reduced inheritance of $1,500,000, compared with the $42,575,000 given to another son, Alfred, although Alfred gave $6,000,000 of it to Cornelius. Alfred died later on the *Lusitania* when it was sunk in World War I.

Of the daughters, Gertrude became Mrs. Harry Payne Whitney, who aided hundreds of New York artists and built the Whitney Art Museum in New York. Gladys, the youngest child, became the Countess Laszló Széchényi. The Countess, widow of a Hungarian nobleman, inherited The Breakers and still has an apartment on an upper floor of the mansion, as well as homes in New York and Washington. It is the countess who leases The Breakers to the preservation society for one dollar a year.

*   *   *   *   *   *   *   *

The Breakers is on Ochre Point Avenue. From May to mid-November the mansion is open from 10 A.M. to 5 P.M., with hours generally extending to 9 P.M. on Sundays in July and August. The admission is $1.75 for adults and 60 cents for children. The stables, open at the same hours from July 1 through Labor Day, have fees of 50 cents for adults and 25 cents for children.

A Watering Place with Bubbles

Oliver H. P. Belmont's Belcourt Castle

NEWPORT · RHODE ISLAND

BESIDES BEING A FOREMOST watering place a generation ago for society's fashionable four hundred, Newport played a major role in popularizing the automobile in America. Today the automobile is returning the favor by making it easy for the public to visit Newport and enjoy some of the city's past glory.

One of the mansions important in perpetuating memories of the old social whirl and also occupying a big niche in history as the birthplace of the automobile's popularity is Belcourt Castle, now open as a museum. This fifty-room "cottage" was built in 1893 by Oliver Hazard Perry Belmont, a son of banker August Belmont. Lavish festivals worthy of the Arabian Nights were held at Belcourt to focus international attention on the "bubbles," as cars were then called. The bubbles became social assets in Newport while Henry Ford was still tinkering with bicycles in Detroit.

Mr. Belmont imported a French car in 1897 and soon Harry Payne Whitney and William K. and Cornelius Vanderbilt followed suit. So did the Goelets, Fishes, Astors, Harrimans, Havemeyers, Flints and most of their millionaire friends. The horseless carriages, sometimes tagged "Red Devil," "White Ghost," "Blue Angel" and other names, were commonplace for the social set to use for afternoon rides along Bellevue Avenue, to the beaches and to dinner parties. Later the fad spread to New York.

By coincidence, Belcourt was especially suited for cars, as visitors at the house still can see for themselves. Mr. Belmont had built the mansion so horses and carriages could enter the front hall through massive doors and allow passengers to step directly into the living room. The bubbles could do likewise.

Newport's first automobile festival was held at Belcourt in 1899. With social leaders at the controls, the cars competed in obstacle races on the broad lawns. The course was lined with dummy figures of horses, dogs, policemen, nursemaids and pedestrians, around which each car had to make its way as a skier would maneuver in a slalom.

Belcourt Castle is of early French design. This bedroom was the one Mr. Belmont occupied.

The Gothic ballroom of Belcourt Castle has leaded-glass windows portraying French provincial scenes. Above the fireplace is a castle.

The cars were bedecked with garlands of flowers, stuffed eagles, flagpoles and colorful streamers, and the drivers wore goggles, dusters and gauntlets as they raced at ten miles an hour around the Belcourt course. Mr. Belmont drove one car and had Mrs. Stuyvesant Fish as co-pilot. Their car was decorated with an arbor of cat-o'-nine-tails. Mrs. Belmont and James W. Gerard were in a car covered with blue hydrangeas and white daisies. Another contained Mrs. John Jacob Astor and Harry Lehr, bon vivant of the resort, with a hydrangea-collared lapdog as mascot.

"We never dreamed," Mrs. Fish said more than a half century later, "that cars would ever become popular with everybody."

Mr. Belmont spent $3,000,000 to build the mansion. He was not married at the time and with little concern for the cost, he installed solid-gold and sterling-silver door hinges and knobs. He imported European craftsmen to perform delicate carvings and make ornate ceilings. He acquired rare furnishings from four continents.

Ironically, the mansion had only one big bedroom and few baths, except for those in the servants' quarters, until Mr. Belmont married the divorced wife of William K. Vanderbilt in 1896. One of the first moves of the new Mrs. Belmont, who had lived just around the corner and was familiar with the oddities of Belcourt, was to add several master bedrooms and big baths. Unlike Mr. Belmont, she liked noisy and extravagant social events and she prepared the house for parties of 500 guests, including many members of European royalty, that were to follow.

One of Mr. Belmont's main considerations in building the house had been to construct a combination mansion for himself and stable for his horses, all under one roof. The architect was Richard Morris Hunt, who already was accustomed to designing "cottages" of sizes up to 250 rooms for the rich but never hitherto had received an assignment such as Mr. Belmont's. After a tour of Europe, Mr. Hunt patterned Belcourt along the lines of Louis XII hunting lodges and early Versailles buildings. Belcourt has stalls for thirty horses on part of the first floor and elaborate living quarters above.

The stables were tiled, upholstered and paneled in the luxurious style of a ballroom. The horses had white linen initialed sheets, embroidered blankets with gold coats-of-arms and harness fittings of sterling silver. They had equipment changes for morning, afternoon and evening. The stable had tastefully furnished barracks for a battery of grooms.

The décor of the social rooms of Belcourt still is splendorous. The grand ballroom on the second floor is seventy feet long and, with adjacent rooms, can and sometimes still does accommodate 500 people. It has a fireplace surmounted by a carved Caenstone castle thirty feet high, with figures of monks, peasants and kings. The chimney is large enough for a half dozen Santa Clauses to pass through simultaneously.

In the ballroom are Gothic stained-glass windows portraying French medieval scenes. As was the custom in Newport society, Mr. Belmont had emblazoned over the windows his decorative coats-of-arms. One on the windows happened to be of Dunois, the Bastard of Orleans. This prompted a friend of Mr. Belmont to say chidingly over cocktails one evening: "My dear Oliver, why proclaim yourself?"

The main dining room of Belcourt is a copy of the mirror room at Versailles. It was here that Thomas A. Edison experimented with indirect lighting, still in use. Mamie Eisenhower spent an hour in it and proclaimed it her favorite room in Newport.

The family dining room of Belcourt Castle is oval and has many mirrors.

Mr. Belmont's original bedroom, of twelfth-century French design, has a massive bed formerly owned by an Indian maharajah. The bed reputedly had taken twenty-five years to be carved. Mrs. Belmont's bedroom, which she installed, has woodwork and paintings originally part of a French castle. It has a split-level bath about the size of a big living room, and near by is an odd circular staircase leading to upper galleries for clothing storage.

Some of the furnishings of the house, collected from fifteen countries, are 800 years old. Rare paintings include seventeenth-century Nicolas Poussin pictures of the life of Christ.

Under Mrs. Belmont's guidance, architect John Russell Pope redesigned the front entrance hall of Belcourt. The massive doors that had accommodated horses and bubbles were closed off. A library and other rooms were developed, without eliminating all signs of the previous uses of the space: visitors turning back the rugs still can see the marks of horses' hoofs on the floors.

Opening onto Belcourt Castle's courtyard are the stables, where the horses had initialed stalls, white blankets and silver harness.

Mrs. Belmont had a budget of $300,000 a year for entertaining at Belcourt. The strain of the social whirl began to leave its mark on Mr. Belmont, although he was five years younger than his wife. At one masquerade party he collapsed under the weight of armor he was wearing, costumed as a knight. He died in 1908 but Mrs. Belmont lived until 1933.

She had been born Alva Smith in Mobile, the daughter of a cotton planter. Besides being noted for her feuds in Newport she was a woman of many "firsts." At Newport she was the first of her social set in bloomers, the first on a bicycle and the first to cut her hair short. She was also the first woman member of the American Institute of Architects. She took up many causes at Belcourt, including soup kitchens for the poor, birth control, model house designing, health clinics and woman suffrage. As a grand dame of Newport's golden age she once told a visitor at Belcourt to forget her troubles and join the fight for women's supremacy. "Brace up," she told the woman. "Just pray to God. SHE will help you."

After the death of the Belmonts the ownership of Belcourt passed through several hands. It was closed for many years, except to an artist who lived there. An industrialist bought it but never moved into the house. An antique automobile museum was to have been set up in Belcourt and plans were made for it to become a fine arts center, but both projects were dropped. It was bought in 1955 as a new home for the Newport Jazz Festivals. Neighboring estate owners recoiled in horror and that scheme was abandoned too.

Since 1957 the mansion and its surrounding four acres, including the site of the early automobile festivals, have been owned and operated as a historic shrine, museum and reception center by Mr. and Mrs. Harold B. Tinney, their son Donald and Mrs. Tinney's aunt, Miss Nellie R. Turner. It is also their home. The size of Belcourt did not faze them a bit, as their previous home had been Seaverge, a forty-three-room "cottage," just around the corner and next door to Doris Duke.

✿　✿　✿　✿　✿　✿　✿　✿

Belcourt is at the corner of Lakeview and Ledge Roads in the Bellevue Avenue section of Newport. It is open from early May to mid-November every year. The visiting hours are 10 A.M. to 5 P.M. daily, and often to 8 P.M. on Sundays. The admission is $1.60 for adults, 60 cents for children six to sixteen years old. Children under six are free.

Steamboat May Lived Here

Ogden Goelet's Ochre Court

NEWPORT · RHODE ISLAND

ONE OF THE "cottages" easily seen by persons strolling along the Cliff Walk is Ochre Court, a luxurious French-style stone château of fifty-two rooms that Ogden Goelet built in 1890. It is located on Ochre Point, also known as Millionaires' Point. The steep embankments rising from the blue surf are the earthy color of yellow ocher. The path near the ocean passes through the front yard of the mansion, which now is the main building of Salve Regina College.

Because of its quiet harmonies, Parisian décor and modern refinements, Ochre Court is a favorite of women visitors in Newport. It is also admired by architects as a classic example of French Gothic design, modeled after the French châteaux of the Middle Ages and the castle that England's Edward VII built in Paris before he ascended the throne of his own country. Its architect was Richard Morris Hunt, who designed The Breakers, the Marble Palace, Belcourt and other Newport mansions. The construction cost was $4,500,000.

Ochre Court has been described as a romantic knight's castle without the outer walls, moats, ditches and subsidiary buildings that similar *maisons grandes* in France's Valley of the Loire possess. Its limestone arches, turrets, ornamental ironwork, walled gardens and ornate wrought-iron fences and towering gates are those of the era when knighthood was in flower.

Mr. Goelet and his wife, the former May Wilson, were sharing the glory of Newport's burgeoning high society when they moved into Ochre Court. Their New York home was at Fifth Avenue and Forty-ninth Street — way uptown in those days. Mr. Goelet had inherited a fortune in Manhattan real estate and parlayed it into an even bigger one. His wife, wealthy in her own right, crossed the Atlantic on luxury liners so often that friends called her Steamboat May. The Goelets' private yachts rode at anchor off Newport with the Morgans' *Corsair*, the Astors' *Nourmahal* and the Drexels' *Sultana*. One of the Goelet craft, *The Mayflower*, later was given to the United States government for Presidential use.

Ochre Court became famous for its lavish parties, some held in not-so-friendly rivalry of those given by Mrs. Stuyvesant Fish at the near-by Crossways. Grand Duke Boris of Russia was such a drawing card at an Ochre Court party that Mrs. Fish gave a competing event of her own with a friend masquerading humorously as the Czar of Russia.

Servants were plentiful, and Ochre Court needed a minimum of thirty-five. There was little fear of overworking or offending the housemaids, butlers and gardeners in Newport and they were openly and cynically classified as "good," "fair" and "rotten." The task of maintaining the mansion and its staff became wearing on Mr. Goelet, however, and it may have affected his health: he became irritable in his later years and lived on a diet of hothouse grapes.

His son, Robert, inherited Ochre Court and soon perceived the growing perils of maintaining the mansion as a private home. He offered it to his daughter but she thought the place was depressing, so in 1947 he gave it to the Roman Catholic Bishop of Providence, the Most Reverend Francis P. Keough, for the establishment of Salve Regina, the first Catholic women's college in Rhode Island. Robert Goelet and his wife had already moved into a snug home, Champ Soleil, that needed only five servants.

The great hall of Ochre Court is three stories high and its balconies, walls and vaulted ceiling have abundant gold leaf, French paintings and marble adornments. The dining room, which accommodates forty guests without crowding, has twin fireplaces side by side, each large enough for five persons to step into, that seem to baffle most visitors. Sister Mary Rose of the college has been known to refer to them, with a twinkle in her eye, as "His" and "Hers."

Experts on manor houses, castles and châteaux were asked by the college to convert Ochre Court into modern academic quarters for 370 students and an administrative staff. The grandeur of its rooms and the task of perpetuating it in functional uses presented such a challenge that one of the experts averred he could not sleep for a week, but the goal was accomplished.

The towering, ornate entrance gates and fences remain as some of the finest examples of wrought-iron artistry in Europe and America. Appearing recurrently in the ornaments, carvings, castings and engravings throughout the estate is the Goelet motto, *Ex Candore, Decus*, ("from splendor comes beauty"). Also frequently seen are the fleur de lis as the symbol of France, the swan as a symbol of grace and the dragon as a representation of the evil monster slain by St. George. The wood carvings were made in Paris.

A $25,000 stained-glass window of the great hall was one of the Spitzen collection in Germany; it probably was taken from a cathedral during the Reformation. In the center of the window is a figure of God holding a scroll of the Ten Commandments. A medieval design of the devil is in the window over the heads of the tempted; on the left is St. George and on the right, St. Maurice. Captions are in quaint Middle German.

The grand staircase of marble and sandstone has balustrades carved with dolphins and cupids — no two alike. The ballroom now is a chapel; it has a white and gold décor, with ceiling paintings in the style of those in the Versailles Palace. The drawing room, now a lecture hall, has Louis XIV paneled walls, a marble fireplace, carved floral wreaths and a chandelier of teardrop crystal. A dining hall also has ceiling paintings and a library has exceptional brass adornments. The Tudor Room, once Ogden Goelet's study, now is occupied by the college registrar; it has Flemish tile decorations and wall paintings resembling those of Holbein.

✿ ✿ ✿ ✿ ✿ ✿ ✿ ✿

The college administrators are proud of Ochre Court and its art treasures. Consequently, they show the more important rooms to visitors when the college schedule permits. The grounds and the exterior of the mansion may be seen at any time. Access is from Ochre Point Avenue, as well as from Cliff Walk.

Architectural Smörgasbord

Swan J. Turnblad's Chateau

MINNEAPOLIS · MINNESOTA

OUTSIDE OF SWEDEN there is no finer collection of decorative porcelainized stoves for heating the front parlors than the eleven in the sumptuous French château that Swan J. Turnblad built on Park Avenue in Minneapolis. Neither is there a finer assortment of carved African mahoganies, European furniture and Swedish rugs of Oriental designs.

When Minnesota was still a wilderness, mustering youths to fight the Confederates at Bull Run, a son was born to the Månson family in the Province of Småland, Sweden. The Månsons were farmers, living in poverty and endless toil. When they heard of the great potential wealth of Minnesota's farmland they migrated there, taking along the boy, Sven, who then was eight years old.

Sven enjoyed handling printing presses more than plows as he grew up at Vasa, Minnesota. Before he graduated from Vasa High School he printed a book on arithmetic that the principal had written. He also changed his name to Swan J. Turnblad. At nineteen he moved to Minneapolis to work for the old *Svenska Amerikanska Posten,* which was in financial trouble. He became the owner of the faltering paper and made it the largest Swedish language publication in America.

Mr. Turnblad created a sensation in Minneapolis in 1900 by driving through the Nicollet Avenue shopping district in a Waverly Electric, the first vehicle of its kind to be seen there. Women scurried for safety and men reined in their horses as Mr. Turnblad clanged the gong of the horseless carriage and cut a path through the crowds.

He created another sensation in 1907 when he completed his $1,500,000 French château of thirty-three rooms at Twenty-sixth Street and Park Avenue, among the lesser mansions that millionaire millers and bankers were building. The massive three-story Turnblad structure, with towers, turrets, terraces and a high wrought-iron fence, was one of the finest and most luxuriously furnished in the Northwest.

Mr. Turnblad, his wife and their young daughter Lillian did not find, however, that the joy of living increased in step with the rise in their standard of living. Managing the servants in the mansion was like commanding a small army The rooms were far larger and more numerous than the family of three either needed or wanted. And the cost of maintaining the property Mr. Turnblad considered excessive.

So the family traveled extensively rather than remain in the mansion. When they were home the three lived just on the second floor, and finally they moved to an apartment across the street, from which they could see the château and not be faced by all the annoyances of operating it.

In 1929, after his wife's death, Mr. Turnblad gave the mansion to the American Swedish Institute, which he had founded. The institute now maintains the property as one of the cultural centers of the Northwest. It is visited by 25,000 persons a year, which would please Mr. Turnblad. Just before his death in 1933 he said:

"It has been my lifelong ambition to foster and preserve Swedish culture in America. I hold dear many things that are Swedish, although I am an American now, and it seems to me to be desirable for both countries if products of Swedish culture are shown here."

The grand entrance hall is paneled in African mahogany and has ornate carvings that craftsmen worked on for seven years. Flanking the staircase are two mahogany griffins – half lion and half eagle, as used in Greek and Roman art. On either side of a fireplace, Viking figures support pedestals for candelabra.

A huge fireplace on the first floor is faced with onyx and has a massive mantel, designed and carved by Albin Polasek, noted Polish artist, that reaches

Extensive wood carvings in the Turnblad house include two griffins beside the staircase. Ulrich Steiner was the carver.

to the ceiling. It has two carved Atlases that, seeming to hold all the weight on their heads, signify eternal strength.

Recessed between Corinthian pillars above the Polasek creation is a large timepiece flanked by carved statues of two women, one with eyes open and the other with eyes closed, to indicate day and night. Overhead, a mahogany Viking is looking out calmly over endless space.

One of the last surviving craftsmen who worked on the carvings was Swiss-born Ulrich Steiner. He fell so deeply in love with the creations that he kept returning for fifty years to see them again and again. Son of a wood carver, Ulrich started in the craft as a boy and continued in it after migrating to Minnesota. The same was true of many of the craftsmen Mr. Turnblad hired.

All the rugs in the house are seamless carpets of Swedish wool, woven in Sweden, with one exception. The big rug covering the floor of the grand hall was made in Austria, since Sweden at that time had no looms large enough for it. The rugs have different Oriental patterns.

The dining room has a table for twenty-four persons and massive chairs that roll on ball bearings. Among the dinner guests there have been former President Dwight D. Eisenhower, Dag Hammarskjöld, Edgar Bergen, Chief Justice Earl Warren and members of the royal family of Sweden.

In eleven of the elegantly furnished rooms are the porcelainized stoves, known as *kakelugnar*. The Swedes used them instead of fireplaces to heat houses and they are as decorative as big chests of drawers. White-birch logs were the common fuel. One loading of the logs would keep a stove hot for thirty hours and warm an entire room. Each stove had its own flue to the roof. Although central heating systems became common in Sweden and Minnesota after 1910, the *kakelugnar* continued to be used in homes as curiosities in the manner that New Englanders used cobblers' benches.

The *kakelugnar* were first used in Europe in the seventeenth century, chiefly by aristocrats with large castles but later by middle-class families. Scandinavians brought a few of the stoves to Colonial America. Benjamin Franklin's achievements with iron stoves increased the interest in replacing the traditional fireplace as a heating device.

Over the years the styles of the *kakelugnar* reflected the fashions in decorations. When tastes switched to Chinese, French or German décor, so did the design of the stoves. The Turnblad collection indicates the changes in tastes. Some experts feel that those of German influence are too heavy, those of French influence too fragile and those that are strictly Swedish are just right. Several of the stoves represent an age of grace in furniture designing that led to the Swedish Modern of today.

The Rörstrand Company, one of Sweden's most famous ceramics manufacturers, absorbed Marieberg, one of the finest makers of porcelainized stoves. The stoves with the Marieberg insignia are among the most prized by collectors, and Mr. Turnblad acquired several. Researchers report that more than half of the stoves in the Turnblad collection probably were made in the last part of the nineteenth century.

A stained-glass window on the landing of the grand staircase of the château shows a historical scene from a painting in the National Museum in Stockholm. The window, made in Sweden for $15,000, depicts the sacking of Gotland's capital, with the conqueror in the marketplace directing inhabitants to contribute jewels, gold and silver.

A carving in one of the rooms illustrates a Swedish legend that elves, trolls and other mysterious inhabitants of the forests can lure young maidens from earthly homes into the splendor of an enchanted universe.

On the third floor of the mansion is the Turnblads' ballroom, currently used for displays of Swedish Modern furniture, paintings and other art objects. In the ballroom and adjacent rooms are the furnishings of a century-old Swedish kitchen and 200 gifts donated to the American Swedish Institute by the parishes and municipalities of Värmland Province, Sweden.

The château also has a general assembly room, now used for public concerts, lectures, exhibits and motion-picture shows related to Scandinavia, early Minnesota and travel. The library has 12,000 books, many relating to Scandinavia.

❋ ❋ ❋ ❋ ❋ ❋ ❋ ❋

The Turnblad château is at 2600 Park Avenue, a mile from downtown Minneapolis. It is open from 2 to 5 P.M. Tuesday through Friday and on Sunday, and from 10 A.M. to 5 P.M. on Saturday. Admission fees are nominal.

The Turnblad mansion has massive fireplaces of German design and several colorful porcelainized stoves.

Mrs. O'Leary's Cow + *Gunpowder* = *a Marble Mansion*

The Home of Samuel M. Nickerson

CHICAGO • ILLINOIS

NOT MANY OF THE MANSIONS of Old Chicago remain on the landscape today. Those that Mrs. O'Leary's cow did not destroy when she kicked over a lantern and set fire to the city in 1871 have largely been erased by the builders of skyscrapers and turnpikes in recent years. Famous dwellings of the financial and social elite have vanished by the hundreds. One that remains, however, probably will continue in perpetuity. It was built for one family but 24,000 of the world's foremost surgeons now call it their headquarters.

The mansion, known as Nickerson's Marble Palace, was built by Samuel M. Nickerson. Affable, dignified and cultured, Nickerson was a Civil War profiteer and one of the business leaders who spurred Chicago into becoming a great rail and business center. He built the mansion at 40 East Erie Street, adjacent to Wabash Avenue and not far from Lake Michigan. The land was part of the 2,024 acres cleared of 13,500 buildings when the balky bovine of legend caused the horrendous conflagration on that bleak October night.

Fire had played an earlier part in Mr. Nickerson's life. A descendant of Puritan settlers from Norwalk, England, he was born at Chatham, Massachusetts. At the age of seventeen he left home to work in his brother's general store at Apalachicola, in the upper panhandle of Florida. Four years later, in 1851, he opened his own general store there. In 1857 the store burned to the ground and Mr. Nickerson was financially ruined.

Thoroughly discouraged, he borrowed a few dollars and moved to Chicago to start life anew. He also married Matilda P. Crosby, a childhood friend from his old home on Cape Cod, and they had one son, Roland.

With meager funds Mr. Nickerson became a distiller of liquors and alcohol in Chicago. The first shots of the Civil War signaled the turning point of his business career; he became a producer of huge quantities of a type of alcohol needed for making black gunpowder for the Union Army.

At the age of thirty-four he had amassed a fortune so large that he could have retired, but instead he went on to become president of the Chicago City Horse Railway, the First National Bank, the Union Stock Yards National Bank and several Chicago industries. With his enterprises producing money faster than he could easily spend it in the Windy City, he started his mansion in 1881 and took a trip around the world with his wife to collect art treasures for the home.

The mansion took three years to build and another year to settle on its foundations before the interior was decorated. Lake Michigan once had covered the site of the mansion; excavators discovered that the sand extended down sixty feet to a bed of clay and that limestone was ninety feet below the surface. Consequently a "floating foundation" was built, such as later were used successfully for some of the largest buildings and bridges in the world. But a long period had to be allowed for settling in those days, before the era of scientific compaction.

The architect, Edward Burling, was told to count no costs — and he didn't. The three-story stone house of twenty-eight rooms cost $450,000, which at today's prices would mean an expenditure of more than $2,000,000.

Something of the values then are indicated by the pay received by A. Fiedler, a designer of wood carvings in the house. He had been a designer for one of the leading furniture manufacturers in New York at a salary of $1,800 a year before undertaking the Nickerson contract for about the same income.

The exterior of the house now is soot-darkened and unattractive. The structure is crowded up against other buildings on two sides and flanked by sidewalks and heavy traffic on the other sides. But inside, the mansion is breath-taking in its extensive use of eleven varieties of marble on walls, floors and sometimes even ceilings. The spacious rooms have onyx pillars, elaborately carved woodwork of Cuban and South American mahogany, alabaster banisters, a dining room with leather-paneled walls, halls with ornate beamed ceilings, mantels with delicate inlays, Dutch-tile fireplaces and crystal-and-brass chandeliers.

"It is architecture gone crazy," one architect said after visiting the mansion.

(Left) The entrance hall of the Nickerson house has eleven varieties of marble. (Right) Nickerson had a "gentlemen's wine room" for poker, smoking and drinking. The skylight is of Tiffany glass.

"But seeing is believing — you just can't imagine the beauty of some of the rooms and the magnificence of the marble and the carvings without seeing them."

A secretary who now works in the mansion has said: "It's like living in a palace seven hours a day. It's like a dream. I almost expect some beautiful society lady to come swooping down the great marble staircase any minute."

There were beautiful women "swooping down the staircase" when the Nickersons did lavish entertaining there. A grand ballroom is on the third floor and a billiard room is in the basement. On the first floor, adjacent to the parlors, is a "gentlemen's wine room," or card and game room. A large poker table is under a Tiffany chandelier and skylight, and beside the mantel are built-in humidors for cigars — now used for some of the priceless books of a medical library dating back to 1620.

Rooms with Turkish décor and carvings of teak and ebonized black cherry add to the interest of the house. The Nickersons had furniture, paintings, statues and curios collected from many countries, but most of these objects now are in public art galleries. They were a main topic of discussion at the parties in the home, especially when Mrs. Nickerson entertained on Thursday afternoons. To the Chicago Art Institute, of which he was a trustee, Mr. Nickerson gave several hundred art objects from his home, along with $50,000 to maintain the collection.

In 1901 the Nickersons sold the house and moved to New York City, where Mr. Nickerson died in 1914. The purchaser of the mansion was Lucius G. Fisher, a paper-bag manufacturer and Chicago civic leader.

The Fishers continued to maintain the house as a social center. Their two daughters were married there to brothers, Homer and William Dixon. Few alterations were made to the house, although the Fishers added a new element of decoration — stuffed heads of buffalo, deer and other animals. Mr. Fisher collected such heads and also old-fashioned weapons. The weapons were displayed in cabinets.

In 1919 the mansion was so highly respected by civic leaders that they bought it and gave it to the American College of Surgeons for use as a permanent headquarters. Among the donors were the McCormicks, the Rosenwalds, the Swifts, the Wrigleys, the Logans, the Spaldings, the Posts and the Fords. Edward L. Doheny later gave bronze doors for an annex as a memorial to his doctor.

Dr. Franklin H. Martin, who was secretary general of the college, said 4,200 surgeons who then were members had voted to accept the gift and convert the mansion into a headquarters. "The donors have brought to Chicago a prize comparable only to the Royal College of England, in London. Chicago now bids fair to become the medical center of the world."

The success of Nickerson's Marble Palace in its new role is beyond dispute. Without changing walls or making other major alterations, offices have been fitted into the rooms of the three floors. Conferences on medical problems often are held in the game room where dice once rolled for $100 bets and poker chips clattered far into the night.

Adjacent to the Nickerson building the college has built an impressive annex of French Renaissance design as a memorial to the great Chicago surgeon, Dr. John B. Murphy, and this structure has a large meeting room and the main library of the college. The headquarters sometimes is a base for 10,000 surgeons at clinical congresses in Chicago, with several hundred of the surgeons meeting in rooms of the mansion where waltz music once resounded.

❖　❖　❖　❖　❖　❖　❖　❖

Nickerson's Marble Palace is at 40 East Erie Street, a few minutes by car from the center of downtown Chicago. The American College of Surgeons has no regular schedule for visitors but several of the main rooms may be seen from 9 A.M. to 5 P.M. Monday through Friday.

To the left is the Alster Tower, Boldt Castle's recreation house. On the right is a stone arch over a waterway. (Opposite page) Boldt Castle was inspired by castles on the Rhine. The mansion is in the center, the powerhouse on the right and recreation house on the left.

Ecstasy in Granite at the Thousand Islands

George C. Boldt's Castle

ALEXANDRIA BAY · NEW YORK

MANY OF THE 1,000 persons who roam through Boldt's Castle each summer day consider the massive $2,000,000 pile of stone the Taj Mahal of North America, although a guidebook of the American Automobile Association describes it as "a neglected ruin of little interest."

However, the ruins of Pompeii and the crumbling pyramids of Yucatan may also be viewed with a jaundiced eye that would prefer polished splendor.

Not far from its source, the St. Lawrence River broadens into the size of a big lake and in this sprawling body of water are the Thousand Islands, which actually total 1,700. The international boundary line between the United States and Canada follows a serpentine path through the lush islands, dotted with the summer homes of industrialists, social leaders, artists and writers. Ocean-going vessels pass near by in the billion-dollar St. Lawrence Seaway.

George C. Boldt was born in poverty in Prussia. In his boyhood he often saw the ivy-covered castles on the Rhine and he dreamed of someday owning a home like them. He came to the United States at the age of thirteen and in a Horatio Alger career became one of the most successful hotel men in the world.

As the proprietor of the Waldorf-Astoria in New York and the Bellevue-Stratford in Philadelphia he taught the new strata of millionaires how to spend their money. Quality of service became his watchword, and he accumulated a $25,-000,000 personal fortune from the hotels and as an official of banks, cigar companies, import houses and insurance corporations.

The Thousand Islands, which reminded him of the Rhine, became his favorite resort, and his wife shared his enthusiasm. Deciding to build a castle there for her, Boldt bought a six-acre island near Alexandria Bay from G. K. Hart. Rearranging its contour by blasting rock and building new breakwaters, Boldt made the island into the shape of a heart and changed its name from Hart to Heart.

It was only a summer castle that Mr. Boldt wanted to build for his wife but he wanted it to be a regal one, with facilities for 100 guests and their servants. He retained Hewitt, Stevens and Paist of Philadelphia as architects.

The construction of the castle and ten related buildings was begun in 1897. Granite for the outer walls was quarried ten miles away at Oak Island. Terra cotta for the roofs and the fountains was brought from the mainland. Marble for the mantels and bathrooms was brought from Italy, along with Italian craftsmen to carve and install it. From other countries were brought choice mahogany, walnut, oak, mosaics, tapestries, furniture and sculpture.

The castle rises five stories and is topped by a tower and high gables. It has ninety rooms and thirty-one baths, although guides on the tourist boats say with straight faces that it has 372 rooms and 55 baths.

On the shore of the island Mr. Boldt built Alster Tower, a recreation house for his two children, George and Clover. (The daughter now is Mrs. Clover B. Johaneson.) Alster Tower is a reproduction of a small castle Boldt had seen on the Rhine. It has a library, theater, bowling alley, billiard room and the Shell Room, which has a ceiling in the shape of a shell, for dancing.

Mr. Boldt also built a stone powerhouse to generate electricity and to contain chimes that could be played from an organ in the castle. He constructed a stone arch resembling the Arc de Triomphe in Paris as an entrance to a lagoon on the island. There were a stone arcade and runway for transporting household supplies from the waterfront to the castle.

But the romance of Mr. Boldt's never-never land really began on the main floor of the castle. The entrance hall is twenty-two by twenty-two feet and rises sixty feet to a dome that was to be covered with leaded glass and have fountains of water playing upon it. The grand staircase was to have been sufficiently elegant for the lords and ladies of yesteryear. Off the entrance hall is the main drawing room, which has a recess for the organ. Near this room are a ballroom, library, dining room, billiard room, kitchen and butler's pantry.

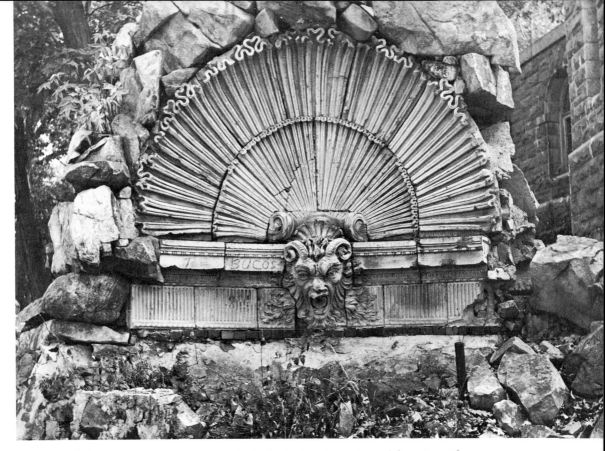

(Above) A terra cotta fountain was built by Boldt. Recent vandalism is evident. (Below) Boldt's powerhouse has a tower with chimes that could be played electrically from the mansion.

Upper floors have balconies overlooking the entrance hall and its high dome. The second floor has master bedrooms and suites for the Boldts' children and guests, and the higher floors are replicas of the second. Other rooms for guests and servants are in the auxiliary buildings.

The buildings were about to be completed and occupied in 1903 when Mrs. Boldt suddenly died. The castle had risen as a tribute to her, and in his grief Mr. Boldt ordered the construction work halted. He never had it resumed. Neither did he ever visit Heart Island again, although he did return to the Thousand Islands.

The castle remains today a huge stone shell. The ornately carved woodwork and mantels that were to have adorned the interior are still piled in open storage in some of the rooms — so open that tourists hack them with penknives to obtain souvenirs to take home. Bats, birds and cobwebs occupy the quaint niches of medieval design.

"It reminds me of Longwood," one visitor commented, referring to the octagonal residence at Natchez, Mississippi, that was almost completed when the Civil War halted its construction, but was never finished.

Vandals have recently added to the desolation at Boldt's Castle, smashing the few glass panes remaining in the hundreds of windows. The elements have played a part in shattering some of the ornate plaster ceilings, which had been carved with cupids, medallions, flowers and big hearts.

The castle was still unoccupied when Mr. Boldt died in 1916. Two years later it was sold to Edward J. Noble of Greenwich, Connecticut, manufacturer of Life Saver candies, chairman of the American Broadcasting Company, of the Civil Aeronautics Authority and of St. Lawrence University, and the owner of vast properties at the Thousand Islands. Another Island enthusiast, he flew his own planes and helicopters to them and was president of the Thousand Islands Club.

Mr. Noble never intended to live on Heart Island. He opened it to the public. New piers were built to accommodate boats that brought thousands of tourists from the Canadian and United States mainlands.

In 1959 Mr. Noble died. His heirs continued the operation of Boldt Castle as a tourist attraction and in 1962 its operation was taken over by the Treadway Corporation. Thousand Islanders hope that someday the appalling stillness at the castle after tourists have left at nightfall may be replaced by the gay music and laughter of hotel patrons that Mr. and Mrs. Boldt would have thoroughly enjoyed.

✧ ✧ ✧ ✧ ✧ ✧ ✧ ✧

Boldt Castle is ten minutes by excursion boat from the docks at Alexandria Bay. It is open every day in the week from Memorial Day to October 1, from 8 A.M. to 7 P.M. in July and August and from 8 A.M. to 6 P.M. in the other months. The admission fee is 60 cents for persons over twelve; others are free. The boats, running every half hour, charge 75 cents for round trips to the castle. Free stops are included on $3 tours of the Islands.

"Henry VIII Should Be Here!"

Frank A. Seiberling's Stan Hywet Hall

AKRON · OHIO

FRANK A. SEIBERLING, the Napoleon of the rubber industry, was only five-feet-three-inches tall but he had big ideas. He was an entrepreneur, with imagination, bounce and follow-through, both in business and in private life. He built Stan Hywet Hall and its picturesque gardens in the style of an English manor home of centuries ago but with the comforts of today.

Born in Ohio, he was a descendant of the Seiberlings who had migrated from Germany in 1741. After trying his luck at milling, manufacturing reapers, operating a trolley car company and producing twine, he borrowed $3,500 in 1898 to found the Goodyear Tire and Rubber Company. He named the company for Charles Goodyear, who had died in 1860 after perfecting vulcanization.

F. A., as Mr. Seiberling was known, developed cord tires, military balloons, raincoats and other rubber items that originally were experimental but now are taken for granted. He was president of the Lincoln Highway Association and one

F. A. Seiberling, the master of Stan Hywet Hall, made a fortune in rubber.

of the most articulate advocates of the Pan-American Highway. When he lost a $20,000,000 fortune in 1921 and was washed out of the Goodyear board chairmanship, he founded the Seiberling Rubber Company at the age of sixty-one to make another big fortune.

Stan Hywet (pronounced Stan Hee-wet) is the estate that F. A. developed on a large woodland tract on the outer rim of Akron. He began building the block-long mansion in 1911 and completed it in 1915. He managed to retain the estate, which had eighteen servants, even through the financial debacle of the early nineteen twenties, and he died at the mansion in 1955 at the age of ninety-five.

F. A. set something of a record in a race with other rubber-company barons to build the biggest, costliest and most spectacular mansion in the region. He won hands down, and his rivals never quite forgave him either for having the biggest business or for having the largest home.

The construction costs on the mansion ran to $2,000,000. F. A. and his wife, who was an amateur painter, patroness of music and admirer of great architecture, traveled extensively overseas while the mansion was being built to spend more millions for furnishings and art treasures from many lands and several centuries. The objects they acquired are still in the mansion.

All the spending had one thing in common — the production of an English-type manor like those of the Elizabethan era. The efforts were so successful that visitors have been heard to exclaim: "I feel as though Henry VIII should come walking through the front door!" Adding to the illusion in summer months are

Shakespearian dramas and musical events on the terraces. When *Romeo and Juliet* is presented, Juliet leans appropriately from one of the balconies of the mansion.

The thirty-two-acre estate and sixty-five-room mansion now are open to the public, operated by an educational and cultural foundation, set up by the family and friends of F. A. Bordering the Cuyahoga Valley, the estate is near Sand Run Park and the Portage Country Club.

The exterior of the mansion is typically Tudor, with some Italian influences. The builders avoided Americanization as much as possible. The walls are of hand-made English red bricks, with white sandstone moldings. The roofs are slate. In design the building is long and narrow, extending 300 feet in one direction. It has wings projecting from a central axis. At the entrance is a square tower four stories high, with an elevator. The remainder of the mansion is three stories high, with the third floor obtaining light chiefly from dormer windows.

Besides being one of the finest examples of English Tudor Revival architecture, Stan Hywet is a memorial to America's period of great personal wealth. In its heydey it had as frequent house guests the leaders of American industry; Presidents William Howard Taft, Warren G. Harding, Calvin Coolidge and Herbert Hoover; Will Rogers; Thomas A. Edison; Helen Keller; Senator William Borah; opera stars Rosa Ponselle, Ernestine Schumann-Heink and Amelita Galli-Curci; pianist Ignace Jan Paderewski; and others. And while cutting a broad swath themselves in society, music, art and commerce, Mr. and Mrs. Seiberling reared their six children in the great mansion.

Stan Hywet, inspired by Ockwells Manor, forty miles from London, has extensive ornamental stripwork, long galleries and big windows. The architects, the

Only in the winter, with trees stripped of foliage, can the vastness and details of Stan Hywet be seen.

decorators and the landscape designers were taken to England several times by Mr. and Mrs. Seiberling to see Ockwells Manor and other old mansions before a stone was turned for Stan Hywet in 1911. On these journeys the Seiberlings began collecting the furnishings for the mansion, five other buildings and two tea houses of the estate.

The name Stan Hywet is Anglo Saxon for "stone quarry." There formerly were stone quarries on the estate; they now are filled with water to provide attractive lagoons for boating, swimming, fishing and skating.

The entrance of the mansion was inspired by one at Henry VIII's castle Compton-Wynyates. Over the door is a stone coat of arms inscribed with "Non Nobis Solum" (Not for Us Alone), which represented the Seiberlings' intentions in building Stan Hywet. The vaulted ceiling of the entrance is centered with a Tudor rose.

Other entrance features that set a pattern for what follows are massive hand-carved doors in an evolutionary form of a portcullis, the heavy iron gate that guarded ancient castles. Torches illuminate a stone carving that reads: "Welcome, as thy need may be; find here gladness, happiness, peace and sanctuary."

Floors are stone, teakwood and rosewood. A reception room is an exact copy of the one in Haddon Hall in England, with carvings of Tudor roses and welcome messages. There also are elaborate stained-glass windows, carvings of the fleur-de-lis of the Bourbons and intricate Gothic ceilings of molded plaster. The great hall is three stories high and has a minstrels' balcony, from which the Seiberlings had minstrels singing as in yesteryear. Two large tapestries which portray Flemish Biblical studies were made in the sixteenth century.

Stan Hywet has three things that F. A. especially desired — a big game room and a forty-foot swimming pool for his cronies and a spacious gymnasium in a remote part of the house for children to play in as noisily as they wanted. He also built a large library, which now has on its shelves rare masterpieces of the book-binder's art. A secret door behind shelves of books leads into the great hall. The music rooms, seating 400 persons, has sculpture by Paul Manship and a harpsichord that Handel owned and Haydn used. There are bowling alleys and a billiard room. English galleries have the coats of arms of feudal barons. On windows are, in color, the heraldic designs of English nobility.

There also are Chinese rooms, dining and breakfast rooms and Tudor bedrooms that are copies of those several centuries old. In a children's dining room are scrolls of inspirational poems. Paintings, sculpture, Persian rugs, Royal Doulton china, antique silver, Gobelin tapestries, an allegorical frieze of Chaucer's *Canterbury Tales*, prayer chairs and fine linens are among the furnishings.

The museum objects include a Boule chest made by Charles Goodyear that is veneered in hard rubber and inlaid with brass. Mr. Goodyear made the chest, which has been exhibited extensively in Europe, when he was searching for new uses for rubber.

The music room of Stan Hywet is entirely English.

In the spring, summer and fall the gardens of Stan Hywet are a spectacle of color. The Birch Allee leading from the mansion to the north meadow is especially alluring. There are hundreds of rhododendrons, 40,000 tulips, quiet dells and a peaceful English walled garden. The garden clubs of Akron and some of the churches help to maintain the flowers. Some of the gardens have pools, fountains and sculpture.

A professional Shakespeare company generally performs on the terraces in July and August. Minstrel groups and string ensembles are supplemented by modern concert and jazz bands. Occasionally the estate has an antique-car show. Flower shows include displays of hemerocallis in July, gladioli in August, roses in September, African violets and house plants in early October and chrysanthemums in late October.

The Seiberlings' children hold Stan Hywet in awe and look upon it as a priceless museum, hoping that it will remain a pillar of Americana and that the property will not be cut up into building lots. Fred Seiberling, one of the sons, has lived in recent years on one of the upper floors, but the mansion is one that modern living makes impractical for family life. Its furnaces once consumed a carload of coal a week and their current use of oil is correspondingly large. The six main buildings and two tea houses are rather more than most families want to cope with.

The Stan Hywet Hall Foundation was incorporated in 1957 to operate the estate as a tax-free public shrine. The title to the property is temporarily held by the First National Bank of Akron, which rents the property to the foundation for one dollar a year. The directors are bankers, labor leaders, lawyers, civic league heads and others. They hope ultimately to gain full control of the property and perpetuate it in public use.

❈   ❈   ❈   ❈   ❈   ❈   ❈   ❈

The mansion is at 714 North Portage Path, an easy ten-mile drive from the Ohio Turnpike. It is open in the summer from 1:30 P.M. to 8 P.M. from Tuesday through Sunday, and the grounds are open every day from 10 A.M. to 8 P.M. The admission fee to the mansion is $1.50 for adults and 75 cents for children. Special rates and hours are arranged for school groups and organizations. If precedents are followed, the mansion will be open regularly on week-ends in the spring and fall and for twelve days in each Christmas season.

An English walled garden adjoins the Stan Hywet mansion.

The Model T Mansion

Henry Ford's Fair Lane

DEARBORN · MICHIGAN

ON A SCENIC BEND of the River Rouge in Dearborn, ten miles west of Detroit, is a massive residence of marblehead limestone that Henry Ford built on his 2,150-acre estate in 1914-16. Architects refer to the design of the sprawling, ivy-covered structure as Dearborn Gothic. More definitely it could be called Grass-roots Ford, since it is as distinctive as the Model-T car. The man who did the most to put tens of millions of people on rubber-tired wheels dictated details of its construction and lived there through the thirty-two most productive years of his life.

More than most mansions, Fair Lane has the personality of its owner embedded in its 31,770 square feet of living space, four-story powerhouse, twenty-car garage, secluded laboratory and vast gardens. While parlaying a $28,000 investment into a billion-dollar industrial empire, the man of Irish-English-Dutch-Scandinavian ancestry found time to perfect innovations for easy living that only an ingenious person of strong convictions would conceive. They included a master

Fair Lane's dining room, where Thomas A. Edison and other notables were entertained, has mahogany paneling and sterling silver fixtures.

bedroom with nineteen convenient electric-light switches and sixteen closets; a private telephone system with sixty-five dial extensions; a river dam to run dynamos and pumps for electricity, water and refrigeration; a "water piano" of 160 valves as neatly arranged as West Point cadets at attention; built-in vacuum tubes for hair drying; and leaded-glass windows and intricate fireplaces etched and carved with the owner's philosophy of life.

Fair Lane is two miles downstream on the Rouge from the birthplace of Mr. Ford. It was in the heart of his industrial empire that he chose to build his fifteenth and final home. In this area he spent his childhood, went to school and courted and married Clara Bryant. Although he chose to leave his father's farm to start his career as an apprentice machinist, he never really left home in his life.

Mr. Ford began acquiring the Fair Lane acreage in 1902. It was when he was perfecting his 999 Racer, which frightened the countryside by spurting flame from huge cylinders and splashing oil from its open crankshaft. At the time, one witness said of the embryonic squire of Fair Lane: "Mr. Ford was a daub of oil from head to foot. His collar was yellow, his tie looked as though it had been boiled in lard, his shirt and clothes were spattered, while his face looked like a machinist's after twenty-four hours' work."

As his fortunes rose, Mr. Ford added to Fair Lane until by 1909 he had more than 2,000 acres. At first he built only a small bungalow beside the meandering Rouge, using it as a retreat. At the entrance once stood the venerable Ten Eyck Tavern and toll gate for the plank road to Detroit, now busy Michigan Avenue (U. S. Route 112).

Mr. Ford made a wildlife sanctuary of the acreage. He had 300 deer released on it. The Michigan Audubon Society helped him install 500 bird houses and feeding stations to attract flickers, bluebirds, goldfinches and cardinals, which are still there. Woodchuck, fox, opossum, raccoon and rabbit also remain. English friends sent 500 chaffinches, larks, linnets and thrushes but few survived.

When he started the mansion Mr. Ford said he wanted nothing lavish and would not spend more than $100,000. He explained: "I don't want an army of servants. I still like boiled potatoes with the skins on and I don't want a man standing in back of my chair laughing up his sleeve at me." But by 1915 the bills for the house of fifty-six rooms and fifteen baths reached $1,032,818 and ultimately the costs of the estate reached $2,000,000.

The peony, blue, English, iris, lilac and rose gardens are large but reflect Mr. and Mrs. Ford's simple tastes. Mrs. Ford said she slept with a seed catalog under

Henry Ford collected 10,000 books for his library. His preferences included Mc-Guffey Readers, Gray's Anatomy *and books on mechanical arts.*

her pillow. She disliked garden statues, favored blue flowers, raised chickens and developed areas of sumac, witch hazel, flowering hawthorn and crabapple that still thrive.

The gardens were the scene of Mr. Ford's frequent strolls and his long meetings with Thomas A. Edison, who laid the cornerstone of the mansion, and with John Burroughs, the naturalist. Mr. Edison had a permanent room in the house. A Burroughs grotto and garden are beside the house. When Burroughs died in 1921, Mr. Ford ordered a vigil lantern kept lighted in the grotto for ten years. The main rose garden of three acres has 10,000 hybrid tea roses, 1,000 climbers and 500 pillar roses. A continuous flow of water reaches pools and lily ponds.

Among guests at Fair Lane have been Edward Prince of Wales and other notables. The Fords, who did not drink, kept ample supplies of liquor on hand for guests. They also had an indoor swimming pool, a bowling alley and a ballroom in which old-fashioned square dancing became famous on radio. The house has two-foot walls, some 200 feet long, and it conforms to the contour of the land in a manner common to more modern structures — including some of Frank Lloyd Wright.

An avid reader, Mr. Ford had 10,000 books at Fair Lane and occasionally spent $4,000 a month on limited editions. Many were unread and still crack when opened. His favorites were books such as Dickens' novels, the McGuffey readers, Gray's *Anatomy* and scientific articles. He often jotted on the pages of these his thoughts, such as:

Henry Ford was photographed in 1914 when he started to build Fair Lane. (Right) The upper level of Fair Lane's staircase has elaborate carvings and a window etched with Ford's "don't waste time" legend.

"The man who cuts his own wood warms himself twice."

"I don't read newspapers; they confuse me."

"The man who smokes in the dining room needs his mother again."

"We must make milk out of something."

"We should call in all the money and issue new; we would be able to tell where the money is and tax the hell out of it."

"Any fool can save a dollar. It takes a smart man to spend it wisely."

In like manner Mr. Ford's philosophy is etched and carved on the mansion. In a leaded-glass window of the main staircase is his "don't waste time" admonition, which reads:

> "To no one is given right of delay.
> Noted in heaven passeth each day.
> Be not thou fruitless, work while ye may.
> Trifling were bootless, watch thou and pray."

Archivists report that Mr. Ford "blew his top" one day when he returned home to find that his wife had let decorators paint costly imported mahogany and walnut paneling in main downstairs rooms to "brighten them up." Not concealed on an oversize walnut fireplace in the music room, however, is this admonition:

> "Gather ye roses while ye may.
> Old time is still aflying,
> For the same flower which blooms today,
> Tomorrow will be a dying."

Connecting the residence with the powerhouse is a 300-foot tunnel that contains in neat array some of the 40,000 feet of brass pipe of the establishment. Mr. Ford used the tunnel as a passageway to his laboratory, garage and powerhouse machinery. The machinery includes two huge water-powered generators and an emergency steam generator, linked to the 135 miles of conduit and 1,160 fuses and switches in the mansion.

Mr. Ford's demand for perfection caused him to change architects while the mansion was being built and to discharge plumbers for sloppy workmanship. Two details escaped him, however. A short length of iron pipe, instead of brass, was used underground; to locate and correct the error recently cost $25,000. And the powerhouse is so low that the river can flood it.

On April 6, 1947, a spring flood sent the Rouge cascading over its banks, smashing walls, toppling trees and crippling the generators. Although eighty-three years old, Mr. Ford inspected the damage and planned repairs for the next day. He went to bed at 9 P.M. as usual. Two hours later he called to his wife, "Clara, I feel ill." She was instantly at his side, as she had been for fifty-nine years. The telephone system was flooded and she sent the chauffeur for a doctor but when he arrived Mr. Ford was dead. On a wall of the powerhouse workmen have chalked the high-water mark, with a notation concerning "the boss."

As he was born, he died by candlelight.

Mrs. Ford remained in the residence until her death in 1950. Edsel, the son of the Fords, had lived in the mansion only until his marriage in 1916.

In 1958 the Ford Motor Company, controlled largely by the grandsons of Henry Ford, gave the mansion and 200 of the acres, with $6,500,000 in cash, to the University of Michigan for a Dearborn campus supplementing the main one at Ann Arbor. The first academic buildings now have risen on the new campus. The mansion is scheduled to be used in perpetuity for seminars, research and as a guest center.

Fair Lane is ten miles west of Detroit and just north of Old Chicago Road, now renamed Michigan Avenue. The grounds and gardens may be seen by the public. Tours of the rooms of the mansion are dependent on the convenience of the university.

The bedroom of Mr. and Mrs. Henry Ford has nineteen electric light switches, sixteen closets and a Wedgwood china mantel.

Acres of rolling countryside lead up to Meadow Brook Hall, a mansion built in the style of old English manor houses.

Tin Lizzies and a Tudor Duo

The Abodes of Edsel B. Ford and Alfred G. Wilson

GROSSE POINTE SHORES
AND ROCHESTER · MICHIGAN

WHILE HENRY FORD was becoming a billionaire in the early manufacturing of tin lizzies, he coincidentally made millionaires of several persons who were associated with him. Some of these persons were relatives, such as his son, Edsel B. Ford, who received paternal birthday gifts of $1,000,000 in gold and was made head of the automobile concern.

Others on the "ride" were business associates, such as John F. Dodge. With his brother Horace E. Dodge, he made parts for Mr. Ford's early cars. The brothers invested $5,000 in the Ford concern, sold their interest to Mr. Ford in 1914 for $27,000,000 and then went on to manufacture the Dodge Brothers cars in a company later absorbed by the Chrysler Corporation.

Mansions that the second-generation fortunes paid for were as different from Henry Ford's Fair Lane residence at Dearborn as the modern Thunderbirds are

Meadow Brook Hall has 200 rooms and paneling carved in the manner of Grinling Gibbons, the seventeenth-century sculptor.

*The baronial dining room of Meadow Brook Hall has an ornately carved plaster
ceiling that craftsmen worked on for many months.*

from the old Model-T roadsters. The later builders chose the Tudor design of the
old rambling mansions of the English countryside, with multiple chimneys, gables,
turrets, abundant carved woodwork, ornate plaster ceilings and stonework inter-
laced with heavy timbers.

On a grand scale is Meadow Brook Hall, built by Mr. and Mrs. Alfred G.
Wilson at Rochester, twenty-five miles north of Detroit. Mrs. Wilson, the former
Matilda Rausch of Canada, had been John Dodge's secretary when he was making
bicycles for Detroiters and thinking about producing parts for Ford cars.

After his first wife died, leaving three children, Dodge married Miss Rausch
in 1907, and there were three more children of this marriage. Then Mr. Dodge
died in 1920. He had almost completed a sumptuous new marble mansion at
Grosse Pointe for his family, with a $50,000 organ and new furnishings on order.
The widow inherited most of Mr. Dodge's $44,000,000 but she lost all interest in
completing the mansion. It stood empty for years and finally was demolished
without ever having been occupied.

Mrs. Dodge, known as the wealthiest widow in America, met Alfred Wilson
at socials and other events of Presbyterian churches in which both were active.

Mr. Wilson, a lumberman and the son of a clergyman, married Mrs. Dodge in 1925. The bride said all the six Dodge children were "very fond" of him. The Wilsons went to Europe for their honeymoon and began looking at famous English manor houses. In the same year, the Dodge Motor Car Company was sold for $146,000,000, which greatly increased Mrs. Wilson's wealth and turned the thoughts of her and her husband to building a castle that would make other millionaires gape.

As a site they chose 1,600 acres of farmland and woodland that Mr. Dodge had acquired near Rochester, Michigan. At a cost of $3,128,000 they built a 200-room home that is 410 feet long. Sometimes Elizabethan and Jacobean in its décor, it has wood-paneled galleries and oversize rooms furnished with Oriental rugs, antique silver, imported chandeliers, rare furniture and a collection of paintings by Rembrandt, Gainsborough, Murillo, Reynolds and Van Dyck.

William E. Kapp of the architectural firm of Smith, Hinchman and Grylls traveled extensively in this country and Europe to plan the Wilson residence. He noted that many American millionaires had imported entire rooms from European castles to install in their new homes and that the change in atmospheric conditions had caused the paneling to crack and disintegrate. He encouraged the Wilsons to have all wood carvings made locally from materials that could be imported but were seasoned locally before being used.

The Wilsons did buy, however, a twenty-foot table of heavy oak from England. Within a few years it developed a crack in its top large enough for fingers to enter.

Mrs. Wilson had kept the measurements of the huge rooms in the Grosse Pointe mansion that she had never occupied, and over the objections of the architects she had some of the rooms at Meadow Brook Hall made the same size.

Mr. Kapp also obtained the measurements of famous rooms of English castles and duplicated some of them in the Wilson residence. He bought considerable oak in England for use in the rooms but made certain it was seasoned in the Michigan climate before it was carved and installed.

The mansion, begun in 1926, was completed in 1929. On property a mile and a half wide, it has subsidiary farm buildings, a riding hall and a golf club that John Dodge developed. He reportedly built the club after having been refused membership in near-by private clubs because of his mule-skinning diction and diamond-in-the-rough mannerisms.

The Wilsons installed in Meadow Brook Hall the $50,000 organ that John Dodge had bought for the Grosse Pointe home. The living room is forty by twenty feet. The grand staircase is decorated with elaborate carvings in the style of Grinling Gibbons, the noted seventeenth-century English sculptor. It has a landing large enough for two davenports, four chairs and several tables.

Meadow Brook Hall has twenty-six fireplaces, two elevators and a secret stairway. It also has hidden alcoves for commonplace items such as typewriters. The dining room is fifty-two by twenty-two feet and has carved wood paneling on the walls and a carved plaster ceiling that is one of the finest in the world. Craftsmen worked for two months to perfect the delicate carvings in the plaster.

The recreation room is two stories high; it rises from the basement and has balconies off the first-floor rooms. There are nine maids' rooms, suites for house-keepers and butlers and a nine-car garage.

As in the case of many such mansion builders, the Wilsons ultimately began to wonder what to do with so much space and all the servant problems that the maintenance entailed. After the heirs of Henry Ford had given Fair Lane to the University of Michigan as a supplement to its Ann Arbor campus, the Wilsons gave Meadow Brook Hall and its vast acreage to Michigan State University, as a supplement to its East Lansing campus.

The gift of the Wilsons, made in 1957, was valued at $10,000,000, which included $2,000,000 cash for development of the new campus. The Wilsons re-tained, however, life occupancy of the mansion and of 127 acres on a corner of the tract. On this corner they built a comparatively modest home of contemporary design for themselves, calling it Sunset House. The college began constructing academic buildings on the new campus and dreaming of the public cultural events that some day would be held in Meadow Brook Hall itself.

In 1926 and 1927, while the Wilsons were building Meadow Brook Hall, Edsel Ford was constructing a mansion of somewhat similar English manor house design on the shore of Lake St. Clair at Grosse Pointe Shores, fourteen miles from downtown Detroit. It has sixty rooms and a tract of sixty-five acres, with 3,000 feet of shoreline.

Henry Ford had believed that his son should continue to live in Dearborn, but Edsel's tastes were different from his father's in matters of housing as well as cars. Edsel wanted to develop an eight-cylinder car, while his father contended that " a motor car should not have more spark plugs than a cow has teats." Edsel preferred the cartoons in *The New Yorker* to the comic strip "Orphan Annie," which was his father's favorite. Edsel desired the schools and the social climate of Grosse Point Shores. He was boat-minded, keeping an eighty-eight-foot schoon-er, a houseboat, several sloops and a few speedboats, all of which made the acqui-sition of the property with Lake St. Clair moorings most logical.

In England, Edsel and his wife visited delightful old rambling Cotswold houses. They soon decided they wanted a "modest and picturesque home — not a palace or fortress — as a residence" for themselves and their four children, Henry II, Benson, William and Josephine.

Albert Kahn, retained as the architect for the residence, did extensive research in England, making innumerable sketches and photographs of the Cotswold houses that the Fords admired. The Fords themselves made several more trips to England to share in the planning, and the houses at Worcestershire especially held their attention.

Edsel B. Ford built a home in the style of the Cotswold houses of England. On the left is the family's art gallery.

The Fords brought from England some of the old weathered stones from demolished buildings to mix with newly cut Michigan stones to produce in their home something of an ancient effect. They also brought back entire stairways of weathered oak, large carved mantels, paneling and other items — some centuries old — for use in the new home.

Stone shingles for the roof were imported from England, along with English craftsmen to shape and install them in the authentic Cotswold manner. To the sorrow of Mr. Ford, the shingles never accumulated in the Michigan climate the green moss that they commonly did at Worcestershire.

The Tudor entrance hall of the mansion opens onto a gallery sixty feet long, leading to a drawing room twenty-five by forty feet, a library twenty-two by thirty-three feet, a morning room eighteen by twenty-two feet and a dining room twenty-two by thirty-two feet.

The Fords also built a gate lodge, a recreation center, greenhouses, a boathouse, dog kennels, swimming and lily pools, tennis courts and an art gallery. A playhouse, a coal-burning train, a steam-operated threshing machine and an assortment of automobiles were provided for the children. In his life at Grosse Pointe Shores, Edsel was a living contradiction of William K. Vanderbilt's declaration that "inherited wealth is a big handicap to happiness, and it is as certain death to ambition as cocaine is to morality."

Edsel Ford won his fight for eight-cylinder cars but he could not win a fight against cancer. He died in 1943 at the age of forty-nine. His widow, Mrs. Eleanor Clay Ford, continued to live for several years in the house beside Lake St. Clair. Her children, now grown and married, lived near by and returned frequently to the mansion for visits.

Finally Mrs. Ford decided the house was too big and presented too many maintenance problems. She posted it for sale at $500,000, which she said was "only a fraction" of the original cost.

✿   ✿   ✿   ✿   ✿   ✿   ✿   ✿

Meadow Brook Hall, at Rochester, is bounded by Pontiac, Adams, Butler and Squirrel Roads. The new Michigan State University campus there may be seen any time but the mansion is open to the public only on special occasions, such as garden-club benefits with $2.50 admission charges. The house Edsel Ford built is at 1100 Lakeshore Drive, Grosse Pointe Shores, and may be seen from the highway and Lake St. Clair.

Even Edsel B. Ford's gatehouse was built in the Cotswold manner. Gardeners, chauffeurs and other servants lived in it.

ACKNOWLEDGMENTS

On trips to mansions throughout the United States to obtain materials for this book, the author received painstaking cooperation from mansion owners, civic leaders, foundation officials, newspaper editors, archivists and librarians. Deep gratitude is expressed to all, and the wish is given that this book will help to perpetuate the mansions.

The picture credits are as follows:

Frontispiece — Ringling Museum. 2-7 — Miami-Metro News Bureau. 9 — John Singer Sargent painting. 11-13 — Whitehall. 15 — Morgan Studio. 18 — Whitehall. 20 — Sarasota Herald-Tribune. 21 — Ringling Museum. 23 — Savely Sorine paintings. 24-27 — Ringling Museum. 29 — the author. 30 — Wide World. 31 — the author. 33-37 — Frank Lloyd Wright Foundation. 39 — Wide World. 41 — Carolina Art Association; Samuel Chamberlain. 43 — Historic Charleston Foundation. 45 — Carolina Art Association. 47 — Historic Charleston Foundation. 48 — Boone Hall. 49 — Louis H. Frohman. 50 — Tryon Palace. 51 — North Carolina State; Louis H. Frohman. 52 — Tryon Palace; Louis H. Frohman. 55-62 — Biltmore. 63-69 — Thomas Jefferson Foundation. 70-73 — Stratford Hall. 75 — U. S. Navy. 77-83 — Mount Vernon Ladies Association. 85 — The New York Times. 86-92 — Abbie Rowe-National Park Service. 93-97 — Winterthur Museum. 101-105 — Monmouth College. 107-112 — Frick Collection. 115-117 — Chatham College. 120-121 — California State. 124 — the author; United Press International. 126 — California State. 127-129 — the author. 130-131 — California State. 133-135 — Union Pacific Railroad. 139 — Frashers. 141 — Union Pacific Railroad. 143-145 — Huntington Art Gallery. 155-160 — Hawaii Vistors Bureau. 163-164 — Bellingrath Mansion. 166-170 — Knabb-Lane-Prince. 172-173 — Daughters of the American Revolution. 174-175 — Knabb-Lane-Prince. 177-179 — Ladies Hermitage Association. 182 — the author. 183 — Wide World. 185 — the author. 186 — Connecticut State. 188-189 — National Park Service. 200 — Wide World. 202-203 — The New York Times. 207 — J. Henry Hills painting. 208-212 — Sleepy Hollow Restorations. 213-214 — Louis H. Frohman. 215-217 — Danny Wann. 220 — The Reader's Digest. 221 — Danny Wann. 222 — Manhattanville College. 225-227 — Ogden R. Reid. 228 — Manhattanville College. 229-243 — the author. 244-247 — Newport Preservation Society. 248 — the author; Newport Preservation Society. 250 — the author. 251-255 — Newport Preservation Society. 257-262 — Belcourt Castle. 264 — the author. 267-271 — American Swedish Institute. 272 — American College of Surgeons. 274 — Chicago Daily News. 276-279 — New York State. 281 — Stan Hywet. 282 — Wide World; Stan Hywet. 283-286 — Stan Hywet. 287-289 — Ford Motor Company. 290 — Wide World; Ford Motor Company. 292 — Ford Motor Company. 293-295 — Detroit Times. 297-299 — Ford Motor Company.

INDEX

(Page numbers in italics refer to illustrations)

grand staircase of, *112*, 113; marble used in, 113; organ in, 113; paintings in, 113
Fritz, Herbert, 37
Froebel, Friedrich, 33
Frost, Mary Pringle, 43, 44
Frost, Rebecca Motte, 44
Frost, Susan Pringle, 44, 45

Gainsborough, Thomas, "Blue Boy" by, 144, 151, 154
Garber, Ben, 219
Garfield, James A., 89
Garner, John Nance, 128
Georgian architecture, 42, 50, 86, 168, 172, 175, 205
Gerard, James W., 259
Gerard, Julian, 136
Gerome, Jean Leon, 128
Gerry, Peter G., 58
Gershwin, George, 184
Gibbons, Grinling, 296
Gibbs, James, 86
Gibson, Charles Dana, 171
Gibson, Walter Murray, 158
Gillette, William, *183*, 183-84, 185, 186-87
Gillette castle (Hadlyme, Connecticut), *182*, 183-87; art gallery of, 187; cost of, 184; furniture of, 185; Gillette's bedroom at, 186, *186*; "Grand Central Terminal" at, 184, *185*; granite walls of, 184; living room of, 185; number of rooms in, 184; oak doors of, 184-85, *185*; open to public, 187
Gish, Lillian and Dorothy, 5
Goelet, May Wilson, 265
Goelet, Ogden, 252, 264, 265
Goelet, Robert, 265
Gonzales, Jean Flagler, 12, 14, 19
Goodyear, Charles, 284
Gospel Foundation of California, 141
Grahame, Charles, 99
Grant, Ulysses S., 89, 101, 171, 172
Gréber, Jacques, 245
Greek Revival style of architecture, 46, 168, 173, 174, 175, 177, 240, 243
Greeley, Horace, 143
Greenhut, J. B., 102
Gresham, Walter Q., 172
Grey, Elmer, 146, 154
Griffin, James S., 172
Grigg, Milton L., 69
Grosse Pointe residence, of Edsel Ford, 297-99, *298*, *299*
Guggenheim, Solomon R., 46, 101
Gumpertz, Sam, 29
Gutenberg Bible, 144, 151, 152, 154

Hadwen, William, 243
Hale, George E., 154

Hals, Frans, 26
Hammarskjöld, Dag, 270
Hammond, John Hays, Jr., 234
Hancock, John, 151
Harding, Warren G., 117, 282
Harriman, E. H., 146
Harris, Luther, 164
Harrison, Mrs. Randolph C., 76
Hart, G. K., 278
Harvey, George, 210
Hastie, J. Drayton, 46
Hastings, Thomas, 14, 110
Hawks, John, 50, 53, 54
Hayne, Isaac, 44
Hearn, James A., 101
Hearst, George, 123, 145
Hearst, Millicent Willson, 122
Hearst, Phoebe Apperson, 83, 121-22, 123
Hearst, William Randolph, 83, 121-32 *passim*, *124*, 125
Hearst San Simeon State Historical Monument, 132
Henry, Patrick, 74
Henry Morrison Flagler Museum, 14; *see also* Whitehall
Hermitage of Andrew Jackson (Nashville, Tennessee), *177*, 177-82; back parlor of, *179*; furniture and furnishings of, 180; open to public, 181
Hertrich, William, 149
Historic Charleston Foundation, 41, 42, 46, 48
Hoban, James, 86
Hobby Club, 152
Hoffman, F. Burrall, Jr., 7
Hoffman, Mathilda, 209
Holder, Fred W., 165
Holladay, Ann, 223, 224
Holladay, Ben, 223, 224
Hollyday, James, 98
Holmes, Oliver Wendell, 246
Homestead (Pennsylvania) battle, 108, 110
Hoover, Herbert, 283
Horlbeck, John, 48
Hosack, David, 199
Houdon, Jean Antoine, 82
Howard, Esme, 150
Howe, Deering, 10
Hudson River Conservation Society, 218
Hughes, Charles Evans, 103
Hunt, Myron, 146, 154
Hunt, Richard Morris, 33, 58, 248, 252, 260, 264
Hunter, William, 246-47
Hunter House (Newport, Rhode Island), *245*, 246-47; hallway of, *248*; parlor of, 247
Huntington, Arabella Duval, 145, 146, 148, 149

Rogers, George B., 162
Rogers, Will, 27, 139, 283
Roosevelt, Anna, 191
Roosevelt, Eleanor, 190
Roosevelt, Eliot, 191
Roosevelt, Franklin (son of Franklin D. Roosevelt), 191
Roosevelt, Franklin D., 76, 90, 91, 181, 189-95 *passim*
Roosevelt, Isaac, 191
Roosevelt, James (father of Franklin D. Roosevelt), 190, 191, 192
Roosevelt, James (son of Franklin D. Roosevelt), 191
Roosevelt, John, 191
Roosevelt, Sara, 190
Roosevelt, Theodore, 89
Roosevelt Foundation, 193
Roosevelt Library, *193*, 194-95
Roper, Robert William, 46
Roper house (Charleston, South Carolina), *45*, 45-46, 48
Rosalie mansion (Natchez, Mississippi), *172*, 172-73, *173*
Rosenbach, A. S. W., 150
Rubens, Peter Paul, 22
Russell, Nathaniel, 47
Rutledge, Edward, 47

Sansovino, Jacopo, 8, 128
Sargent, John Singer, 5, 9
Schad, Robert O., 153
Schiff, Mortimer, 150
Scott, Walter, 210
Scott, Walter Perry, 133-42, *135*, *139*
Scotty's Castle (Grapevine Canyon, California), 38, *133*, 133-42, *135*, 141; cost of, 134; dining room of, 140; music room of, 139; number of men employed in building, 137; number of rooms in, 136; open to public, 142; Will Rogers Room at, 139
Seiberling, Fred, 285
Seiberling, Mr. and Mrs. Frank A., 281, 282, *282*, 283, 284
Shadow Lawn (West Long Branch, New Jersey), *101*, 101-06; Aztec solarium of, 102, *105*; electronic communications at, 106; gardens of, 103, *105*; hall of, 102, *104*, 105; materials used for, 102; mirrors at, 102, 106; and Monmouth College, 106; number of rooms in, 101; organ at, 102, 105; petrified wood used at, 102, 105; rebuilt after fire, 103
Shakespeare manuscripts, in Huntington residence, 151, 154
Shamrock Cliff (Newport, Rhode Island), 246, 249-50
Shaw, George Bernard, 128

Sheraton, Thomas, 99
Sherman, William Tecumseh, 11
Shorb, J. de Barth, 146, 154
Siegling, Rudolph, 46
Skelton, Martha Wayles, 67
Sleeper, Henry Davis, 229, 230, 231, 232, 233, 234
Sleeper, J. Henry, 230
Sleeper, Jacob, 230
Sleepy Hollow, mansions at, *207*, 207-14, *211*, *213*
Sloan, Samuel, 168
Smith, Alfred E., 27
Smith, Myra Virginia, 174, 175
Smithsonian Institution, 91
Society of Architectural Historians, 221
Society for the Preservation of New England Antiquities, 233
Somerville, William C., 75
Spreckels, Claus, 158
Staircase, flying, in Russell house, 47
Stamper, John, 98
Stan Hywet Hall (Akron, Ohio), *281*, 281-86, *283*; cost of, 282; entrance to, 284; exterior of, *283*; furnishings of, 284; gardens of, 285, *286*; guests at, 283; music room of, 284, *285*; open to public, 286
Stan Hywet Hall Foundation, 286
Stanton, Frederick, 169, 170
Stanton Hall (Natchez, Mississippi), *169*, 169-70
Starbuck, Eunice, 243
Starbuck, Joseph, 240, 242
Steiner, Ulrich, 270
Stephenson, Harvey, 218
Stiles, Edward, 98
Stillington Hall (Gloucester, Massachusetts), 234
Stone, Thomas A., 48
Storke, Henry, 76
Stow, Bill, 145
Stratford Hall (Westmoreland County, Virginia), *70-71*, 70-76, *75*; bricks for, made on property, 73; children killed in accidents at, 75; design of, 73-74; dining room of, *72*; furniture and furnishings of, 74; Ha-Ha wall at, 74, *75*; hall of main floor at, 74; Mother's Room of, *73*, 74; number of rooms in, 73; open to public, 76; restoration of, 76; site of, 73
Stuart, Charles E., 76
Stuart, Charles E., Jr., 76
Stuart, Gilbert, 87, 98, 99, 151, 191, 238
Stuart, Richard, 75
Stuart, Richard H., 76
Stuyvesant, Peter, 209
Suarez, Diego, 7
Sullivan, Louis, 33

Washington, John, 80
Washington, John A., Jr., 79
Washington, Lawrence, 80
Washington, Lund, 81, 82
Washington, Martha, 81, 83
Waves (Newport, Rhode Island), 246, 247-48
Webster, Daniel, 91, 238
Wedgwood Company, 219
West, Benjamin, 98, 151
West Brick (Nantucket, Massachusetts), 240, 242
Westchester County Park Commission, 218
Westchester Historical Society, 218
Weston, Ernest, 37
Weston, William, 35, 37
White, John A., 102
White, Stanford, 24, 198, 225, 247
White House, *85*, 85-92; *92*; age of, 86; Blue Room of, *89*, 90, 92; burned by British, 86, 87; East Room of, *87*, 89, 90, 92; furniture and furnishings of, 88; gardens of, 88; Green Room of, *91*, 92; Lincoln Room of, *88*, 91; main entrance to, 2, *92*; reconstruction of, 90, 91; Red Room of, *90*, 92; State Dining Room of, *86*, 92; tourists' entrance to, 92
Whitehall (Palm Beach, Florida), *11*, 11-19; architects for, 14; ballroom of, *13*, 17; bedrooms of, 17; cost of, 12; design of, 16; dining room of, 17, *18*; entrance to, 16; furniture and furnishings of, 12, 17; hall of, 17; library of, 17; marble used for, 16; as museum, 12, 14, 19; music room of, 17; salon of, *15*, 17; site of, 16; solarium of, 19; "stone area" of, 19
Whitney Art Museum, 256
Whitney, Harry Payne, 258
Whitney, Mrs. Harry Payne, 256
Widener, Mrs. George D., 250
Williams, Julia, 168
Williams, Mr. and Mrs. Winthrop, 242

Williams, William, 99
Wilson, Gilbert, 212
Wilson, Mr. and Mrs. Alfred G., 295, 296, 297
Wilson, Mrs. Andrew L., 173
Wilson, Woodrow, 19, 89, 101, 102, 103
Winans, Celeste, 249
Winfield Foundation, 233
Winslow, Lorenzo S., 90
Winterthur (New Castle County, Delaware), 91, 93, 93-100; antiques at, 96, 98; art objects at, 96, 97; Baltimore Rooms of, 99; Candlestick Room of, 99; carpets at, 98; Chinese Parlor of, *94*, 99; du Pont Dining Room of, 99; furniture and furnishings of, 94, 98; gardens of, 99; Latimeria Room of, 98; Marlboro Room of, 99; materials used for, 98; as museum, 93; number of rooms in, 93; open to public, 100; paintings at, 98; periods portrayed by, 98, 99; Phyfe Room of, *95*, 99; Port Royal Entrance Hall of, 98; Readbourne Stair Hall of, *96*, 98; spiral staircase of, *97*, 99; Stamper-Blackwell Porch and Parlor of, 98; valuation of, 97
Winterthur Corporation, 96, 100
Winterthur Museum, 97
Wisconsin, 32
Woolworth, Frank W., 103, 233
Wren, Christopher, 86
Wright, Anna Lloyd-Jones, 32, 33
Wright, Catherine, 33, 34
Wright, Frank Lloyd, 9, *30*, 31-40 *passim*, 136, 290
Wright, Miriam, 38
Wright, Olgivanna, *30*, 38, 40
Wright, William R. C., 32

Young, Brigham, 223
Young, Robert R., 246

Ziegfeld, Florenz, 6, 27